The State of Democratic Theory

The State of Democratic Theory

❖

Ian Shapiro

PRINCETON UNIVERSITY PRESS

PRINCETON AND OXFORD

Library of Congress Cataloging-in-Publication Data

Shapiro, Ian.
The state of democratic theory / Ian Shapiro.
p.   cm.
Includes bibliographical references and index.
ISBN 0-691-11547-8 (alk. paper)
1. Democracy. I. Title.
JC423.S466 2003
321.8—dc21   2002193070

British Library Cataloging-in-Publication Data is available

This book has been composed in Galliard, Gill Sans, and Gill Sans Light

Printed on acid-free paper. ∞

www.pupress.princeton.edu

Printed in the United States of America

1   3   5   7   9   10   8   6   4   2

FOR ZANDRA RATHBONE

❖ Contents ❖

❖ *Preface* ❖

AN EARLIER VERSION of parts of this book appeared as my essay "The State of Democratic Theory" in *Political Science: The State of the Discipline*, edited by Ira Katznelson and Helen Milner, and published jointly by the American Political Science Association and W. W. Norton & Company in 2002. I am grateful to Ira and Helen for the initial invitation; to the participants in two conferences they organized at which our contributions were discussed, for their comments; to the publishers who hold the copyright for permitting me to make use of that material here; and to Ira in particular for talking me out of abandoning the venture on the grounds that I lacked the time to do it—which indeed I did. Ira and Helen's mandate to us was to offer an evenhanded elucidation of a piece of the terrain of political science from a distinctive point of view. The instruction might seem oxymoronic, requiring us to be opinionated and dispassionate at the same time. I took it to mean that I should assess the state of democratic theory from my point of view, but in a way that a reader with a different point of view might find helpful. A map of a country prepared for an invading army depicts hills, valleys, and other sites of strategic interest; yet it might nonetheless be useful to a recreational hiker. I tried to act on this mandate in the original article and have done so in the book as well.

In the course of expanding the original essay into the book, I have added new material on power and democracy, democratic transitions, deliberation, courts and judicial review, and the impact of democracy on the distribution of income and wealth. These discussions incorporate and build on material from the following previously published pieces: "Elements of Democratic Justice," *Political Theory* 24, no. 4 (November 1996): 579–619, copyright © 1996 by Sage Publications; "Group Aspirations and Democratic Politics," *Constellations* 3, no. 3 (January 1997): 315–25, and "Optimal Deliberation?" *Journal of Political Philosophy* 10, no. 2 (June 2002): 196–211, copyright © 1997 and 2002, respectively, by Blackwell Publishing; "Enough of Deliberation: Politics Is about Interests and Power," in *Deliberative Politics: Essays on Democracy and Disagreement*, edited by Stephen Macedo, 28–38, copyright © 1999 by Oxford University Press, used by permission of Oxford University Press, Inc.; introduction to *Abortion: The Supreme Court Decisions*, 2d ed., 1–26, copyright ©

2001, reprinted by permission of Hackett Publishing Company, Inc., all rights reserved; "Why the Poor Don't Soak the Rich,"reprinted by permission of *Daedalus*, Journal of the American Academy of Arts and Sciences, from the Winter 2002 issue (vol. 131, no. 1) "On Equality"; and "Democracy and Rights," in *The Moral Foundations of Politics*, 207–23, copyright © 2002 by Yale University Press. I am grateful to all these copyright owners for permission to draw on said material here.

Versions of the inexorably expanding paper were presented at a conference on the social sciences in Villa Lana, Prague, in May 2000, the annual meeting of the American Political Science Association in September 2000, and at faculty workshops at Yale, Ohio State, the University of Cape Town, and Texas A&M between 2000 and 2002. Other parts of what was to become the rest of the book were presented at annual meetings of the American Political Science Association in August 1997, the Columbia Political Theory Workshop in September 1999, the New School for Social Research in October 1999, the conference on Democracy and Distribution at Yale in November 1999, the conference on Deliberating about Deliberative Democracy at the University of Texas, Austin, in February 2000, the Nuffield College political theory workshop in March 2000, as the Porthemus Lecture at the University of Georgia in April 2000, as a Tercentennial De Vane Lecture at Yale in January 2001, as a keynote lecture to a joint session of the Danish and Norwegian Democracy and Power Project, Copenhagen, May 2001, and at the annual meeting of the Brazilian Political Science Association in Niteroí in July 2002. Numerous participants in these various venues made worthwhile suggestions, some of which have been heeded.

The book was written in the summer of 2002 with the indispensable help of Jeffrey Mueller, who occupies a position somewhere in the zone between multitasking research assistant par excellence and para–political theorist. The research assistance of Jennifer Carter is also gratefully acknowledged. The entire manuscript was read by José Cheibub, Bob Dahl, Clarissa Hayward, Nancy Hirschmann, Courtney Jung, Joseph LaPalombara, Vicky Murillo, Mark Stein, and Peter Swenson. Their comments all helped improve it, though the usual caveats apply. I should also like to record my thanks to Ian Malcolm at Princeton University Press for encouraging the project from the outset and shepherding it efficiently into print. He belongs to the vanishing breed of acquisitions editors who actually read manuscripts and make informed substantive suggestions. He is a pleasure to work with.

While writing the book, I received research funding from Yale's Institution of Social and Policy Studies and the Carnegie Corporation of New York. I am particularly grateful to Carnegie for its ongoing support of the larger project on democracy and distribution on which I am working, and for which chapter 5 is the prolegomenon.

The State of Democratic Theory

❖

THE DEMOCRATIC IDEA is close to nonnegotiable in today's world. Liberation movements insist that they are more democratic than the regimes they seek to replace. Authoritarian rulers seldom reject democracy outright. Instead they argue that their people are not ready for democracy "yet," that their systems are more democratic than they appear, or that the opposition is corrupt and antidemocratic—perhaps the stooge of a foreign power. International financial institutions may be primarily interested in countries' adopting neoliberal market reforms, yet they also feel compelled to call for regular elections and other democratic political reforms. Of course, different people understand different things by democracy, and every democratic order will be thought by some not to be functioning as it should, in the corrupt control of an illicit minority, or otherwise in need of repair. But the very terms of such objections to democracy affirm its obligatory character, since it is the malfunction or corruption of democracy that is being objected to.

Within democratic systems it is accepted that people are free to despise the elected government, but not its right to *be* the government. Christian fundamentalists may believe they are acting on God's orders, but the fact that they claim to be a "moral *majority*" indicates that, as far as *political* legitimacy is concerned, they understand democracy's nonoptional character. Constitutional arrangements sometimes limit democracy's range, particularly in separation-of-powers systems such as the United States. But constitutions generally contain entrenched guarantees of democratic government as well. Moreover, they are themselves revisable at constitutional conventions or via amendment procedures whose legitimacy is popularly authorized. Even liberal constitutionalists like Bruce Ackerman (1993b) agree that critical moments of constitutional founding and change require popular democratic validation if they are to be accepted as legitimate over time.

Nonetheless, democracy's nonnegotiable political status has long stood in contrast to the widespread skepticism about it among political theorists. Generations of scholars following Kenneth Arrow (1951) have questioned the rationality of its inner logic, and many others have been deeply skeptical of its desirability as a political outlook. John Dunn (1979: 26) captured this skepticism well with the observation that although most people think

I

of themselves as democrats, democratic theory oscillates between two variants, "one dismally ideological and the other fairly blatantly utopian." The oscillation Dunn had in mind was between Cold War rhetoric masquerading as theory and arguments for egalitarian and participatory democracy that lacked convincing attention to how they might actually be deployed. Despite its legitimacy in the world, democratic theory did not then seem to be going anywhere interesting or worthwhile.

In the years since Dunn wrote there has been a revival of interest in the study of democracy, fed by the dramatic and unexpected increase in the number of democracies in the world in Africa, Asia, and Latin America—not to mention the countries of the former Soviet Empire. Between 1980 and 2002, some eighty-one countries moved from authoritarianism to democracy, including thirty-three military dictatorships that were replaced by civilian governments (United Nations 2002). Yet if the turn of events has rendered Dunn's opposition anachronistic, it is far from clear that democracy's underlying theoretical difficulties have been addressed satisfactorily. The time seems ripe for a reassessment of the state of democratic theory in light of the actual operation of democratic politics. That is the enterprise attempted here.

Assessments of this sort require yardsticks, two of which suggest themselves. One is normative, implied when we ask how persuasive the theories are that seek to justify democracy as a system of government. The other is explanatory, prompted by asking how successful the theories are that try to account for the dynamics of democratic systems. Normative and explanatory theories of democracy grow out of literatures that proceed, for the most part, on separate tracks, largely uninformed by one another. This is unfortunate, partly because speculation about what ought to be is likely to be more useful when informed by relevant knowledge of what is feasible, and partly because explanatory theory too easily becomes banal and method-driven when isolated from the pressing normative concerns that have fueled worldwide interest in democracy in recent decades. Accordingly, I take an integrative tack, focusing on what we should expect of democracy, and on how those expectations might best be realized in practice.

Sharpening this focus, one inevitably confronts dissensus on both issues. The book is organized around these disagreements. I begin, in chapter 1, with a discussion of the main contending views of democratic purposes, and more specifically the normative claim popular among theorists in what I describe as the aggregative and deliberative traditions that democracy should be geared toward arriving at some notion of the general will that reflects the common good. This is Rousseau's formulation of the problem as set forth in *The Social Contract*, and aggregative theorists follow his lead in trying to discover the general will by "taking men as they are and laws as they might be" (Rousseau [1762] 1968: 49). They regard preferences as given and concern themselves with how best to tot them up. The aggregative tradition has bequeathed a view of democracy in which competing for the majority's vote is the essence of the exercise, and the challenge for democratic theorists as they conceive it is to come up with the right rules to govern the contest. Deliberative theorists, by contrast, are more Aristotelian in taking a transformative view of human beings (see Aristotle [ca. 330 B.C.] 1977: bk. 2). They concern themselves with the ways in which deliberation can be used to alter preferences so as to facilitate the search for a common good. For them the general will has to be manufactured, not just discovered.

Proponents of aggregation and deliberation thus operate with different views of the human condition and the possibilities of collective life; indeed, each group often defends its views as much by pointing to the demerits of the other as by putting forth constructive arguments on its own behalf. Yet both camps share Rousseau's assumption that democracy's task is to express a general will that reflects the common good. For aggregative theorists the alleged impossibility of doing this is said to be proof of democracy's impossibility, whereas for deliberativists the goal is to get people to engage in deliberation so as to forge, and sometimes also implement, policies that serve the common good. I argue that both groups overestimate the importance of the idea of the common good for democracy. Instead, democracy is better thought of as a means of managing power relations so as to minimize domination. My view embodies a view of the common good, to be sure, but it is a stripped-down one: less demanding in its assumptions about collective rationality than either the aggregative or the deliberative view, and more sensitive to considerations about power. Indeed, taking my cue from Machiavelli's ([ca. 1517] 1970: 1.5) intimation at the start of the *Discourses*, I define the common good in a democracy as that which those with an interest in avoiding domination share. In chapters 2 and 3, I revisit conceptions of politics as deliberation and competition for a majority of votes from this perspective, exploring the conditions under which they can be advantageous once Rousseau's construction of the enterprise has been jettisoned.

If a central task for democracy is to enable people to manage power relations so as to minimize domination, the following questions arise: what is domination? how do we know it when we see it? and how effective can democratic governments aspire to be at reducing it? These questions shape much of the ensuing discussion, but some prefatory comments are in order here. Weber ([1914] 1968: 53) defined domination as "the probability that a command with a specific content will be obeyed by a given group of persons," insisting that "the existence of domination turns only on the actual presence of one person successfully issuing orders to others." I conceive of domination differently, as resulting from the illegitimate exercise of power. In some respects this is a broader conception than Weber's because domination as I conceive it can occur without explicit orders emanating from identifiable agents. Although I do not go all the way with Foucault (1977, 1982) in thinking that domination can be entirely divorced from human agency, I do agree that domination can result from a person's, or a group's, shaping agendas, constraining options, and, in the limiting case, influencing people's preferences and desires. Domination can also occur without the need for explicit commands when one person or group secures the compliance of another as a by-product of their control of resources that are essential for the second person or group, or, in the terminology I will deploy, is in a position to threaten their basic interests.

My conception is narrower than Weber's in that I regard domination as arising only from the illegitimate exercise of power. Compliance is often compelled in armies, firms, sports teams, families, schools, and countless other institutions. Indeed, political theorists from Plato to Foucault have often noted that the ineradicably hierarchical character of much social life makes power relations ubiquitous to human interaction. But this does not mean that domination is. There is a world of difference, for instance, between a teacher's requiring a student to do her homework and his taking advantage of his powerful position to engage in sexual harassment of her. The latter is domination, but the former is not. Hierarchical relations are often legitimate, and, when they are, they do not involve domination on my account. Yet hierarchical relations must concern democratic theorists nonetheless because there is always the possibility that, left unchecked, they can facilitate domination. This is why I have argued elsewhere (Shapiro 1999a) that hierarchies should generally be presumed suspect and be structured so as to minimize the likelihood that they will atrophy into systems of domination.

To be sure, this is often difficult to achieve, partly because governments frequently lack the necessary information and partly because they act with notoriously blunt instruments—creating the danger that the cure can be worse than the disease. Accordingly, there are good reasons for structuring social life, where possible, so that people will discover incentives to democratize things for themselves by creating mechanisms through which those who wield power are held accountable to those over whom it is wielded. Where this fails, I argue, government legitimately intervenes, but one of the more important creative challenges involves calibrating the intervention by reference to the seriousness of the possibility of domination, so as to avoid self-defeating efforts at democratic reform.

Governments can help structure the power dimensions of human interaction so as to ameliorate domination in many walks of life, but since they wield power willy-nilly, they are also potential agents of domination themselves. Indeed, for much of the twentieth century governments were arguably the most fearsome sources of domination in the world, and they continue to be so in many places. The appalling excesses of fascism and communism may have led some political theorists to adopt too governmentalist a view of politics, missing the ways in which governments underwrite domination throughout civil society, however implicitly, and undervaluing the ways in which they can ameliorate it. Yet there is no doubt that governments continue to be major exercisers of power in the world, and that a central task for democratic theorists is to devise ways of making them more accountable to those over whom their power is exercised—servants of the people rather than their masters.

If the task for democratic theorists is to devise better ways for governments to render the exercise of power legitimate, then democratic theory should be informed by considerable attention to the nature of power. Unfortunately, at the same time as the democracy literature has been oddly innocent of the research on power, the power literature been preoccupied with epistemological issues to the virtual exclusion of their implications for the theory and practice of democracy. I try to redress this mutual blindness in my discussions of deliberation and electoral competition, by showing how insights from the power literature can help us specify the conditions under which these practices can operate to minimize domination.

In chapter 2, I argue that although deliberation can sometimes be inimical to undermining domination, there are settings in which it can be helpful. Because people cannot really be forced to deliberate or to pursue any particular goal when they do deliberate, the challenge for democratic institutional designers is to structure the incentives so that people will want to deploy deliberation to minimize domination in the course of their collective endeavors. The best way for government to try to foster this is to strengthen the rights of appeal, delay, and in extreme cases even veto—but only of those who are vulnerable to the power of others because they have basic interests at stake in a given setting. Strengthening these rights may lead to the reduction of domination through deliberation, and, even when it fails to achieve this result, it nonetheless makes sense from the perspective of a stripped-down conception of the common good geared to reducing domination. Strengthening the hand of the vulnerable in such settings is desirable, even if they end up using it to bargain or negotiate rather than to deliberate.

In chapter 3, I turn to the literature on majoritarian competitive democracy. The classic power-centered analysis of it is Joseph Schumpeter's *Capitalism, Socialism, and Democracy*, published in 1942, and I organize my discussion around an examination of the debates between Schumpeter and his critics. Like many liberal constitutionalists, Schumpeter was keenly aware of the potential for the legitimate exercise of power to atrophy into illegitimate forms of domination. The liberal constitutionalist impulse is to try to wall power off by limiting the sphere of collective action. This is not an approach, I argue, that is attractive or even coherent when viewed through the prism of the power literature. More plausible is the Schumpeterian impulse to control power by making it the object of electoral competition. In this, I argue, he delivers more effectively than anything that can be found in *The Federalist* on the Madisonian aspiration to ensure that "ambition will be made to counteract ambition" (Hamilton, Madison, and Jay [1788] 1966: 160).

Schumpeter's critics fall into two groups: those who think his competitive democracy desirable but insufficient and those who think it undesirable. I argue that, when compared with the going alternatives, wholesale rejections of Schumpeterianism are unpersuasive. Those who are hostile to Schumpeterian democracy usually value agreement and consensus more than competition, whether because of beliefs about what deliberation can do, or convictions that unanimity is inherently desirable, or because competition is thought to lead to destabilizing conflict. I argue that all three rationales for preferring consensus-based to competitive conceptions of democracy are wrongheaded. We do better, instead, to conceive of bipartisan agreement in antitrust terms as collusion in restraint of democracy. This is not to say that Schumpeterian democracy is without flaws, but I argue that the more fruitful path to addressing them involves exploring ways to make democracy more genuinely competitive than it is, to expand its reach beyond governmentalist institutions, and to supplement it with complementary institutional devices. I discuss a variety of ways in which this can be done, better to structure power relations so as to minimize domination. Inter alia, this involves supplementing the idea of nondomination with a principle of affected interest, geared to ensuring that there is genuine competition by decision-makers for the votes of those who are actually affected by their decisions.

If Schumpeterian democracy needs supplementation, questions arise: what should it consist of, and who should do the supplementing? Debates about these issues are taken up next. Because there are no perfect decision rules, a purely procedural scheme like competitive majority rule can produce self-defeating results. Most obviously, majorities can use their power to undermine democratic freedoms by abolishing opposition and undermining future political competition. The evidence suggests that the likelihood of this occurrence is often exaggerated, but the possibility exists and democratic procedures can in any case have perverse consequences in a host of subtler ways. Yet the difficulty with those who would question the procedural results of majority rule is that they do not—and in all likelihood cannot—agree on a "substantive" standard by reference to which those results can be measured. In this situation I argue that the best solution is to agree with those who propose a middle-ground approach, in which courts or other second-guessing institutions should play a reactive, escape-valve, role in limiting the perverse consequences of democratic procedures when they produce results that foster domination. Defending this view leads me into a discussion of alternative ways for courts to behave in democratic systems. I argue that their legitimacy appropriately varies with the degree to which they act in democracy-sustaining ways, and I supply a variety of examples of what this means in practice in the American context.

This is followed, in chapter 4, by a consideration of the literatures on democratic transitions and consolidation. The scholarship in this area prompts the thought that the state of democratic theory is a bit like the state of Wyoming: large, windy, and mainly empty. It reveals that we know something about some of the necessary conditions for some democratic transitions, but that there are numerous possible paths to democracy, and that we should not be looking for a single general theory—certainly not a predictive one. The scholarship also reveals that we know something about the economic preconditions for viable democracy, but, notwithstanding the confident assertions of numerous commentators, we are mainly in the dark about the cultural and institutional factors that influence democracy's viability. Prudence suggests that it is nonetheless wise to try to inculcate support for democracy among those who operate it, though it is far from clear just how important this is, or, indeed, how best to accomplish it.

It is often claimed that certain types of societies, to wit, "deeply divided" ones, are inherently incapable of democracy. I explore this claim in some depth, finding it unsupported by either evidence or convincing theoretical argument. Too often, arguments about divided societies operate as rationalizations for resisting democratization and sustaining domination. Nonetheless, I argue for an incremental approach, given the dearth of reliable knowledge about the adaptability of politicized identities to the requirements of competitive democracy, and I survey the different ways in which reform of electoral systems might be pressed into the service of this goal. This raises normative questions about the circumstances under which group aspirations merit deference in democratic polities. I take these questions up in the final section of chapter 4, analyzing them from the interest-based perspective geared to limiting domination developed in chapters 2 and 3.

Some potential sources of domination come from within the political system; others come from outside it. Perhaps the most important one of these derives from economic vulnerability to the power of others. This subject is of particular interest from the standpoint of democratic theory because many nineteenth-century thinkers—both defenders and critics of democracy—believed that imposing majority rule with a universal franchise on democracy in highly inegalitarian societies would lead the poor to soak the rich. This intuition was formalized in the twentieth-century political science literature via the median voter theorem, which predicts that in highly inegalitarian settings the median voter will vote for downward redistribution. In chapter 5, I take up the puzzle presented by history's having demurred. This is reflected in the reality that in the United States today the bottom fifth of the population either lives in poverty or is in imminent danger of so doing. Not only is there no systematic relationship between expanding the franchise and downward redistribution of income or wealth, but democracies often engage in regressive redistribution—sometimes with strong bipartisan support.

Whatever justice-related reasons one might have for concern about this, I argue that we have democratic reasons as well—given that so large a segment of the population is vulnerable to domination. I examine the relationship between democracy and distribution first from the supply side, where I explore institutional and other factors that impede the kinds of political competition that would be expected to lead to more redistribution to the bottom quintile of the population. Then I turn to the demand side, looking to issues concerning beliefs, information, ideologies, framing effects, and the psychology of interpersonal comparisons in accounting for the relative dearth of demand for downward redistribution. I also consider the counterintuitive hypothesis that the more unequal a society, the less likely it is that there will be effective demand for downward redistribution, for reasons having to do with the physical separation between rich and poor, the opening up of what I describe as empathy gulfs between them, and structural incentives for the rich and the middle classes to marginalize the poor. Like many other areas in the study of democratic politics, this is one in which a great deal of research remains to be done. But, in light of what we do know and can reasonably surmise, I advance a variety of suggestions for viable reforms that would make the American political system more responsive to the interests of the poor, undermining their vulnerability to domination. By that token at least, these reforms would move us a little closer to a genuine democracy than can the system we have at present.

Aggregation, Deliberation, and the Common Good

Underlying the normative literature on democracy is a series of debates about rationality. They revolve around the question whether the classic democratic notions of a "will of the people" or "common good" have any coherent meaning. The idea that democracy does or should converge on a rationally identifiable common good finds its locus classicus in Jean-Jacques Rousseau's *Social Contract,* and in particular in his contention that decision procedures should reveal a general will that embodies the common good. Rousseau ([1762] 1968: 72) famously, if vaguely, characterized this by saying that we start with "the sum of individual desires" and subtract "the plusses and minuses which cancel each other out"; then "the sum of the difference is the general will." Attempts to make sense of this formulation have spawned two literatures, an aggregative literature, which has been geared to finding out just how we are supposed to do the relevant math, and a deliberative literature, which has been partly motivated by impatience with the aggregative one. Deliberative theorists are concerned with getting people to converge on the common good where this is understood more robustly than as a totting up of exogenously fixed preferences.

In §1.1 I make the case that proponents of aggregative conceptions of the common good are right that Rousseau's formulation of the problem cannot be solved, but that considerably less turns on this failure, for democratic politics, than they often suppose. The expectation that a general will should be discoverable rests upon implausible expectations of collective rationality and a misconstrual of what stable democratic politics requires. Turning to proponents of deliberative conceptions in §1.2, I argue that they share a touching faith in deliberation's capacity to get people to converge on the common good. Sometimes people's interests are irreducibly at odds, precluding this possibility. Moreover, in the world of actual politics people confront one another in massively unequal power contexts—in the United States most obviously owing to the role of money in politics. Deliberation theorists tend to confuse problems associated with the unequal power contexts in which deliberation occurs with a deliberative deficit, mistaking the doughnut for the hole. Some contend that what is of interest for democratic politics is what deliberation would produce under ideal, noncoercive, conditions. I doubt that we can answer such questions. In any case I argue that, if such conditions prevailed, the facts about politics that lead people to call for deliberation would no longer obtain.

1.1 AGGREGATIVE CONCEPTIONS OF THE COMMON GOOD

At least since Plato's time, political theorists have warned that democracy fosters mob rule rather than the common good. As the franchise expanded over the course of the nineteenth century, Alexis de Tocqueville ([1835] 1969: 246–61) and John Stuart Mill ([1859] 1978: 4) also cautioned against democracy's propensity to lead to the "tyranny of the majority." In this they echoed Rousseau's concern that a majority might satisfy its members' interests at the expense of the minority ([1762] 1968: 73) and Madison's (Hamilton, Madison, and Jay [1788] 1966: 122–28) discussion of the dangers presented by "majority factions" in *Federalist* No. 10.

1.1.1 Democracy's Alleged Irrationality

Modern social choice theorists have held that the problem is worse than these classical authors realized in that majority rule can lead to arbitrary outcomes and even to minority tyranny. They agree that the goal of democratic decision procedures should be to discover something like a general will, referred to in the modern idiom as a social welfare function, but, following Kenneth Arrow (1951), they argue that this is impossible. Extending an old insight of the Marquis de Condorcet ([1785] 1972), Arrow showed that under some exceedingly weak assumptions, majority rule leads to outcomes that are opposed by a majority of the population. For instance, if voter I's ranked preferences are A > B > C, voter II's are C > A > B, and voter III's are B > C > A, then there is a majority for A over B (voters I and II), a majority for B over C (voters I and III), and a majority for C over A (voters II and III). This outcome, known as a voting cycle, violates the principle of transitivity, generally taken to be an essential feature of rationality because it permits a self-contradictory ranking of societal preferences. Moreover, it opens up the possibility that whoever controls the order of voting can determine the outcome, provided she knows the preferences of the voters. Even if outcomes are not consciously manipulated, they might nonetheless be arbitrary in the sense that, had the alternatives been voted on in some order other than they actually were, the result would have been different. In short, democracy might lead to tyranny of the majority, but it might also lead to tyranny of a strategically well placed minority or to tyranny of irrational arbitrariness.[1]

Notice that power relations enter into aggregative conceptions of the common good only implicitly, and then in an implausible fashion. The presumption behind trying to render the Rousseauist project coherent is that if it cannot be done, then collective decisions that *are* taken amount to illicit impositions masquerading as democratic decisions. And since there is a wide consensus in the literature that the project cannot be rendered coherent, the libertarian implication, that collective action of all kinds should be limited as much as possible, is held by libertarians such as Riker, Weingast, Buchanan, and Tullock to follow from this result (see Shapiro 1996: 30–42).

Fear of tyranny by majority factions led Madison and the Federalists to devise a political system composed of multiple vetoes in order to make majority political action difficult: a separation-of-powers system in which "ambition will be made to counteract ambition" (Hamilton, Madison, and Jay [1788] 1966: 318). This included an independent court with the power to declare legislation unconstitutional and a president whose election and hence legitimacy are independent of the legislature; strong bicameralism in which legislation must pass both houses and in which two-thirds majorities in both houses can override the president's veto power; and a federal system in which there is constant jurisdictional tension between federal and state governments. The findings in the post-Arrovian social choice literature have led commentators such as Riker and Weingast to endorse this multiplication of institutional veto points on the possibility of governmental action, arguing that courts should hem in legislatures as much as possible, lest they compromise individual rights, particularly property rights, with irrational and perhaps manipulated collective decisions.[2]

Yet we can grant Arrow his victory over Rousseau without being persuaded of the merits of these ossifying institutional arrangements. The decisive question, after all, is compared to what? Arrow's finding deals not merely with majority rule. His theorem shows that, given the diversity of preferences he postulates, his modest institutional conditions, and his unexceptionable constraints on rationality, *no* mechanism will produce a

---

[1] The most comprehensive and accessible, if somewhat dated, review of this literature is Mueller (1989). See also Shapiro (1996: 16–52) and Przeworski (1999).

[2] Riker (1982), Riker and Weigast (1988). On the ways in which multiplying veto points limit the possibilities of governmental action, see Tsebelis (2002).

rational collective decision. Libertarians suppose that the alternative is to minimize governmental action as much as possible, but that is inadequate for two reasons. First, it is mistaken to suppose that making governmental action difficult limits collective action. Perhaps owing to their proclivity for thinking in a social contract idiom, libertarian commentators often write as if "not having" collective action is a coherent option in societies that nonetheless have private property, enforcement of contracts, and the standard panoply of negative freedoms. The recent experience of postcommunist countries such as Russia should remind us that these are costly institutions requiring continual collective enforcement (see Holmes and Sunstein 1999). The libertarian constitutional scheme is a collective action regime maintained by the state, one that is disproportionately financed by implicit taxes on those who would prefer an alternative regime. The more appropriate question, then, is not "whether-or-not collective action?" but rather "what sort of collective action?"

Second, liberal constitutionalists like Riker and Weingast (1988) tend to focus on potential institutional pathologies of legislatures, while ignoring those of the institutions that they would have curb legislative action. At least in the United States, courts are themselves majoritarian institutions. There is every reason to believe they would be at least as vulnerable to cycles as legislatures, and possibly even more susceptible to manipulation. Chief justices, who have considerable control over court agendas and the order in which issues are taken up, know a good deal about their colleagues' preferences, owing to the fact that they decide many closely related cases, and personnel turnover is incremental and slow. In theory judges are constrained by doctrines and precedents, but, as Oliver Wendell Holmes insisted, much of the time these can be rendered consistent with any outcome by a sufficiently enterprising judge.[3] Indeed, it may be that less of the information pertinent to manipulation is available in a Senate of 100, a third of whom are up for election every two years, or a House of Representatives of 435, all of whom are up for reelection every two years—not to mention the population at large. True, high incumbent reelection rates slow down turnover of legislators, and much of their work is done in smaller committees. Granting this, there is still no reason to

---

[3] Holmes used to taunt his colleagues on the bench by challenging them to name any accepted judicial rule or precedent they liked; he would then show it could be rendered consistent with either outcome in the case at hand. See Menand (2001: 339–447).

believe them more susceptible than courts to the potential for arbitrary or manipulated outcomes identified by Arrow.[4]

1.1.2 Competing Views of Rational Collective Decision

More important, perhaps, than these weaknesses in the liberal constitutionalist critique of democracy are the expectations about what would be a nonarbitrary decision-making outcome. Arrow may have established that often there may be no such thing as a Rousseauian general will, but why should we be troubled by that? Transitivity may well be a reasonable property of individual rationality, but it is far from clear that it makes sense to require it of collective decisions. If the New York Giants beat the Dallas Cowboys, who in turn beat the Washington Redskins, no one suggests that the Redskins should not play the Giants lest the principle of transitivity be violated. Deadlocked committees sometimes make decisions by the toss of a coin—arbitrary, perhaps, but necessary for collective life to go on. In such circumstances it matters more that each contest or decision mechanism was perceived to be fair than that a different outcome might not have occurred on a different day (see Mueller 1989: 390–92).

If we abandon the expectation that there is a Rousseauian general will or social welfare function waiting out there to be discovered like a Platonic form floating in metaphysical space, we might nonetheless be persuaded of the merits of majority rule for decision making in many circumstances. As I argue below, one reason to favor it is that it promotes competition of ideas. Another is that majority rule can contribute to political stability just because it institutionalizes the perpetual possibility of upsetting the status quo. Theorists such as Di Palma (1990: 55) and Przeworski (1991: 10–12) note that it is institutionalized uncertainty about the future that gives people who lose in any given round the incentive to remain committed to the process rather than reach for their guns or otherwise become alienated from the political system. This will not happen when there is a single dominant cleavage in the society, as when a majority of the population has identical preference orderings. Such a preference structure will forestall an Arrovian cycle, but at the price of turning loyal opposition (where the democratic system is endorsed though the government of the day is opposed) into disloyal opposition, where those who lose try to overthrow the system itself.

[4] See Easterbrook (1982) and Murphy (1964). For a more general argument that if voting really is as meaningless as Riker claims, this undermines his "liberalism" just as much as the "populism" he attacks, see Coleman and Ferejohn (1986).

Generalizing this, Nicholas Miller (1983: 735–40) has noted that there is a tension between the notion of stability implicit in the social choice literature since Arrow, where various restrictions on preferences are intended to prevent cycling, and the pluralist idea of stability that turns on the presence of crosscutting cleavages of interest in the population. The periodic turnover of governments is facilitated by just the kind of heterogeneous preferences that create the possibility of cycling. Indeed, students of comparative politics often contend that competitive democracy does not work when heterogeneous preferences are lacking. If the preference-cleavages in the population are not sufficiently crosscutting to produce this result, they propose alternative institutional arrangements, such as Arend Lijphart's "consociational democracy" (1969, 1977), which includes entrenched minority vetoes and forces elites representing different groups to govern by consensus as a cartel, avoiding political competition.[5]

1.1.3 The Likelihood of Cycles

Closer inspection thus reveals that the possibility of voting cycles is not especially troubling, and it may even be advantageous for the stability of democratic institutions. How likely it is that cycles actually occur is another matter. I have already noted that they are ruled out if an absolute majority has identical preferences. Various other constraints on preferences will also reduce their likelihood or eliminate them (Mueller 1989: 63–66, 81–82). At least one theoretical result suggests that cycles are comparatively unlikely in large populations even when preferences are heterogeneous (Tangian 2000), and an exhaustive empirical study by Gerry Mackie (2003) has revealed almost every alleged cycle identified in the social choice literature to be based on faulty data or otherwise spurious.[6] It may be that democracies turn out to enjoy the best of both worlds. The possibility of cycles gives those who lose in any given election an incentive to remain committed to the system in hopes of prevailing in the future, but the fact that cycles are actually rare means that government policies are not perpetually being reversed (Tullock 1981).[7] In the area of tax policy, for instance, there is undoubtedly a potential coalition to upset every

[5] I leave for §§4.1.3 and 4.1.4 discussion of the empirical difficulties associated with determining whether preferences in a population are mutually reinforcing or crosscutting, and how, if at all, they can be transformed from the former into the latter.

[6] See also Green and Shapiro (1994: 98–146).

[7] For the argument that institutions reduce the likelihood of cycles, see Shepsle and Weingast (1981).

15

conceivable status quo, as one can see by reflecting on a society of three voting to divide a dollar by majority rule: whatever the distribution, a majority will have an interest in changing it. Yet tax policy remains remarkably stable over time (Witte 1985).

In short, despite the considerable attention to the possibility of voting cycles in the social choice literature, there are few reasons to see them as undermining the attractiveness of majoritarian democracy. Once we abandon the Rousseauist expectation that collective action should be guided by a general will or social welfare function, we can see numerous reasons for thinking that democratic constraints on collective action might nonetheless be desirable. This becomes evident once we remind ourselves that power is exercised willy-nilly in social life; that hamstringing government privileges one set of collective arrangements, however implicitly; that institutions for containing democracy's "irrationality" may be no less susceptible to "irrational" behavior than the legislatures they are intended to limit; that it is unclear how likely cycles are in fact; and that in any case we have not been given good reasons to think that the rational stability prized by democracy's post-Arrovian critics is desirable. On the contrary, there may be good reasons to avoid it.

1.1.4 Privileging Unanimity Rule

If the findings in the public choice literature are less threatening to democracy's legitimacy than is often assumed, what of the more traditional worry about the tyranny of the majority associated with the arguments of Tocqueville and Mill and the countermajoritarian elements that the Framers built into the American Constitution? Tocqueville's forecasts were particularly apocalyptic on this point. "Formerly tyranny used the clumsy weapons of chains and hangmen," he noted, yet "nowadays even despotism, though it seemed to have nothing more to learn, has been perfected by civilization." The possibility of majority tyranny struck him as the greatest threat posed by democracy in America. Quoting Madison's worry in *Federalist* No. 51 that "in a society under the forms of which the stronger faction can readily unite and oppress the weaker, anarchy may truly be said to reign," Tocqueville opined that "if ever freedom is lost in America, that will be due to the omnipotence of the majority driving the minorities to desperation and forcing them to appeal to physical force." The result might be anarchy, as Madison said, "but it will have come as a result of despotism" (Tocqueville [1835] 1969: 255, 260).

An influential theoretical response to this danger put forward by James Buchanan and Gordon Tullock builds on the Framers' impulse to make some rights and liberties more difficult than others to change by majority rule. Deploying the style of reasoning that John Rawls would later make famous, they asked what decision rules mutually disinterested citizens would choose at a constitutional convention where everyone is uncertain "as to what his own precise role will be in any one of the whole chain of later collective choices that will actually have to be made." Whether selfish or altruistic, each agent is forced by circumstances "to act, from self-interest, *as if* they were choosing the best set of rules for the social group" (Buchanan and Tullock 1962: 78, 96).[8] Thus considered, they argued, there is no reason to prefer majority rule to the possible alternatives. Collective decision making invariably has costs and benefits for any individual, and an optimal decision rule would minimize the sum of "external costs" (the costs to an individual of the legal but harmful actions of third parties) and "decision-making costs" (those of negotiating agreement on collective action). The external costs of collective action diminish as increasingly large majorities are required; in the limiting case of unanimity rule, every individual is absolutely protected since anyone can veto a proposed action. Conversely, decision-making costs typically increase with the proportion required, since the costs of negotiation increase. The choice problem at the constitutional stage is to determine the point at which the combined costs are smallest for different types of collective action, and to agree on a range of decision rules to be applied in different future circumstances (Buchanan and Tullock 1962: 63–77).

At least three kinds of collective action can be distinguished, requiring different decision rules. First is the initial decision rule that must prevail for other decision rules to be decided on. Buchanan and Tullock "assume, without elaboration, that at this ultimate stage . . . the rule of unanimity holds." Next come "those possible collective or public decisions which modify or restrict the structure of individual human or property rights after these have once been defined and generally accepted by the community." Foreseeing that collective action may "impose very severe costs on him," the individual will tend "to place a high value on the attainment of his consent, and he may be quite willing to undergo substantial decision-

[8] One indicator of the work's influence is that when Buchanan was awarded the Nobel Prize for economics almost a quarter-century after its publication in 1986, the citation singled out "his development of the contractual and constitutional bases for the theory of economic and political decision-making." http://www.nobel.se/economics/laureates/1986/ [9/3/02].

making costs in order to insure that he will, in fact, be reasonably protected against confiscation." He will thus require a decision rule approaching unanimity. Last is the class of collective actions characteristically undertaken by governments. For these "the individual will recognize that private organization will impose some interdependence costs on him, perhaps in significant amount, and he will, by hypothesis, have supported a shift of such activities to the public sector." Examples include provision of public education, enforcement of building and fire codes, and maintenance of adequate police forces. For such "general legislation" an individual at the constitutional stage will support less inclusive decision rules, though not necessarily simple majority rule, and indeed within this class different majorities might be agreed on as optimal for different purposes. "The number of categories, and the number of decision-making rules chosen, will depend on the situation which the individual expects to prevail and the 'returns to scale' expected to result from using the same rule over many activities." Requiring high levels of agreement enables people to protect their interests, they say, but this takes time that could be spent on other activities. In effect they come up with a sliding scale. Democracy is best suited to issues of moderate importance on their account. Issues of high importance should be insulated from it, while issues of low importance might even be delegated to administrators (Buchanan and Tullock 1962: 73–77).

This argument is defective in various ways that need not concern us now (see Shapiro 1996: 19–29). The point to note here is that Buchanan and Tullock's initial bias in favor of unanimity rule turns on two dubious assumptions that make democracy look less attractive than it should. First there is the social contract fiction already alluded to: that there could be an initial stage in which only private action prevails in society—without being underwritten by collective institutions. The second defect arises even if we engage in the thought experiment Buchanan and Tullock propose. Unanimity as a decision rule has the unique property, they argue, that if decision-making costs are zero, it is the only rational decision rule for all proposed collective action.[9] But this argument confuses unanimity

---

[9] This is not strictly true if vote trading is allowed. Under that assumption, and also that there are no decision-making costs, there is no optimal decision rule for the same reason as Coase showed that, in the absence of information costs, wealth effects, external effects, and other blockages to exchange such as free riding, no system of tort liability rules is more efficient than any other. Whatever the system, people will then make exchanges to produce Pareto-optimal results. See Coase (1960: 1–44). Assuming, however, that a pure market in votes does not exist, and Buchanan and Tullock acknowledge that some constraints on it are

qua decision rule with unanimity qua social state, that is, a condition in the world where everyone actually wants the same outcome. Douglas Rae has pointed out that from the standpoint of their constitutional convention it makes more sense to assume that we are as likely to be ill disposed toward any future status quo as well disposed toward it, and that in cases where we are ill disposed, a decision rule requiring unanimity will frustrate our preferences. Buchanan and Tullock assume throughout that it is departures from the status quo that need to be justified, but Rae shows that this is not warranted. Externalities over time, or "utility drift" (Rae's term), may change our evaluations of the status quo. We may feel in certain circumstances that failures to act collectively, rather than collective action itself, should shoulder the burden of proof (Rae 1975: 1270–94).[10] People may change their minds for other reasons, foreseen or unforeseen, or someone might be opposed to, and not wish to be bound by, a status quo that was the product of the unanimous agreement of a previous generation. Indeed, Rae has shown formally that if we assume we are as likely to be against any proposal as for it, which the condition of uncertainty at the constitutional convention would seem to require, then majority rule or something very close to it is the unique solution to Buchanan and Tullock's choice problem (Rae 1969: 40–56, 51).[11]

1.1.5 The Likelihood of Majority Tyranny

Ultimately it is an empirical question whether majoritarian democracy is more likely than the going alternatives to produce tyranny. Robert Dahl (2002) has recently reminded us that in the century and a half since Tocqueville articulated his fears, the individual rights and political freedoms that he prized have turned out to be substantially better respected in democracies than in nondemocracies. The countries in which there is meaningful freedom of speech and of association, respect for personal and property rights, prohibitions on torture, and guarantees of equality before the law are overwhelmingly the countries that have democratic political systems. Even if we expand the definition of individual rights to include social and economic guarantees, one could not make a credible case that

---

inevitable, they maintain that unanimity would uniquely be chosen in the absence of decision-making costs (1962: 270–74).

[10] See also Barry ([1965] 1990) and Fishkin (1979: 69).

[11] When the number of voters is odd, the optimal decision rule is majority rule, n over two, plus one-half; when n is even, the optimal decision rule is either majority rule (n over two plus one), or majority rule minus one (simply n over two).

nondemocracies supply these better than do democracies.[12] This subject is, of course, difficult to study empirically, because most of the world's wealthy countries, with the resources for meaningful socioeconomic guarantees, are also democracies, and the failures of the communist systems arguably had at least as much to do with their economies as with their political systems. Yet one would scarcely want the Tocquevillian case to rest on the communist example, where civil and political freedoms were substantially less well respected than in democracies, and the level of social provision was generally low. At a minimum one is bound to conclude that the Tocquevillian case has not been established, and that the converse of it seems more likely to be true, to wit, that democracy is the best known guarantor of individual rights and civil liberties.

On the question whether constitutional courts make a difference among democracies, in the United States there have certainly been eras when the federal judiciary has successfully championed individual rights and civil liberties against the legislative branch of government, that of the Warren Court being the best known.[13] But there have also been eras when it has legitimated racial oppression and the denial of civil liberties (see Smith 1997: 165–409). Until recently there has been surprisingly little systematic study of this question beyond the trading of anecdotes. As early as 1956 Dahl had registered skepticism that democracies with constitutional courts could be shown to have a positive effect on the degree to which individual freedoms are respected when compared to democracies without them, a view he developed more fully in his seminal article "Decisionmaking in a Democracy: The Supreme Court as National Policymaker" (Dahl 1997:

[12] The sociologist Terence Marshall (1965: 78) famously distinguished three types of increasingly comprehensive rights. *Civil* rights include "the rights necessary for individual freedom—liberty of the person, freedom of speech, thought and faith, the right to own property and conclude valid contracts, and the right to justice [the right to assert and defend one's rights]." *Political* rights include "the right to participate in the exercise of political power, as a member of a body invested with political authority or an elector of the members of such a body," and by *social* rights Marshall meant "the whole range from the right to a modicum of economic welfare and security to the right to share in the full social heritage and to live the life of a civilized being according to the standards prevailing in the society." Marshall was more optimistic than the historical record has turned out to warrant in that he conceived of societies as moving from civil to political to social citizenship rights as they modernized.

[13] There are terminological issues at stake here on which substantive issues turn. For instance, in the *Lochner* era the Supreme Court struck down much legislation in the name of protecting individual freedoms, but the legislation in question was aimed at increasing social and economic guarantees—promoting civil rights at the expense of social rights, in Marshall's terminology discussed in footnote 12 above. See *Lochner v. New York*, 198 U.S. 45 (1905). For discussion of the *Lochner* era, and for a general discussion of the evolution of American constitutional law through the years of the Warren Court (1953–69), see Tribe (1978).

279–95). Subsequent scholarship has shown Dahl's skepticism to have been well founded (see Dahl 1956: 105–12, 1989: 188–92, Tushnet 1999, Hirschl 1999). Indeed, there are reasons for thinking that the popularity of independent courts in new democracies may have more in common with the popularity of independent banks than with the protection of individual freedoms. They can operate as devices to signal foreign investors and international economic institutions that the capacity of elected officials to engage in redistributive policies or interfere with property rights will be limited. That is, they may be devices for limiting domestic political opposition to unpopular policies by taking them off the table (Hirschl 2000).

This is not to deny that there may be an appropriate role for second-guessing institutions, such as courts, in majoritarian systems. Ways of thinking about courts that reinforce democracy rather than wall it in are explored in chapter 4. It is to say, however, that the fear that majority rule would become the engine of majority domination has not been borne out historically. Indeed, those on the ideological left who hoped that the "parliamentary road to socialism" would be achieved by the majority appropriation of what they saw as the minority's ill-gotten gains through the ballot box have been sorely disappointed. The reasons for this are taken up in chapter 5.

1.2 DELIBERATIVE CONCEPTIONS OF THE COMMON GOOD

The literature on deliberative democracy is to some extent a reaction to dissatisfaction with the aggregative literature, but not for its inattention to the questions about power and collective action that we have been considering. The aggregative literature concerns itself with how to do the math to solve Rousseau's problem; proponents of deliberative democracy are also in search of the common good. But they hope to get to it by transforming preferences rather than aggregating them. It is not really a Rousseauist project (Rousseau had no faith in deliberation as a useful political device). However, it owes something to his injunction that people should vote not their individual preferences but rather their perceptions of what is good for the society as a whole.[14] The goal is to move us "beyond adversary democracy" (Mansbridge 1980).

---

[14] For Rousseau voting was a means of disciplining private interest by getting people to focus on what is best for society as a whole. As he put it, "When a law is proposed in the people's assembly, what is asked of them is not precisely whether they approve the proposition or reject it, but whether it is in conformity with the general will which is theirs; each, by casting his vote, gives an opinion on this question" (Rousseau [1762] 1968: 153).

People advocate deliberation for different reasons. Some think it inherently worthwhile. More commonly deliberation is valued for instrumental reasons: achieving consensus, discovering the truth, and consciousness-raising are among the usual suspects. Some of the time, at least, deliberation promotes these and related values. But it also has costs. Wasted time, procrastination and indecision, stalling in the face of needed change, and unfair control of agendas are among its frequent casualties. Sometimes by design, sometimes not, deliberation can amount to collective fiddling while Rome burns. If deliberation is not always and everywhere an unmitigated good, how do we determine the conditions under which it is desirable?

Deliberative remedies are put forward in response to various maladies that are perceived as pervading contemporary democracy. Poor quality of decision making, low levels of participation, declining legitimacy of government, and ignorant citizens are among the more frequently mentioned. Advocates of deliberative democracy such as Gutmann and Thompson (1996) and Ackerman and Fishkin (2002) argue for the merits of deliberation by pointing out how little of it there is in contemporary politics dominated by superficial television campaigns and political advertising. The idea is that if we can get away from the soap opera of electoral one-upmanship, more thoughtful and effective political choices will result. Deliberative forums can range from town meetings, to designated deliberation times, to citizen juries and "deliberative polls"—randomly selected groups who become better informed about particular issues and render decisions as to what should be done (Fishkin 1991). On some accounts such entities should inform existing processes; on others they should replace them en route to instituting a more robust participatory politics. The unifying impulse motivating these proposals is that people will modify their perceptions of what society should do in the course of discussing this with others. The point of democratic participation, on this account, is more to manufacture the common good than to discover it. Indeed, deliberative theorists sometimes write as if the activity of searching for the common good is itself the common good (see Shapiro 1996: 109–36). Some deliberative democrats do not go this far, but usually they do assume that if people talk for long enough in the right circumstances, they will agree more often, and this is a good thing.

1.2.1 Reciprocal Deliberation as the Common Good

One influential account of how deliberation might work in practice has been put forth by Gutmann and Thompson in their much discussed book

Democracy and Disagreement. There they argue for a view of deliberation that is designed to minimize disagreement when this is possible, and to get people to accommodate themselves to one another's views, maintaining "mutual respect," when it is not. Drawing on the idea of reciprocity, they argue for a view of deliberation in which citizens "aspire to a kind of political reasoning that is mutually justifiable," each making claims that the others will accept. They do not claim that deliberation will vanquish all moral disagreement in politics, but they expect it to reduce disagreement and help people who disagree better to converge on mutually acceptable policies. Even when it does not resolve disagreement, it can "help citizens treat one another with mutual respect as they deal with the disagreements that invariably remain." Gutmann and Thompson claim that the lack of deliberation is not limited to public debate alone. It is also reflected in academic commentary on democracy, which is "surprisingly silent about the need for ongoing discussion of moral disagreement in everyday political life. As a result, we suffer from a deliberative deficit not only in our democratic politics but also in our democratic theory." Moreover, we are "unlikely to lower the deficit in our politics if we do not also reduce it in our theory" (Gutmann and Thompson 1996: 2–12, 52–53, 346).

To know how effective Gutmann and Thompson's deliberative model would be, at either reducing moral disagreement or promoting accommodation of irresolvable differences in American politics, one would have to see it in action in debates among pro-lifers and pro-choicers, parties to the *Mozert v. Hawkins* litigation over school textbooks that parents believe violate their children's free exercise of religion,[15] or protagonists in debates over redistricting, affirmative action, welfare reform, child-support, and the other contentious political issues that Gutmann and Thompson describe. Their claim is that if the various protagonists "seek fair terms of cooperation for their own sake," committing themselves to appeal, in their arguments, "to reasons that are recognizably moral in form and mutually acceptable in content," then such disagreements will be minimized and accommodation will be promoted (Gutmann and Thompson 1996: 53, 57). They report how they believe these and other public policy debates ought to come out when the model is applied, or, in some cases, that it cannot resolve them. This is different, however, from demonstrating that it would actually happen in practice. Gutmann and Thompson do offer qualified praise of some actual deliberative processes, such as the 1990 meetings that were held in Oregon to help set health care priorities for

[15] *Mozert v. Hawkins County Board of Education*, 827 F.2d 1058 (6th Cir. 1987).

Medicaid recipients (see §1.2.2 below). But they fail to mention any actual deliberative process that does not fall significantly short of their deliberative ideal. Accordingly, the claim that their model would have the beneficial effects claimed for it remains speculative.

Sometimes, perhaps, people might better resolve differences and accommodate themselves to views they reject by more deliberation of the prescribed sort. But what reason is there to suppose that failure to attempt this is the principal reason why the public policy issues they examine are not resolved along the lines Gutmann and Thompson advocate? It is one thing to think that much of what divides people politically is susceptible to rational analysis more often than people realize; quite another to believe that what prevents better resolution of prevailing disagreements is insufficient deliberation of the Gutmann-Thompson sort. They give a plausible account of the nature of some moral disagreements and of possible argumentative strategies for constructive responses to them when protagonists are appropriately inclined, but their account attends too little to the role of power relations and conflicts of interest in politics.

The main reason for Gutmann and Thompson's call for more deliberation is that there seems to be so little of it in the political debate they observe. "In the practice of our democratic politics, communicating by sound bite, competing by character assassination, and resolving political conflicts through self-seeking bargaining too often substitute for deliberation on the merits of controversial issues" (Gutmann and Thompson 1996: 12). But sound-bite politics and media-driven campaigns may well result principally from the powerful American antipathy toward publicly financed elections and the concomitant influence of private money in politics. This would presumably remain in a world of expanded deliberative institutions, given the Supreme Court's 1976 declaration that regulating political expenditures is an unconstitutional interference with free speech.[16] Any credible defense of deliberative democracy in the American context would have to show how deliberative institutions would be any less corrupted than are existing institutions by those with the resources to control agendas and bias decision making, and that it would merit its cost.

Gutmann and Thompson are not alone in treating deliberation as a panacea. Consider, for instance, Bruce Ackerman and James Fishkin's (2002: 129–52) proposal for "deliberation day," to be held a week before

---

[16] In *Buckley v. Valeo*, 424 U.S. 1 (1976), the Court held, inter alia, that although Congress may regulate financial contributions to political parties or candidates, it cannot otherwise regulate private expenditures on political speech. The Court has since allowed some

national elections. On this proposal all citizens would be paid $150 to show up at their local school or community center to deliberate. According to its proponents this would cost $15 billion a year in public funds—not to mention the indirect costs to the economy. It is hard to see what benefit would result from so vast an expenditure of funds once candidates had been selected, platforms chosen, interest groups deployed, and campaign funds expended. By contrast, $15 billion a year spent to support fledgling third parties or publicly financed elections might attenuate many of the pathologies that lead people to call for more deliberation.[17]

These considerations aside, it is far from clear that deliberation exhibits the felicitous political properties that proponents attribute to it. As Gutmann and Thompson concede at one point, sometimes deliberation can promote disagreement and conflict. The cases they have in mind are moral issues that arouse intense passions, paradigmatically the issues liberals have sought to defuse politically since the seventeenth-century wars of religion. Skeptics of deliberation in these areas proceed from the assumption that there are "moral fanatics as well as moral sages, and in politics the former are likely to be more vocal than the latter." Gutmann and Thompson's response is that although moral argument "can arouse moral fanatics," it can also "combat their claims on their own terms." Deliberation undermines moral extremists, who "must assume that they already know what constitutes the best resolution of a moral conflict without deliberating with their fellow citizens who will be bound by the resolution." In the everyday political forums "the assumption that we know the political truth can rarely if ever be justified before we deliberate with others who have something to say about the issues that affect their lives as well as ours." Accordingly, they conclude with a presumption in deliberation's favor: "By refusing to give deliberation a chance, moral extremists forsake the most defensible ground for an uncompromising position" (Gutmann and Thompson 1996: 44–5).

Alluring as this reasoning might be to many of us, it is difficult to imagine a fundamentalist's being much impressed by it—particularly when she

---

minor constraints on corporate expenditures in *Austin v. Michigan State Chamber of Commerce*, 110 S. Ct. 1391 (1990), but for all practical purposes the *Buckley* rule makes it impossible to limit privately funded political advertising.

[17] Ackerman and Fishkin (2002: 148) insist that "it is a big mistake to view the annualized cost of $15 billion through the lens of standard cost-benefit analysis" on the grounds that its "large" benefits "cannot be reckoned on the same scale as other elements in the cost-benefit equation." Even if we were to concede that the benefits could coherently be declared to be large at the same time as they are said to be incommensurable with their costs, their claim ignores the point stressed here: that its benefits surely should be weighed against other ways in which such a sum could be spent to enhance American democracy.

learns that any empirical claims she makes must be consistent with "relatively reliable methods of inquiry." Nor will she be much comforted by Gutmann and Thompson's gloss to the effect that this does not "exclude religious appeals per se" (why not, one wonders?), so long as these do not include taking the Bible literally. The reason for this latter constraint is that "virtually all contemporary fundamentalists subject biblical claims to interpretation, accepting some as literally true and revising the meaning of others. To reject moral claims that rely on implausible premises is therefore not to repudiate religion" (Gutmann and Thompson 1996: 56). If the syllogistic force of this claim was not lost on the fundamentalist in the abstract, surely it would be once it was explained to her that it denies her the right to insist on the literal truth of *any* particular biblical imperative. She will rightly expect to come out on the short end of any deliberative exchange conducted on that terrain. The Gutmann-Thompson model works only for those fundamentalists who also count themselves fallibilist democrats. That, I fear, is an empty class, destined to remain uninhabited.

Gutmann and Thompson are plausibly skeptical of those, like Owen Fiss and Ronald Dworkin, who believe that courts are better suited to achieving principled resolution among contending moral perspectives in the public realm than are other political institutions. Neither a compelling theoretical argument nor any persuasive evidence has ever been adduced in support of this view. Contrary to what they seem to suppose, however, this is scarcely relevant to the standard constitutionalist argument for avoiding, or limiting, public deliberation about intense—particularly religious—differences. This does not turn on any illusion that courts can resolve them in a principled fashion, but rather on the recognition that no one can. The idea is that their explosive potential is so great that it is better, for the welfare of both religious adherents and the democratic polity, if they are kept out of organized politics as much as possible, subjected to what Stephen Holmes (1995: 202–35) describes as "gag rules." Hence the First Amendment's Establishment Clause. That is the serious constitutionalist case against promoting attempts to resolve religious disagreements in the public sphere. Perhaps there is a reply to it from the deliberative democratic perspective, but Gutmann and Thompson do not supply it.

1.2.2 Deliberation and Conflicting Interests

Gutmann and Thompson's acknowledgment that deliberation might move politics away from the agreement and accommodation they value skirts the tip of a large iceberg. Beyond the issue of uncompromising religious values, people with opposed interests are not always aware of just how opposed those interests actually are. Deliberation can bring differences to the surface, widening divisions rather than narrowing them.[18] This is what Marxists hoped would result from "consciousness-raising": it would lead workers to discover their interests to be irreconcilably at odds with those of employers, assisting in the transformation of the proletariat from a class-in-itself to a revolutionary class-for-itself. In the event, these hopes proved naive. The general point remains, however, that there is no particular reason to think deliberation will bring people together, even if they hope it will and want it to. A couple with a distant but not collapsing marriage might begin therapy with a mutual commitment to settling some long-standing differences and learning to accommodate one another better on matters that cannot be resolved. Once honest exchange gets underway, however, they might unearth new irreconcilable differences, with the effect that the relationship worsens and perhaps even falls apart in acrimony. Deliberation can reasonably be expected to shed light on human interaction, but this may reveal hidden differences as well as hidden possibilities for convergence. It all depends on what the underlying interests, values, and preferences at stake actually are.

Gutmann and Thompson's inattention to the contending interests at stake is most evidently revealed in their discussion of health care reform in Oregon in the early 1990s. Rationing of health care procedures for the nonelderly poor by the legislature followed a series of "town meetings" in which citizens and various health professionals were asked to rank medical procedures.[19] The object was to find a way of settling disagreements about priorities in health care insurance, given the hard choices that public budget constraints impose. Gutmann and Thompson note that this procedure was flawed because the plan covered only the nonelderly poor. They describe this as a "basic injustice" that "may have adversely influenced the surveys and community meetings, which in any case fell short of the delib-

---

[18] See Simon (2000) and Sunstein (2002) for discussion of empirical conditions under which deliberation leads to divergence rather than convergence of opinion.

[19] The participants were asked to rank categories of treatment by importance and articulate the values that guided their decisions. The state legislature then used the list as a yardstick to appropriate Medicaid funds. The Oregon Plan was intended to expand Medicaid eligibility from 68 percent of those at the federal poverty level to 100 percent, and to finance the increased cost by prudent rationing of procedures. Although Oregon did end up expanding coverage to some 126,000 new members by February 1997, much of this was actually achieved by appropriation of new funds by the legislature rather than from savings generated by the deliberations about rationing priorities. See Daniels (1991) and Montague (1997: 64–66).

erative ideal." Yet they commend the process on the grounds that it "forced officials and citizens to confront a serious problem that they had previously evaded—and to confront it in a cooperative ('first person plural') spirit." They go on to claim that the process helped ameliorate the underlying injustice, because when the legislators "finally saw what treatments on the list would have to be eliminated under the projected budget, they managed to find more resources, and increased the total budget for health care for the poor" (Gutmann and Thompson 1996: 143–44).

Notice that the legislature's decision to appropriate additional funds was unrelated to the substance of the deliberative meetings, which never dealt with what the overall budget should be or how health care resources should be traded off against other demands on the state treasury. It was not a product of reciprocal deliberative exchange whereby citizens with moral disagreements came closer together. It was, rather, a fortunate externality, for the uninsured poor, of the deliberative process—such as it was—in that the publicity it generated helped spotlight their plight in the media and the legislature. If this is the proffered defense of the Oregon process, one would have to compare it to other ways in which the condition of the uninsured poor might have been publicized with similar or better effect—such as publicity campaigns, public protests, or class action lawsuits. This issue, however, does not bear on Gutmann and Thompson's defense of deliberation: that it reduces disagreement and increases mutual accommodation of differences that cannot be resolved.

In fact, as a device for settling disagreements about how hard choices should be made in the rationing of health care resources, the Oregon deliberative process was a notable failure. Gutmann and Thompson acknowledge, as have others, that it is hard to find a relationship between the final rankings of medical procedures and the results of the deliberative process, which eventually became little more than a vehicle for public outrage at attempts to introduce a measure of prudence into Oregon's health care priorities (see Hadorn 1991). Nonetheless, Gutmann and Thompson conclude that the deliberations "evidently helped citizens, legislators, and health care professionals arrive at an improved understanding of their own values—those they shared and those that they did not." But whose values are we really talking about? The "citizens, legislators, and health care professionals" by and large excluded those who would be covered under the Oregon plan: the nonelderly poor. This is not to speak of the injustice which Gutmann and Thompson acknowledge—that in effect this choice was really about "making some poor citizens sacrifice health care that they need so that other poor citizens can receive health care they need even more urgently, while better-off citizens can get whatever treatment they need." Rather, the question is this: why should we attach any legitimacy at all to a deliberative process that involved very few of those whose health care priorities were actually being discussed?[20] Gutmann and Thompson themselves make a similar point in criticizing workfare and welfare reform later in the book. There they suggest the need for participatory processes that "encourage the participation of economically and educationally disadvantaged citizens" (Gutmann and Thompson 1996: 143–44, 303–6). That seems right so far as it goes. But, as I argue in §1.3 below, it needs to be taken further.

Only part of the infirmity in these cases is that those who must live with the results go more or less unrepresented in the decision making; the other part is that most of those making the decisions know that they will never depend on the good whose rationing or provision is under discussion. In countries like Britain and Canada, where the great majority of the population use collectively rationed medical services, their participation in democratic decision making through the political process lends legitimacy to the resulting policies. By contrast in Oregon, upwards of 80 percent of the population is unaffected by the rationing program (see Daniels 1991: 2233–34). The general point here is that the legitimacy of decision-making processes varies with the degree to which they are both inclusive and binding on those who make them. Deliberative processes are not exceptions. Gutmann and Thompson acknowledge this in principle. They define political decisions as collectively binding, adding that "they should therefore be justifiable, as far as possible, to everyone bound by them" (Gutmann and Thompson 1996: 13). However, their discussion is not sensitive to the reality that different people are differently bound by collective decisions. When there is great variation in the impact of a decision, then interests diverge in ways that are relevant to the assessment of the decision's legitimacy.

This is most obviously true when there are substantial differences in the capacities of different groups to escape the effects of policies on which they are deciding. Those who can easily avoid them do not have the same kind of interest at stake in a decision as those whose exit costs are prohibitively high. The story of apartheid in American public schools

---

[20] Daniels (1991: 2234) reports that the meetings were attended predominantly by "college educated, relatively well off, and white" audiences, half of which consisted of health professionals. Of the attendees 9.4 percent were uninsured (whereas 16 percent of the state's population was uninsured at the time), and Medicaid recipients (among other things the only direct representatives of poor children) were underrepresented by half.

attests eloquently to what happens when this goes unrecognized. Urban public schools are starved of resources by white middle-class voters who opt out either fiscally, to private schools, or physically, to suburban schools (see Hochschild 1984). It should be added that the latter may live in towns that are paragons of deliberative democracy. In 1995, for instance, a statewide Connecticut plan to reduce school segregation was duly deliberated upon at great length in New England town meeting after New England town meeting in which the inner-city residents of Hartford and New Haven had no effective voice at all. As a result, their interests were simply ignored and the plan was easily defeated (see McDermott 1999: 31–53). Gutmann and Thompson place great stress on the importance of adequate elementary and secondary education, like adequate health care, in providing the necessary basic opportunities for living in a democracy. But they seem not to appreciate that as deliberation operates on the ground in what Douglas Rae (1999: 165–92) has described as the "segmented democracies" that Americans increasingly inhabit, it is often an obstacle to providing these goods. When there are great differences in capacity for exit, what is often needed is not widespread deliberation but action to protect the vulnerable.

1.2.3 The Context of Deliberation

Another weakness in the deliberative literature concerns its relative inattention to what shapes the terms of deliberation in modern democracies. To the extent that more deliberation would be a healthy thing in the formation of public policy, the principal obstacle often is not the lack of will on the part of people with differing moral convictions to deliberate in ways that can minimize their differences. Rather, the obstacle results from decisions by powerful players who make it their business to shape the terms of public debate through the financial contributions they make available to politicians and political campaigns. Engels once described ballots as "paper stones." In the post–*Buckley v. Valeo* world, when all credible political campaigns require multimillion-dollar war chests to buy the requisite television time to do political battle, public deliberation all too often consists of verbal stones hurled across the airwaves, with victory going to whoever has the most bountiful supply. Granted, this is a long way from what Gutmann and Thompson have in mind when they advocate deliberation, but it is surely curious that a book about the importance of enhancing deliberation in contemporary American politics can ignore the reality it creates.

For instance, in their discussion of the failure of the Clinton administration's attempt at national health care reform, Gutmann and Thompson seek to lay blame on the secret meetings of Hillary Clinton's Task Force on National Health Care Reform, along with other unmentioned factors. Endorsing the claims of critics who, at the time, said that support for the plan would be more difficult to achieve "if the policy makers did not show that they were responding to criticisms and taking into account diverse interests in the process of formulating the plan," they conclude that even when "secrecy improves the quality of a deliberation, it may reduce the chances that a well-reasoned proposal will ever become law" (Gutmann and Thompson 1996: 117). Perhaps the secret meetings contributed something to the failure, along with the Clinton administration's ineptitude in failing to enlist the support of essential Capitol Hill barons like Senators Moynihan and Nunn, their inability to come to grips with the sheer economic scope of the proposal (12 percent of a $3 trillion economy),[21] and the structural deficit inherited from the Reagan and Bush administrations.[22] But how can anyone who lived through the huge amounts of public misinformation that contributed to the steady decline in the bill's popularity, and its eventual abandonment by the administration, not be struck by the importance of the $50 million public relations and lobbying campaign that the medical, insurance, and other corporate establishments waged to kill the legislation?[23]

We need not quarrel with Gutmann and Thompson's contention that secrecy is generally a bad thing in government to ask how much it had to do with the failure of health care reform in 1993 and 1994. Secrecy's importance seems *de minimus* when compared to the way the options were presented in the war of words on television and the activities of political lobbyists. They ensured that important options (notably a Canadian-style single payer system) were never seriously discussed, and that the entire debate came to focus on issues that were irrelevant to the bill's basic goal of achieving universal health care coverage. Arguments about the feasibility of managed competition and the freedom people might or might not have in selecting their own physicians dominated the discussion, as the plight of the 40 million uninsured fell by the wayside. It is difficult to see how any aspect of Gutmann and Thompson's "deliberative deficit" was responsible for this, since the problem had nothing to do with reaching

---

[21] See Marmor (1994: 2–3, 184).

[22] For accounts of the failure, see Hacker (1997) and Skocpol (1997).

[23] The $50 million figure is reported by Rinne (1995: 4–5). See also Hamburger and Marmor (1993: 27–32).

agreement among the contending views or finding an accommodation among those who could not agree. Rather, the problem was that some of what ought to have been the contending views never confronted one another in the public mind. How else is one to explain the fact that a single payer system could not be seriously mooted, even at the start of the public debate, despite a substantial body of academic commentary which suggests that it is by far the most cost-effective way of achieving affordable universal coverage?[24]

For anyone perturbed by the Clinton health care debacle, worrying about how money structured the debate should be high on the list of concerns. Yet Gutmann and Thompson never mention it. Perhaps they would say their book is simply not concerned with this subject, but that is difficult to square with their insistence that their focus is on "the everyday forums of democratic politics," differentiating their deliberative perspective from other academic discussion, which is said to be "insensitive to the contexts of ordinary politics: the pressures of power, the problems of inequality, the demands of diversity, the exigencies of persuasion." As my discussion has indicated, their own account pays surprisingly little attention to these very features of politics. They are heartened by the fact that although "the quality of deliberation and the conditions under which it is conducted are far from ideal in the controversies we consider, the fact that in each case some citizens and some officials make arguments consistent with reciprocity suggests that a deliberative perspective is not utopian" (Gutmann and Thompson 1996: 2–3).

We should not be so easily fortified. Unless it can be shown that these arguments can be made on a sufficient scale and can garner enough institutional force to influence the ways politics is structured by powerful interests, it is difficult to accept the suggestion that deliberation will lead people to converge on the common good through reciprocal recognition of one another's valid claims. The decisive role played by money in politics means that politicians must compete in the first instance for campaign contributions and only secondarily for the hearts and minds of voters. By ignoring this, Gutmann and Thompson attend too little to the ways in which power relations influence what deliberation should be expected to achieve in politics.

Likewise with the Ackerman-Fishkin proposal for "deliberation day." The chances that this could have an impact on actual political options seem negligible. In addition to ignoring the role of campaign expendi-

---

[24] See the papers collected in Marmor (1994).

tures, it ignores candidate selection, conventions, platforms, and interest group activities. Perhaps these difficulties might be mitigated if deliberative mechanisms were injected into the political process much earlier than a week before Election Day and structured to have an impact on the ways in which resource inequalities shape political outcomes. That Ackerman and Fishkin do not even consider such possibilities underscores the extent to which they conflate lack of deliberation with power contexts within which deliberation takes place.

1.3 DELIBERATION IN IDEAL SETTINGS?

Fishkin's proposal for deliberative polls raises comparable worries. They differ from his joint proposal with Ackerman in that they are intended to take place in structured settings in which power inequalities are rendered immaterial: participants are randomly selected and paid for their participation. To be sure, such deliberative polls offer certain advantages, particularly with respect to the trade-off between the costs of deliberation in terms of time and the benefits in terms of sophisticated understanding of complex issues. The idea—which actually goes further than Fishkin suggests—that some political decisions might be devolved to such groups is an innovative one. Perhaps they could develop democratic legitimacy for reasons analogous to those attending the legitimacy of juries. Indeed, one group that organizes such polls, the Jefferson Center in Minneapolis, calls them "citizen juries."[25] Yet proponents of deliberative polls and citizen juries fail to address obvious questions that are pertinent to their democratic legitimacy. Who decides which issues should be presented to these groups for discussion, and, possibly, decision? Who sets the agenda? The "experts" who testify before the randomly selected groups are supposed to be "balanced," but who does the balancing, and who decides what criteria they should use? Participation in deliberative polls and citizen juries might alter people's views, but without satisfactory answers to these questions it is hard to see why we should have much confidence that they have been altered for the better, or that they are owed any particular deference in a democracy.

Other deliberative theories have been developed that abstract from actual politics even more thoroughly than do deliberative polls and citizen juries. Jürgen Habermas's (1979, 1984) "ideal speech situation," for ex-

---

[25] See the Jefferson Center's Web site at www.jefferson-center.org [9/3/02].

ample, appeals to a model of uncoerced speech that is divorced from the power considerations of actual politics, as does Bruce Ackerman's (1980) dialogic model of justice. Proponents of these theories believe that they can establish what political institutions, arrangements, and policies would be agreed upon in ideal deliberative conditions. In this their endeavor is analogous to Rawls's (1971) enterprise of trying to determine what basic structure of political institutions people would chose behind a veil of ignorance designed to factor out self-interest. As my discussion of Buchanan and Tullock in §1.1.4 indicated, you cannot derive something from nothing, and it is scarcely surprising that writers in the Rawlsian tradition reach different results depending on the assumptions about human nature and the causal structure of the social world that are fed into their models (see Shapiro 1986). For present purposes notice that these are solipsistic theories, geared to answering this question: what institutions or arrangements would a rational person choose under specified ideal conditions?[26]

The ideal deliberative theories confront the additional difficulty that if, *per impossible*, this question could be answered unequivocally for one person, then presumably it could be answered for everyone. But what, then, would be left for deliberation? Ideal deliberative theorists are caught on the horns of a dilemma. Either they must concede that their speculations about what would be chosen under ideal deliberative conditions are indeterminate, prompting one to wonder, as with Gutmann and Thompson's speculations, what purpose they can serve in the actual world. Alternatively, they might claim that skepticism about their ability to demonstrate what outcomes authentic deliberation would converge on is misplaced. But in that case deliberation adds no value.

[26] On the differences between the Habermas and Rawls, see their exchange: Habermas (1995) and Rawls (1995).

Deliberation against Domination?

T HAT DELIBERATION is not the cure-all proponents often believe it to be does not mean it is worthless in politics. But how should we think about its appropriate role in promoting the common good? Given the difficulties we have confronted with the aggregative and deliberative notions of it considered thus far, I propose that we operate with a stripped-down conception of it—suggested by Machiavelli rather than Rousseau. In *The Discourses* Machiavelli intimates that the common good is that which those with an interest in avoiding domination share.[1] Perhaps a more robust notion of the common good can plausibly be defended, but this is a bedrock commitment that most plausible theories of justice and democracy share (Shapiro 1999a: 1–63). If we embrace it, the question whether deliberation promotes the common good is reframed as the question whether it diminishes domination.

To begin answering it, I turn, in §2.1, to the power literature. It is more suggestive than instructive because for the most part its practitioners have ignored institutional arrangements. Either they have seen them as irrelevant to power's operation, or the preoccupation with epistemological questions has diverted theorists of power from exploring the institutional implications of their own views. Even theoreticians who agree on a particular theory of power have not been much moved to explore its implications for institutional design or normative theory. Rather, they have been concerned to defend their theories against critics—for instance, by showing that the so-called second and third faces of power that deal with the shaping of agendas and preferences can be studied in empirically rigorous ways, or that structural theories capture features of power that have been missed in the "faces" debate. Worthwhile as these activities might be, they leave unanswered the question: how should considerations about power feature in theorizing about democracy? I begin addressing it in §2.2 by developing an account of a potential role for deliberative institutions that piggybacks on significant insights gleaned from the power literature. My account

---

[1] See his consideration, in *The Discourses*, of the Roman argument that the common people should be made the guardians of freedom because, unlike the aristocracy whose desire is to dominate, their desire is not to be dominated. Machiavelli ([ca. 1517] 1970: 1.5).

turns on the recognition that although power relations are involved in everything we do, they are never the totality of what we do. The challenge is to devise ways to manage the power dimensions of human interaction that limit domination while minimizing interference with the nonpower dimensions. Both prudence and the myriad disadvantages of imposed solutions suggest that, where possible, deliberation should be pressed into the service of this goal.

Strengthening deliberative rights and institutions poses a double risk, however, that concerns me in §§2.3 and 2.4. They can be used by the powerful to prevaricate and procrastinate, in effect furthering domination rather than undermining it, and the institutional means to promote deliberation might merely lead to bargaining. I argue that the second danger becomes less troubling to the extent that we deal well with the first: by limiting the right to demand increased deliberation to those who are vulnerable in a given situation because their basic interests are at stake. If this leads merely to increased bargaining, there may be a cost in that better solutions that might have come about through the creative cooperation characteristic of deliberation will be missed. But at least that cost will not have to be internalized by those most vulnerable to domination; in that sense it remains a desirable, if suboptimal, outcome. This conclusion sets the stage for a more general discussion of political institutions, in chapter 3, from my power-centered perspective.

2.1 THINKING ABOUT POWER

One group of theorists, perhaps best dubbed epiphenomenalists, ranges from Marx ([1844] 1972: 26–52) to Mosca (1939), Michels (1962), and Mills (1956). For all their manifold differences, they share an assumption that power always trumps institutional arrangements, rendering the latter inherently uninteresting as an object of study. On their views, domestication of power relations is impossible. Power relations evolve, displacing one another over time, but they are never eliminated. As a result, collective life remains power and domination all the way down.[2] Indeed, it is notable that even those who challenged them, such as Dahl (1961), had little to say about democracy in connection with that challenge. *Who Governs?* seeks to establish that different elites make different decisions in American

[2] See Laclau and Mouffe (1985), and Hayward (2000) for illustration and discussion of this view.

cities, but it is scarcely the place one looks for a defense of Dahl's democratic principles. And Dahl's "behavioral" theory of power, like the critical and supplementary literatures it spawned, is exclusively concerned with how to define power and how to identify it empirically.

To be sure, the different theories in the faces-of-power debate have implications for thinking about institutional design. Adherents of the first "face" will attend principally to decision making, while those of the second "face" are more likely to focus on questions about agenda setting, and those of the third "face" to the factors that might repress preferences that would otherwise be expressed and acted on.[3] Yet even within the constraints of these competing ontologies of power, adherents have not spelled out the institutional implications of their views—on how decisions *should* be made, how agenda-setting power *should* figure into the debates about institutional reform, or how quiescence *should* be dealt with when it is identified. One scarcely needs to work through the intricacies of these debates to reach the conclusion that any credible democratic theory will need to attend to decision making, agenda control, and the conditions under which preferences are formulated and expressed.[4] Beyond this, perhaps specific implications for institutional design could be drawn out of the faces-of-power debate, but no one has actually done so.

The recent European tradition of thinking about power has also largely ignored institutional arrangements, partly because of its roots in Marxism, and partly because it, too, has operated almost exclusively on the terrains of ontology and epistemology to define and identify power. Moreover, the substantive claims that have come out of this literature, from Marcuse's (1965: 81–117) discussion of repressive tolerance to Foucault's (1977, 1980, 1982) insistence that power is ubiquitous and ineliminable, have not led to, or even facilitated, discussion of better and worse ways of managing power relations. Perhaps toleration is a desirable feature of democracy even if it is repressive, but critical theorists like Marcuse never con-

[3] For theorists of the "first face" such as Dahl (1956) and Polsby (1960, 1963), power is usually understood in terms of prevailing in a decision-making process. Following Bachrach and Baratz (1962, 1970), theorists of power's "second face" point out that control of, and access to, the agenda often shapes outcomes. Finally, such "third face" theorists as Lukes (1974) note that power can determine people's very perceptions of the preferences they can articulate. This debate is well surveyed in Lukes (1974), Gaventa (1980: 3–32), and Hayward (2000).

[4] Nor, it should be said, is it true that proponents of the second face, such as Bachrach and Baratz, held that democratic theory could ignore issues concerning the expression of preferences (they were silent on this subject), or that proponents of the first face thought agenda setting or preference expression could be ignored. Dahl explicitly takes both into account in his writings on democracy. (For a concise summary, see Dahl 1979: 97–133).

37

cerned themselves with such questions. Similarly, Foucault's writing has made an effective case in support of the proposition that power relations are ubiquitous and ineliminable, but it is not clear what, if anything, follows from this for discriminating among alternative institutional possibilities. True, commentators in the Foucauldian tradition have sometimes defended democracy for the "agonistic" reason that it promotes contestation (Hayward 2000: 173–74). However, if relations of domination, hydralike, defy all attempts to domesticate them, as Foucault argues, it is far from clear that there is any point to contestation. Even if, *per impossible*, one was persuaded of the contrary, there is nothing in Foucault's corpus to tell us which institutional arrangements are better, and which worse, at producing the requisite contestation.

A partial exception to this generalization is Clarissa Hayward's *De-Facing Power*, based on an impressive synthesis of a Foucauldian view of power as inhering in networks of social boundaries and the systematic case-study research characteristic of the Anglo-American power literature. Hayward makes a convincing case that domination is minimized to the degree that freedom is enhanced, where this is understood as enabling people to shape their own fields of possible action. Following from this, she argues that political institutions "should be structured such that their effects on other social practices and institutions are freedom-promoting." But she says nothing about how this is to be achieved, beyond noting that the state "has significant influence over which social practices and institutions survive and flourish," and that democratic norms and practices "are defined in part by social boundaries to action, including egalitarian values and norms of respect for self-determination, that promote both inclusiveness in the collective determination of social possibility and some degree of mutability in power relations" (Hayward 2000: 177).

We can agree with Hayward's contention that democratic and egalitarian norms "can be invoked to draw attention to the contradictions between the constitutive principles and the practical effects of these particular practices and institutions" (2000: 177). Nonetheless, this is a slim beginning for thinking about just how this should happen in particular contexts, and which norms might be more and less effective in enabling people to enhance their freedom to shape the fields in which they act collectively so as to limit domination. Taking that next step, or series of steps, is one of the more important challenges for democratic institutional engineering.

I deploy the formulation "series of steps" to emphasize that the view that power relations are ubiquitous overreaches in two respects: by failing to discriminate among different ways in which power is exercised (the subject I take up in chapter 3), and by equating the valid observation that power suffuses all collective life with the implausible claim that all collective life is reducible to power relations. To say that power relations suffuse contexts as various as workplace, family, and church is not to deny that things go on in all these areas other than exercises of power. Producing goods and services may often, and perhaps inevitably, involve power relations; as may pursuing intimacy, affection, education, and spiritual fulfillment. But they are not themselves power relations. The challenge for democratic theorists in this area is to devise mechanisms for structuring the power dimensions of human interaction so as to minimize domination while limiting interference with these other activities as much as possible. The conditions under which deliberation might be expected to facilitate this goal are taken up in §2.3. First, we must more fully explore the distinction between power relations and the activities they infuse.

2.2 INSIDERS' WISDOM AND SUPERORDINATE GOODS

Deliberation's benefits are not unequivocal, as I have noted. They depend on many contingencies of circumstance, and sometimes deliberation creates costs that outstrip its advantages. This reality leads to difficulties for would-be third-party institutional designers: often they do not know how much and what sorts of deliberation will enhance other activities. For instance, even if increasing certain types of deliberation within firms would make them more efficient, why suppose that a government planner will know what these are? It seems better to suppose that those involved in operating firms will know this, or have an incentive to find it out. Should they fail, while their competitors succeed, they will succumb to market discipline. Likewise with sports teams. If certain kinds of deliberation enhance performance, teams that engage in them will win, and those that fail will pay the price. These examples suggest the wisdom of opting for a presumption in favor of insiders' wisdom: we should assume that those skilled in a particular activity are more likely than anyone else to know how to do it well, and, a fortiori, to know how much and what sorts of deliberation are most likely to enhance it. Insiders' wisdom is pertinent, we may say, to the pursuit of superordinate goods: the purposes for which people strive from which they derive meaning and value.[5]

[5] For elaboration, see Shapiro (1999a: 12, 80–81, 92, 116, 132).

A presumption in favor of insiders' wisdom is not a presumption against insisting that the pursuit of collective activities be accompanied by deliberative institutions. It requires only that the purpose, and hence the justification, for such insistence is not enhanced pursuit of the activity in question. There are other reasons for requiring deliberation, as we will see, linked to the reality that we exercise power over one another in the course of pursuing superordinate goods. Managing the power dimensions of our activities well requires a distinctive kind of insiders' wisdom about what I describe as the subordinate good of democratic control. Government should aspire to be knowledgeable about this, and deliberation is sometimes pertinent to it. But that claim differs from the thesis that the superordinate goods people pursue are to some degree distinguishable from the power relations in which they are enmeshed, and that, to the extent that this is so, they should be immune from government's reach.

Now it might be objected that my discussion so far depends on the misleading examples of economic efficiency and winning at sports. They have comparatively uncontroversial bottom lines by which success and failure can be judged: the firm makes, or fails to make, profits; the team wins or loses. But the purposes of many collective activities are more contentious and at any rate less clear. Evaluating scholarship in the context of tenure promotions at universities is notorious in this regard, at least in the social sciences and the humanities. One person's brilliant insight is the next person's banal truism, and the bottom line—such as it is—is measured by slippery reputational rankings that come loaded with performative freight: the best people are the best people because those reputed to be the best people declare that they are, and sometimes for no reason other than that. Apparently objective criteria, such as citation indexes, are easily manipulated by cliques of insiders, controlling the definitions of their own success. An external bottom line might at some point substantiate or undermine their judgments, but this can take decades or even generations to eventuate, and in some instances it will not be forthcoming at all.

This is a serious concern, not least because many collective human activities may have more in common with academic evaluation than with winning at sports or making firms profitable. But it cuts no ice with respect to my present argument. There are no more good reasons to believe government officials capable of second-guessing evaluations of Elizabethan poetry or different kinds of social science, however difficult this might be, than there are reasons to believe them capable of knowing how best to run firms or sports teams. Again, government may have a legitimate role to play in ensuring that these evaluations do not masquerade as something other than they are; that topic is taken up in §2.3. Contentious as it might be for insiders to agree on what makes for the best literature or social science, this is scarcely a reason to suppose that someone lacking insiders' wisdom will do a better job. Textualists and contextualists disagree on how to read books; postmodernists and statisticians disagree on how to conduct social research. Serious as these disagreements may be, they will not be diminished by supposing that Jesse Helms can know which side, if either, is right.

Another possible objection to the preceding argument takes off from the observation that even when those who control firms generally agree on how they should be run, they could be wrong. Arguments to the effect that economywide investment decisions are destructively geared to the short term, that managers systematically undermine the interests of share-holders, and that buyers loot and destroy profitable firms in certain types of corporate buyouts all rest on convictions that this can be the case. Such possibilities should not be discounted. It is important, however, to distinguish arguments for intervention designed to protect the interests of vulnerable employees from arguments that assume outsiders know how to run firms most efficiently—let alone that they know when increased deliberation within the firm contributes to this goal. Too little deliberation might lead to inefficiencies, but so might too much deliberation (see Hansmann 2000). Asking the question whether deliberation is a good thing is a bit like asking the question whether a saw is a good tool. If you are making shelving, it is, but not if you are trying to repair a watch.

What about the institutions of government? In a democracy people are supposed to govern themselves. Perhaps the government should be severely constrained in requiring deliberation of us, but it does not follow that we should be similarly constrained in requiring deliberation of the government. This view implausibly hearkens back to the ancient Greek comprehension of democracy as ruling and being ruled in turn. The doctrine of representative government developed as a response to the impracticality of that notion in a world of large nation-states, populations in the tens and hundreds of millions, and an advanced division of labor. It also reflects a partial concession to the idea that governing is an activity within the division of labor that involves distinctive competencies. The modern term *democratic control* suggests an independent activity that is subjected to democratic constraint. In this respect, democratic control of the government is not qualitatively distinct from democratic control of the firm: there are insiders, often but not always career professionals, who are expected to have expert competence yet also to be constrained by democracy.

Outsiders are no more thought competent to insist that Supreme Court justices should deliberate before voting to grant or deny certiorari than to insist that managers should deliberate before investing in a new line of products. Likewise with the jealously guarded House and Senate rules, the frequency or duration of cabinet meetings, or the arcane practices surrounding the Senate filibuster. Such practices may be reformed from time to time in ways that make them more or less deliberative, but this is scarcely in response to outside pressure for more deliberation. These types of rules for conducting government business are part of the superordinate good about which those with the experience are assumed to have the relevant insiders' wisdom.

However, governing does differ from running firms, families, churches, and other collective endeavors in that a substantial part of the superordinate good involved *is* the exercise of legitimate power in a given territory or domain. This provides the warrant, discussed in §3.2, for control of politicians via democratic competition for power. It also suggests one reason for valuing opposition rights that might issue in increased deliberation, taken up in §2.3: to protect the vulnerable from imposed solutions. But this differs from mandating increased deliberation on the theory that it promotes good government generally. Outsiders are no better placed to know that this is true than what amounts and kinds of deliberation are optimal in any other walk of life.

What of the suggestion that increased deliberation among citizens should be instituted by government on the grounds that it is inherently, rather than instrumentally, valuable? It may well be good for people to deliberate more rather than less, up to some point, depending on what else they seek to, or must, accomplish. We should expect this to vary from person to person. The argument that more deliberation is always good calls to mind a group of political junkies sitting in a meeting discussing the dynamics of their last meeting, or the therapist who declares that in the best of all possible worlds everyone would always be in therapy.

No doubt there are plausible conceptions of the human condition supporting the idea that deliberation is inherently worthwhile. For instance, someone might endorse a neo-Hegelian philosophical psychology according to which intersubjective recognition is the highest stage of being.[6] We become truly human, on such views, only in justifying ourselves to one another. Deliberation is then seen as intrinsic to that activity, rather than to be evaluated by reference to whether it contributes to, or detracts

[6] On Hegel's account of recognition, see Hegel ([1807] 1949: 229, 645, 650, 660).

from, other activities. This is one credible view of the human condition, to be sure, but there are others, and it is difficult to see why it should be privileged over those other views. Dissidents might not want to embrace the robust demands on citizenship it suggests, and there is no reason that they should be compelled to do so. This is not to prevent true believers from deliberating with like-minded others for whom this is an important, perhaps even the most important, superordinate good.

Deliberation that is defended for its inherent benefits is best seen by government, then, as a consumption good; people should be free—but not forced—to engage in it. This is not to say that government should have no interest in it. People with intense preferences for deliberation might be able to exert disproportionate influence on outcomes by monopolizing control of agendas, or simply by virtue of the comparatively large amount of time they devote to politics (see Sirianni 2001, 1993: 283–312). When such thresholds are crossed, we have too much deliberation, but it is difficult to know just when this occurs. From the perspective developed here, this type of deliberation should be treated like any other superordinate good. How to approach it, given the advantages of insiders' wisdom and government's cognitive limitations, is taken up next.

2.3 LIMITING DOMINATION THROUGH DELIBERATION

Decisions about how to pursue superordinate goods are best left to those with the relevant insiders' wisdom, but their freedom to make them should not be unfettered. The warrant for this claim has already been noted: superordinate goods are bound up with power relations. This suggests an additional role for government in regulating the pursuit of superordinate goods. It is a conditioning role, however, not sought after for its own sake. Rather, it is pursued in order to limit, if it cannot eliminate, the possibility of domination in the course of people's pursuit of superordinate goods.

A helpful way to think about the appropriate circumstances in which government should try to institute deliberative mechanisms is Hirschmanesque: as the costs of exit increase, so does the importance of voice (Hirschman 1970). From this perspective we might say that the right to deliberative participation should vary with the degree to which people are trapped. If a stockholder is adversely affected by what a firm's management does, she can sell her shares, buying stock in a firm she finds more congenial. An adversely affected employee seldom has the same freedom of action; hence his stronger claim to deliberative participation. From this vantage point it is easy to see why the Oregon town meetings discussed in §1.2.2 were unsatisfactory. The elderly poor for whom the exit costs were high lacked effective voice in the process because most of them did not participate, while the majority of those participating in deliberations faced negligible exit costs because they had alternatives to Medicaid for health insurance. Having an effective voice varied inversely with exit costs instead of covarying with them.

Even when the affected party cannot participate in decision making, there are circumstances in which it is wise to insist on significant deliberation by others. Hence the unanimity requirement for juries in criminal cases, which is intended to encourage exceedingly thorough deliberation before someone can be convicted of a criminal offense. Decisions to terminate life support of the terminally ill belong in an analogous category: insisting that they be preceded by a deliberative process, perhaps one involving judicial oversight, is justifiable to protect the important interests of someone who cannot escape the effects of the decision.

When exit costs are low for everyone, there is no reason to require deliberation; by definition the interests at stake are not hostage to the decision. The same conclusion holds when exit costs are high for all and the interests at stake are the same. If all are equally affected by decisions, then it is reasonable to defer to insiders' wisdom concerning what decision rules to employ and how much deliberation, if any, is required. So long as all have equally strong interests at stake (as in an *ex ante* veil-of-ignorance decision by a healthy population about how to ration future organ transplants), then no one has power over anyone else by virtue of the decision-making procedure, and there is no reason for outsiders to second-guess it.

In reflecting on when it is appropriate to require deliberation, we should attend to the kind of interest at stake, not merely differences in exit costs. This becomes apparent when we consider the limitations of a rule that would link the right to insist on deliberation to the latter exclusively, perhaps by entitling those bearing the greatest costs to rights of delay, appeal, and even veto if the difference in exit costs is sufficiently large. To fix intuitions, think of South Africa's white minority before the democratic transition. They stood to lose vastly more than nonwhites (who in fact stood to gain) from the planned transition, because they had vastly more resources, status, and power than nonwhites. For the whites the costs of leaving were in this sense greater, but it does not follow that they should have been entitled to rights of delay, appeal, or veto in virtue of that fact.

Part of the reason for this is perhaps that their gains were ill gotten during apartheid, but that is not dispositive. After all, most gains are ill gotten if we go back far enough.

My suggestion is that it is when basic interests are at stake that such protections should be activated. We can think of people's basic interests by reference to the obvious essentials that they need to develop into and survive as independent agents in the world as it is likely to exist for their lifetimes. This conception belongs in the family of resourcist views, such as those put forward by Rawls (1971), Dworkin (1981), and Sen (1992), all of which affirm the importance of a list of basic or instrumental goods from the perspective of achieving multiple conceptions of the good life. These and other resourcist views differ from one another in ways that need not concern us here. Suffice it to say that even though they are self-consciously more pluralist with respect to competing conceptions of the good life than are views, such as utilitarianism, that impose a single conception, they invariably favor some conceptions and disfavor others and are for that reason not neutral among conceptions of the good life, as is sometimes claimed by their adherents (see Shapiro 1999a: 80–99, 186–90).

But we need not resolve these issues here, since my focus is limited to how the resources needed to vindicate basic interests are relevant to democratizing power relations. Anyone in a position to threaten a person's basic interests evidently has great power over him. An employer who can fire an employee in a world where there is no unemployment compensation has power of this kind. The employer may have vast interests at stake in the governance of a particular business, so that her exit costs might be greater in dollar terms should both decide (or be forced) to leave. But the employee has basic interests at stake in this example, whereas the employer is presumed not to; this is the justification for strengthening the employee's voice. It was embodied in the National Labor Relations Act of 1935, which rested on explicit recognition of "the inequality of bargaining power between employees who do not possess full freedom of association or actual liberty of contract, and employers who are organized in the corporate or other forms of ownership." The act responded to this situation by "encouraging the practice and procedure of collective bargaining and by protecting the exercise by workers of full freedom of association, self-organization, and designation of representatives of their own choosing, for negotiating the terms and conditions of their employment." It also imposed affirmative duties on employers to bargain with elected union representatives, and contained protections of closed shops, and other collective rights.[7]

Notice that it was not merely the bargaining-power disparity but the fact that employees were found to lack "full freedom of association" and "actual liberty of contract" that was decisive in the determination to enhance employee voice in this way. Employees were found to face what Marxists like to think of as structural coercion. In my terms, their basic interests were at stake. If we consider other areas where the law limits contractual freedom, similar considerations apply. Courts will not enforce prenuptial agreements that leave spouses destitute (though they will often enforce unequal agreements that do not have this effect). Nor will they enforce rental leases that void certain statutory protections for tenants, or agreements to sell one's body organs, or to sell oneself into indentured servitude or slavery.

How much "voice" such regulation creates varies. Some agreements (such as selling oneself into slavery) so obviously compromise basic interests that they are treated as void *ab initio*, regardless of the views of the parties. Others, such as certain types of leases, may be suspect and for that reason be challenged in court. This creates the possibility of obligatory deliberation, should the tenant feel aggrieved. In other settings, such as those covered by the NLRA, government seeks to mandate deliberation through an affirmative duty to bargain. Generally, we can think of institutional devices that seek to force deliberation as an intermediate form of regulation between proscriptive intervention and full deference to insiders' wisdom. As a normative matter we can say that the more one's basic interests are threatened, the stronger one's claim is to insist on deliberation, but that beyond some threat threshold even this is insufficient.

Saying just where that threat threshold lies is more difficult and often depends on contextual factors. Cases like slavery are conceptually easy. Most of the time, however, the tensions between protecting people's basic interests so as to limit domination and pursuing superordinate goods are more nebulous. Indeed, even when basic interests are threatened, it is not self-evident that governments are well placed to do much about it. This is one reason to press for deliberative solutions where they can be successful. The considerations adduced in my earlier discussion of the limitations on what governments can know will often extend, in practice, from the pur-

---

[7] Quotations from the Wagner Act taken from the *Legislative History of the National Labor Relations Act, 1935*, vol. 2 (Washington, D.C.: National Labor Relations Board, 1959), §§ 1, 7, 8, arts. 1–5, pp. 3270–74.

suit of superordinate goods to the protection of basic interests. In many situations, those with the relevant insiders' wisdom might well be better placed than external regulators to discover how best to accommodate tensions between the two. The difficulty arises when there are conflicts of interest about this matter, and those with the power lack the incentive to engage in deliberation to facilitate the relevant accommodation. By strengthening the hand of those whose basic interests are threatened, government can shift the balance of incentives indirectly without itself proposing solutions.

In this spirit we might, for example, replace proscription of voucher schemes in education with a solution in which parents of those who do not opt out of the public schools are given delay, appeal, or perhaps even veto rights, enabling them to insist on guarantees that promised benefits for their children's education do in fact eventuate. Those proposing voucher schemes would then have to engage in deliberation with them, take account of their concerns, and persuade them that these concerns could be dealt with. How strong their deliberative rights should be would still require an independent judgment as to how seriously threatened the children's basic interests in fact were, but not an exogenous adjudication of the merits of voucher schemes.[8] The goal would be to strengthen the hand of those whose children remain in the public schools sufficiently (but only sufficiently—that is the institutional design challenge) to ensure that they could extract the relevant guarantees, or compensation, from those advocating the change, while interfering as little as possible with its benefits for others. This, in turn, would supply those who wanted the change with the incentive to design it in ways that would work to the benefit of all, to provide fail-safe guarantees in case it did not, and to persuade those whose basic interests are at stake that they have done this. Achieving that would be a triumph for subordinate deliberation.

This approach recognizes the cognitive limitations of governments without abdicating their responsibility to regulate the power dimensions of social life so as to limit the possibility of domination. Rather than have government try to evaluate the merits of innovative funding schemes, in this example, it would use its power to make those who advocate them persuade those whose basic interests are most plausibly at stake. Structuring things to induce this kind of deliberation is useful because it gives

---

[8] I also assume, for present purposes, that there are not significant conflicts of interest between parents and their children about this matter. The possibility of such conflict is explored in Shapiro (1999a: 64–109).

those with the relevant insiders' wisdom the incentive to turn their creative energy to pursuing superordinate goods in ways that minimize domination over others. When this is successful, it constrains the sacrifice of vulnerable interests to the efficacious pursuit of superordinate goods. Strengthening the hand of the vulnerable in this way is intended to encourage the search for cooperative solutions when interests conflict, while maximizing the odds that these solutions do not come at the price of coerced agreement.

As the example of voucher schemes suggests, the preceding reasoning applies to government agencies no less than to other powerful players in society when their actions threaten basic interests. Rights of delay and appeal force power wielders to take account of threatened interests. An appropriate example of such a right would be the Supreme Court's 1970 decision *Goldberg v. Kelly* that welfare agencies may not terminate public assistance to the poor without a pretermination evidentiary hearing.[9]

Some, such as Pettit (2000: 105–46), would extend strong "contestatory" rights to all minorities in democratic systems to slow down decisions, and would insist that they be "edited in the application" in the interests of moving us closer to a world in which "what touches all" will be "considered and approved by all." Going this far re-creates the difficulties with unanimity discussed in §1.1.4. Unless we limit rights of delay to those whose basic interests are threatened, we privilege the status quo, making it impossible for government to prevent domination (see Van Parijs 1999 and Ferejohn 2000). Of course, defending any mechanism through which courts or other agencies may legitimately obstruct majority rule requires a justification for judicial review that does not appeal to the dubious countermajoritarian arguments discussed in §§1.1.1 and 1.1.5. Providing that justification is deferred to §§3.3 and 3.4.

2.4 DELIBERATION VERSUS BARGAINING

It will be objected that the means proposed here are less than adequate to achieve the end sought. I delimited my concern to the types of deliberation that government should seek to require. My proposal, that it should strengthen the hand of weaker parties whose basic interests are threatened in a variety of circumstances, is sufficient to guarantee more equal bargaining, perhaps, but not deliberation. This is true, but two points should

---

[9] *Goldberg v. Kelly*, 397 U.S. 254 (1970).

be noted in response. It is doubtful, first, that government can ever really insist that people deliberate. Government can try to structure things so as to make deliberation more or less likely, but ultimately deliberation depends on individual commitment. By its terms, deliberation requires solicitous goodwill, creative ingenuity, and a desire to get to the best answer. These cannot be mandated. Even juries sometimes choose to bargain rather than to deliberate when they want to go home, and, when they do, there is little anyone can do about it.

Second, my suggestion is that by strengthening the hand of the weaker party in the types of circumstance discussed, government can increase the likelihood that insiders will deploy their wisdom to search for the deliberative solutions that may be waiting to be discovered. Life has more imagination than us, so the saying goes; it certainly has more imagination than most government officials. This is not to deny that structuring the incentives to promote the search for domination-minimizing solutions through insiders' deliberation may fail. It may often do so in particular cases, so that increasing the voice of weaker parties will amount to no more than increasing their bargaining power. When this is so, we can take consolation from the fact that it will not be those whose basic interests are at stake who must internalize all the costs of the failure. Bargaining may sometimes be inferior to deliberation, but, from the standpoint of the stripped-down conception of the common good I have suggested we should embrace, domination is always inferior to both.

Power and Democratic Competition

Political institutions differ from other sites of collective human activity in that the exercise of power is not incidental in the pursuit of some further goal; it is integral to the nature of the beast. To be sure, governments do many things other than exercise power: they respond to market failures, build infrastructure, provide education, insure banks, supply welfare—the list is long. But what differentiates government's activities from those of other social actors involved in these and other collective activities is the specter of legitimate coercive force. Weber may have gone too far in defining the state as having a monopoly on the legitimate use of force. As Scott (1985, 1990) and others have pointed out, often its monopoly is incomplete and its legitimacy is questioned at least by significant sectors of the population.[1] But if Scott's weapons of the weak were to become too effective, or the state's legitimacy were too widely questioned, it would collapse into the kind of conditions that prevailed in Lebanon in the 1970s or parts of Colombia and the former Soviet Union in the 1990s. Moreover, Weber was surely right to the extent of saying that states *aspire* to maintain a monopoly of legitimate force in a given territory. Because their raison d'être involves the conscious deployment and maintenance of legitimate force, it is inescapably a substantial part of the superordinate good of government.

This reality suggests a different set of institutional design challenges for democratic theorists from those that informed the discussion in chapter 2. Whereas the issue there was to think about domesticating the power dimensions of human interaction while minimizing interference with superordinate goods, here the superordinate good substantially is the exercise of power as a legitimate public monopoly. As a result, the questions revolve less around managing the trade-offs between limiting domination and the pursuit of other goods, and more around better and worse means of con-

---

[1] Even in the United States groups like the Amish have often managed to defy the will of the state with respect to their educational practices. For decades before the famous *Wisconsin v. Yoder*, 406 U.S. 205 (1972), litigation local authorities had all but given up trying to enforce mandatory high school education on them. The *Yoder* litigation came about only as a by-product of a school rationalization plan in Wisconsin that had nothing to do with the Amish. See Arneson and Shapiro (1996: 365–411).

trolling the exercise of power so as to ensure that governments limit domination rather than facilitate it. Following an elaboration of the advantages of this approach to the issue in §3.1, I turn, in §3.2, to the most influential power-centered theory of government developed in the twentieth century, that put forward by Joseph Schumpeter. Noting that his account depends on more attractive and persuasive assumptions about managing power relations than the conventional liberal and republican alternatives, I make the case that the persuasive critiques of Schumpeterianism suggest that it should be supplemented rather than rejected as the best available means of structuring political power. This leads to a discussion of how best to think about supplementation in §§3.3 and 3.4, where I develop a case for democracy-reinforcing judicial review—as distinct from the democracy-limiting view rejected in §1.1.1. Democracy-reinforcing judicial review draws on the notion of minimizing domination as a thin theory of the common good that occupies a middle ground between those, like Schumpeter, who would reduce democracy to a mere set of procedures such as majority rule, and those, like the aggregative and deliberative democrats discussed in chapter 1, who identify it with a substantive conception of the will of the people.

3.1 STRUCTURING POWER TO LIMIT DOMINATION

Conceiving of democracy as a means for limiting domination offers several advantages. First, it poses normative questions about democracy in a "compared to what?" framework, because democracy is now judged not by the either/or question whether it produces social welfare functions or leads to agreement, but rather by how well it enables people to manage power relations as measured by the yardstick of minimizing domination. Second, this approach invites us to avoid another kind of binary thinking: about democracy itself. Ways of managing power relations can be more or less democratic. It is one of the singular contributions of Dahl's idea of polyarchy that it turns questions about democracy into more-or-less questions rather than whether-or-not questions.[2] Third, the power-centered

---

[2] Dahl formulates eight criteria by which to measure the degree to which the conditions of polarchy are met. These conditions revolve around four periods: voting, where votes by members of the political system must have equal weight, and the choice with the most individual votes wins; prevoting, where members have equal chances of presenting alternatives and information about alternatives; postvoting, where those leaders or policies that won the vote displace those with fewer votes, and the orders of elected officials are followed; and the interelection period, where decisions are subordinate to those made during elections—for

approach brings the normative literature on democratic theory into confrontation with the empirical political science literature on democracy. Normative theorists have attended too little to this literature, with the result that their proposals have not been famous for their feasibility, and others have tended to ignore them as a result.

Even when normative theorists take up the first two questions, inattention to empirical practice can mar their arguments. For instance, Buchanan and Tullock (1962) answer the "how much democracy?" question by noting that its benefits must be traded off against other valuable ways of spending one's time. Apart from the difficulties of this view adduced in §1.1.4, Buchanan and Tullock assume, without supplying any evidence, that it is the standard panoply of libertarian protections that people most value. It is these, they argue, that are to be insulated from change by supermajorities or even unanimity rule. If we query that assumption, their substantive claims are all thrown into doubt.

Another advantage of the power-centered approach is that it offers a tractable perspective on long-standing conundrums about the relations between democracy and citizenship. Democratic theory is often said to be impotent when confronted with questions about its own scope. It depends on a decision rule, usually some variant of majority rule, but this assumes that the question "majority of whom?" has been settled. If this is not done democratically, however, in what sense are the results that flow from democratic decision making genuinely democratic? Thus Shapiro and Hacker-Cordón (1999a: 1) observe that "a chicken-and-egg problem lurks at democracy's core." Questions relating to boundaries and membership seem in an important sense prior to democratic decision making, yet paradoxically they cry out for democratic resolution.

If democracy is about structuring power relations so as to limit domination, it becomes unnecessary to think of questions about citizenship as different from questions about any other superordinate good that is conditioned by democratic constraints. The claim to a democratic say in collective decisions, whether or not one is a citizen, appropriately rests on the causal principle of having a pertinent affected interest. The rallying cry of the American revolutionaries, after all, was "No taxation without representation!" not "No taxation without citizenship!" There might be good reasons for restricting citizenship, but this does not mean that noncitizens should be denied rights to vote on matters that affect their pertinent inter-

---

example, an interim senator will be replaced by the senator who wins the next election (1956: 71–76, 84–89).

ests, as when a decision is taken to deny the children of illegal aliens access to the California public schools,[3] or when "guest workers" in foreign countries claim a say in the laws that govern them (see Barbieri 1998). As I argued in §2.3, the legitimate claim to a say in a decision should turn on whether someone's interests are likely to be affected by the result. The claim becomes particularly strong when basic interests are at stake, rendering people vulnerable to domination by others.

The causally based view has been invoked in a number of recent arguments aimed at decentering citizenship as decisive in determining rights of democratic participation, and replacing it with systems of overlapping jurisdiction in which different groups are sovereign over different classes of decisions—as is occurring in the governance of the European Union. At the same time as it might make sense for the United Kingdom to centralize some decision making in Brussels, it might also make sense to devolve other decision making to regional parliaments in Scotland and Wales and even to local governments. The operative thought here is that the appropriate demos should be settled decision by decision, not people by people. Democratic reform is best guided by the aspiration to bring the structure of decision making into closer conformity with the contours of power relationships, not of memberships that are best thought of from this perspective as superordinate goods.[4]

This is a prudent conclusion in light of the difficulties that have been identified by Dahl (1999) and others with the idea of achieving democratic institutions on a global scale. Some, such as Held (1995, 1999), suggest here that the difficulty is merely one of institutional development. Just as the nation-states of the modern world became centralized power monopolies before they were democratized, so too with global institutions. On Held's view the priority should be to create an international *Rechtsstaat* that mimics the development of national states between the seventeenth and nineteenth centuries, pressing later for democratization. The decisive difference is that in today's international arena there are huge obstacles to the formation of global political institutions that had no analogues for state formation, namely, powerful states that command both

---

[3] This was passed as Proposition 187 by a majority of 59 percent to 41 percent in a November 1994 California ballot initiative and subsequently struck down in federal court as violating the constitutional right to education regardless of immigration status, and on the grounds that immigration law is a federal rather than state matter.

[4] See Pogge (1992), Antholis (1993), Wendt (1994), and Benhabib (2001). For other arguments that decisions about membership should not be seen as anterior to democratic decision making, see Shapiro and Hacker-Cordón (1999a: esp. chaps. 6, 10, 12, and 15).

widespread political legitimacy and coercive resources and can ignore global institutions at will (Wendt 1999, Kymlicka 1999).[5] In such a world it seems that working, where feasible, toward democratization decision by decision makes better sense than holding out for the development of a global order that can subsequently be democratized. Moreover, the principle of affected interest and the presumption in favor of insiders' wisdom discussed in §2.2 both suggest that often subnational decision making is more appropriate than world government.

Difficulties are, of course, bound to arise in the endeavor to settle conflicting claims about whose pertinent interests are affected by a given decision. Controversial as this might often be, arguments about who has a legitimate claim to citizenship are scarcely less so (see Smith 1997). Moreover, there is instructive experience with arguments about affected interests in other arenas. In dealing with tort actions, for instance, courts develop rules for deciding who should have standing to sue, for sorting genuine from frivolous claims, and for distinguishing weaker from stronger allegations to have been adversely affected by an action. The comparison illustrates that institutional mechanisms can be developed to assess and manage conflicting claims about how pertinent interests are affected. They may be imperfect mechanisms, but they should be evaluated by reference to the other imperfect mechanisms of collective decision making that actually prevail in the world, not by comparison with an ideal that prevails nowhere.[6]

This is not an argument for turning politics into tort law. The principle of affected interest could be applied through a variety of institutional arrangements. Despite the presumptions behind much academic literature, human beings do not generally design institutions ex nihilo; they *re*design existing institutions along the lines suggested by such metaphors as rebuilding a ship at sea. For this reason the principle of affected interest is best thought of as a guide for the direction of institutional reform. Whatever the inherited system of decision making, positive reform occurs when it changes so as better to reflect affected interests, particularly affected basic interests. In some settings courts might be the best available vehicles for trying to bring this about; in others it might be pursued in other ways—through administrative agencies, labor negotiations, and arbitra-

---

[5] This was dramatically illustrated in July of 2002 when the United Nations Security Council was forced to accept that United States peacekeepers would be exempt from prosecution by the permanent war crimes tribunal that it is seeking to establish. Edith Lederer, "U.S. Exempt for One Year from Tribunal Prosecution," *Miami Herald*, August 13, 2002, p. 1.

[6] For elaboration and defense of this claim, see Shapiro (1999a: 31–39).

tion hearings, not to mention the legislative process itself. Whatever the mechanism, the goal should be to facilitate participation in decision making by those affected by the results, in addition to the opposition rights discussed in §2.3.

3.2 Schumpeterian Competition

The most influential twentieth-century approach to the democratic management of power relations is Schumpeter's (1942) argument in *Capitalism, Socialism, and Democracy*. Although much of the book is a polemical critique of Marxism, in the part that has endured he develops a theory intended to speak to long-standing deficiencies of democratic theory and to realize both decision-making rights and opposition rights as fully as is feasible in the modern world. The underlying logic of his argument is disarmingly simple. It reduces to a double claim: (1) that structured competition for power is preferable both to Hobbesian anarchy and to the power monopoly that Hobbes saw as the logical response to it, and (2) that the choices among anarchy, monopoly, and competition are the only meaningful possibilities. Both of Schumpeter's claims were innovative, and, although they have drawn heavy critical fire, neither has been driven from the field.

3.2.1 Incentives versus Constraints

Schumpeter's view is often said to be conservative. There is substance to this, but focusing too quickly on it obscures the radical dimensions of his argument.

Before Schumpeter wrote, scholarship on institutions and political stability was informed by two conflicting views of power. On the monolithic view, which dates back at least to Hobbes's *Leviathan*, power is assumed to be unitary and indivisible. Unless it is in the hands of an absolute sovereign, Hobbes insisted, there would be anarchical chaos and civil war. For Marx, as for the elite theorists of democracy, power was also always located in one place—whether in the hands of the bourgeoisie or its "executive committee," or in those of some political elite working behind the scenes. Weber (1947: 156, 1998: 310–11) articulates the monolithic view as well when he defines a state as enjoying a monopoly of legitimate coercive force over a given territory, and Nozick (1974: 23–24) makes this view even more explicit when he defines coercive force as (the only) natural monopoly.

Liberal constitutionalists like those discussed in §§1.1.4 and 1.1.5 typically operate with the monolithic view, however consciously. This is why their approach to limiting governmental power involves either hamstringing it through the multiplication of veto points or walling it in: creating a robust "private sphere" that countermajoritarian agencies such as courts are intended to keep the government out of. The difficulties with this, as we saw, are that hamstringing government can preserve domination embedded in the status quo, and that domination and the threat of it often do occur in civil and private institutions. Failure to come to grips with this reality renders liberal constitutionalist views vulnerable to the critiques of feminists and others, even if the solutions proposed by the critics are often less than fully persuasive (see Shapiro 1999a: 64–229). The monolithic view of power does not easily lend itself to creative thinking about regulating the power dimensions of human interaction while otherwise minimizing interference.

Republicans, by contrast, have adopted the more complex view that power is divisible and best managed by being divided. Pocock (1975) traces the lineage of this view to Aristotle's argument that the best regime combines the powers of the one, the few, and the many, though it has exhibited many variants in subsequent centuries. It began to take on its characteristic modern hue in the arguments between Machiavelli and Guicciardini in the Italian Renaissance, and was taken over by Harrington and his followers as a materialist claim that the powers of different social estates must both be reflected in the government and balance one another for a regime to be stable. At the hands of Montesquieu and the American revolutionaries he influenced, this idea of balance was replaced by that of the separation of powers among representatives of the one (now the president instead of the king), the few (now the judiciary instead of the House of Lords), and the many (now Congress instead of the House of Commons). Each branch of government was given a specified sphere of authority, limited by the other two. "Ambition will be made to counteract ambition," in Madison's famous phrase, protecting the citizenry from the possibility of domination (Hamilton, Madison, and Jay [1788] 1966: 160).

The authors of *The Federalist* distinguished incentives from constraints in the pursuit of power, sowing the seed of a third view of the matter. In *Federalist* No. 48 Madison insists that "mere demarcation on parchment of the constitutional limits of the several departments, is not a sufficient guard against those encroachments which lead to a tyrannical concentration of all the powers in the same hands." Such "exterior provisions" are inadequate and must be supplemented, as he elaborates in *Federalist* No.

51, by additional provisions giving "those who administer each department the necessary constitutional means and personal motives to resist encroachments of the others" ([1788] 1966: 150–51, 159–60). Important as this distinction is, it is far from clear that the institutional device of separation of powers is a system of incentives rather than of constraints. It is, after all, no more than a list of powers and jurisdictional limits. As is often pointed out, if the executive branch chose not to enforce a Supreme Court order, there is nothing the Court could actually do about it. In sum, as Dahl (1956: 30–32) noted long ago in his *Preface to Democratic Theory*, the call for incentives to structure the exercise of power was long on rhetoric and short on an account of the mechanisms by which this would actually operate. The Federalist solution was mainly a matter of engineering institutional sclerosis to make all government action difficult and so protect the interests of landed elites. In this it is not qualitatively different from standard liberal justifications of bicameralism, strong constitutionalism, and other types of institutional veto that have often been put forward to limit democracy (see §1.1.1).

Schumpeter's theory was an attempt to deliver more fully on an incentives-based system while remaining agnostic on whether power is divisible or monolithic. The essential point is that power is acquired only through competition and held for a limited duration. Schumpeter's account was a radical departure in that he thought that rather than succumb to power (Hobbes) or hem it in (all these others), a system could control power by turning it into an object of electoral competition. Whereas constraints are geared to limiting politicians' power via rules (such as separation of powers or other constitutional limitations), incentives link what politicians find strategically beneficial to the demands of competitive politics.

Schumpeter forcefully articulated the competitive ideal by pressing the analogy between political and economic competition. He suggested that we think of voters as analogues of consumers, parties and politicians as corresponding to firms, the votes politicians seek as proxies for profits, and the policies governments enact as political goods and services.[7] To be sure, democracy is not reducible to competition. Often it involves other things as well, notably rights to participate in agenda setting and to operate as a "loyal" opposition—to render competition meaningful, if for no other reason. But competition for power is indispensable. Once parties are modeled on firms trying to maximize votes as analogues of profits, then leaders

---

[7] Schumpeter (1942: 269–83). The analogy was in fact first explored by an economist, Hotelling (1929).

can be seen as disciplined by the demands of competition. Attempts by Downs (1957) and others to turn this into a predictive theory of electoral competition have been less than successful (see Green and Shapiro 1994: chap. 7), but as a normative theory Schumpeter's account broke new ground. From his perspective, the value of competition is twofold: it disciplines leaders with the threat of losing power in the same way that firms are disciplined by the threat of bankruptcy, and it gives would-be leaders the incentive to be responsive to more voters than are their competitors.

Schumpeter's consumer analogue to voting displaced the idea of representation in what he thought of as Rousseau's classical theory of democracy. In fact, Rousseau's theory was actually a neoclassical adaptation of the ancient idea of democracy as ruling and being ruled in turn. If the ancient ideal looks problematic to contemporary eyes because of its assumptions about the demos (women and slaves were excluded), the neoclassical idea of representation falters for different reasons. Representative government may seem like a necessary adaptation of the classical democratic ideal for a world in which countries have populations in the tens or hundreds of millions, and nation-states can be continental in size, with vast bureaucracies and complex economies. Yet it has always been vulnerable on normative democratic grounds because representatives represent some better than others, they may be vulnerable to capture by special interests, and there is the ever present danger that they will atrophy into a professional class, concerned more with their own advancement than with their representative role. If representatives follow Burke's ([1790] 1969) admonition not to sacrifice their judgment to the opinions of their constituents, they are vulnerable to charges of elitism, yet if their actions reflect the vicissitudes of public opinion, then they are "pandering." In short, representation is an elusive notion in democracies, a seemingly inevitable practice whose legitimacy is inescapably suspect.[8] Schumpeter's move from the language of representation to that of consumer sovereignty elides these difficulties.

3.2.2 Difficulties with Schumpeterianism

Schumpeterian democracy is often denoted "minimal" for one of two reasons: its exclusive focus is on (usually national) political institutions narrowly defined, and Schumpeter's definition of democracy by reference to competition for power. However, nothing inherent in Schumpeter's rea-

---

[8] The best contemporary treatment of the concept of representation is Pitkin (1972).

soning thus limits it. To say that social arrangements other than national political institutions should be democratized is not to deny that Schumpeterian tools might be useful in that endeavor, as I have illustrated elsewhere (Shapiro 1999a: 64–229). Nor is it to assert that national political institutions could not benefit from Schumpeterian reform even if other reforms are deemed necessary as well.

True, it might be said that at the end of the day Schumpeter's is a system of constraints rather than incentives because the loser of an election could refuse to give up power, just as a political executive or army commander could refuse to enforce a court order he found objectionable. Indeed, just because this is so, the competitive requirement has been read by modern Schumpeterians like Huntington (1991) to mean that a polity is not democratic unless governments have at least twice given up power following electoral defeat. This is a tough test. It would have ruled out the United States until 1840, Japan and India for much of the twentieth century, and most of the so-called third wave democracies in the ex-communist countries and sub-Saharan Africa. It is also why opposition rights are so important in democracies: meaningful political competition requires that there be opposition parties waiting in the wings, criticizing the government and offering voters potential alternatives. Minimal, in short, does not mean negligible.

Despite its attractiveness, Schumpeterianism invites criticism from a power-centered perspective. For one thing, the sense in which Schumpeterian competition produces responsive government is constrained and thus leads to less than fully adequate political competition. In theory at least, the standard left criticism of markets—that they reward those with greater resources—does not apply. One-person-one-vote is a resource equalizer that is widely seen as a nonnegotiable requirement of democracy, despite occasional defenses of markets in votes on efficiency or intensity grounds (see Buchanan and Tullock 1962: 125–26, 132–142). However, as I noted in §1.2.3, particularly in the United States the difficulty is that politicians must compete for campaign contributions in order to be in a position to compete for votes. Perhaps there would be decisive voter support for confiscatory taxes on estates worth over ten million dollars, but no party proposes this. Indeed, in 2000 and 2001, the United States Congress gave strong bipartisan support to a bill that would abolish the existing estate tax—paid by only the wealthiest 2 percent of Americans.[9] It

[9] The Death Tax Elimination Act of 2000 was passed by Congress in the summer of 2000 and vetoed by President Clinton. President Bush signed a similar provision into law as part of a tax cut that was passed with considerable bipartisan support in the summer of 2001.

seems likely that politicians avoid increasing taxes on the wealthy for fear of the funds that would be channeled to their electoral opponents if they sought to do so. Empirical study of such claims is inherently difficult, but it seems reasonable to suppose that the proposals politicians offer are heavily shaped by the agendas of campaign contributors; why else would they contribute? Add to this the fact that the small number of major parties means that what we really get is oligopolistic competition, and it becomes clear that the sense in which parties are as attentive to voters as firms in competitive markets are to consumers is highly attenuated.

Second, it is less than clear that electoral competition provides much in the way of disciplinary incentives, given the high rates at which incumbents are often reelected (Lowenstein 1995: 653–67). But again there is the response: compared to what? The discipline of the electoral constraint might seem modest when compared to an ideal that prevails nowhere, but achieving it would be a substantial gain for the billions who live in countries where it is lacking (see Przeworski 1999: 43–50). Once it has been attained, it is plausible to think that additional constraints will be needed to discipline politicians, ranging from devices to force publicity of their decisions, to term limits that undermine the power of incumbency, to mechanisms, such as permissive opposition rights, to challenge their decisions and "edit" them in the application—subject to the provisos mentioned in §2.3.

However, one can embrace both these critiques without rejecting Schumpeterianism *tout court*. The objections are aimed not at the idea of political competition but rather at the ways in which the system is imperfectly competitive. Disproportionate power of campaign contributors could be reduced (proposals for reform abound),[10] and reforms could be instituted to increase the number of parties, facilitating more competition. Indeed, it is remarkable that public interest litigants, activists, and political commentators (not to mention political theorists) do not argue for attempts to use antitrust laws to attack the existing duopoly. If competition for power is the lifeblood of democracy, then the search for bipartisan consensus (along with the ideal of deliberative agreement that lies behind it) is really anticompetitive collusion in restraint of democracy. Why is it that people do not challenge legislation that has bipartisan backing, or other forms of bipartisan agreement, on *these* grounds? It is far from clear

---

[10] See Ackerman (1993a) and Ayres (2000) for examples.

that there are fewer meritorious reasons to break up the Democratic and Republican parties than there are to break up AT&T and Microsoft.[11]

There are legal obstacles to antitrust action against political parties, but also untested legal possibilities. For instance, the Supreme Court's Noerr-Pennington doctrine rules out applying antitrust laws to "valid governmental action, as opposed to private action."[12] But this does not speak to activities by political parties. Moreover, although the Sherman Act has generally been held not to apply to noneconomic entities such as labor unions, exceptions are made when a conspiracy is alleged between such an entity and a business to injure the interests of another business, or where the agreement sought does not encompass a "legitimate union interest."[13] Analogously, activities by political parties might not be exempted if they allied with corporate contributors to promote anticompetitive practices, or could otherwise be shown to be seeking agreements with one another that went beyond "legitimate party interests."

The constitutional obstacles to applying antitrust principles to politics are rooted in the right of petition and the "ability of the people to make their wishes known to their representatives."[14] But the rationale for this type of political exemption does not go to forms of collusion that undermine the process of free political expression itself, which parties engage in by maintaining prohibitive costs to entry, agreeing to exclude minor parties from political debates, and related practices. Because the Sherman Act has been held to apply only to business combinations,[15] and to organizations that have commercial objectives,[16] antitrust regulation of such behavior might require additional lawmaking. It is hard, for obvious reasons, to envision legislators enacting such laws, but it is less difficult to think of political antitrust measures being adopted as a result of ballot initiatives.

---

[11] The Progressives did advance a version of this critique (see Epstein 1986: 17–71). The lone voice in the contemporary literature seems to be Wittman (1973).

[12] *Eastern R.R. President's Conf. v. Noerr Motor Freight*, 365 U.S. 127 (1961) at 136.

[13] *Connell Constr. Co v. Plumbers & Steamfitters Local Union No. 100*, 483 F.2d 1154, 1164 (5th Cir. App. 1973); see also *Local Union No. 189, Amalgamated Meat Cutters v. Jewel Tea Co.*, 381 U.S. 676 (1965).

[14] *Noerr*, 356 U.S. at 137, 138. Thus the court rejected a claim by the State of Missouri that the National Organization for Women had violated the Sherman Act by organizing a conference boycott in states that had not ratified the Equal Rights Amendment, holding that the participants were engaging in legitimate forms of political organizing rather than undermining commercial competitors. *Missouri v. National Organization for Women, Inc.*, 467 F. Supp. 289, 304 (1979), and cert. denied, 449 U.S. 842 (1980).

[15] *Parker v. Brown*, 317 U.S. 341, 351 (1943).

[16] *Klor's Inc. v. Broadway-Hale Stores, Inc.*, 359 U.S. at 213 n. 7, and *Apex Hosiery Co. v. Leader*, 310 U.S. 469 at 493 n. 5.

There are numerous other areas in which the anticompetitive character of American politics is sustained by the rules and administrative practices built into the system. For instance, the Federal Election Commission, created in 1974 to enforce regulations on campaign finance, consists of six commissioners—three Republicans and three Democrats. Because it operates by majority rule, it has strong incentives to serve the common interests of the political parties rather than what fairness or vigorous competition might be thought to require. As a result, it often ignores the recommendations of its professional staff, as in October 2001 when it overruled the finding of its own general counsel that numerous individual Senate candidates, both the Republican and Democratic Senatorial Campaign Committees, and numerous state political parties had apparently engaged in illegal schemes during the 2000 campaign to funnel soft money into their races.[17] The example underscores how important it is for bipartisan institutions not to be confused with nonpartisan ones. The former have incentives to behave as a duopoly, exempting themselves from the law and undermining political competition. Bipartisan debate commissions often operate with similar effect, limiting the terms of political debate, and sustaining overwhelmingly high entry costs to third parties.

In all these areas the difficulty lies not with the Schumpeterian analogy but rather with the failure to press it sufficiently far. Just as parties do in the political realm, in the economy individual firms strive to increase their market shares and to become monopolies if they can—even though this is deleterious to the competitive system. This is one of the reasons that markets stand in need of regulation by institutional players who are independent of the firms that operate in them. The difficulties that arise from bipartisan political regulation would be mimicked in the economy if the Securities and Exchange Commission, the Federal Reserve, and related agencies were turned over to the largest brokerage firms to run as they saw fit, rather than being run by career professionals or appointees who are otherwise insulated from partisan political influence. To be sure, the insulation is often less effective than it might be, but in the political realm the need for it is not even perceived. Small wonder that the two-party system retains a vicelike grip on the terms of political debate.

Arguments about the merits of party proliferation, usually to be achieved via proportional representation, are sometimes advanced on the quite different ground that this would lead to fairer outcomes. Here the operative idea is that they would be more representative, not merely that

[17] See www.commoncause.org/publications/oct01/102401.htm [9/2/02].

the system would be more competitive if there were more viable political parties. Notice that such arguments can be oversold. Proportional representation may lead to more representative electoral outcomes by offering voters a broader array of parties, but it need not lead to more representative governments. Frequently we see this in Israel when small extremist parties needed for a viable governing coalition exert disproportionate influence on government policy, leading to highly unrepresentative government. Nonetheless, trying to ensure that the parties competing with one another are more representative of the electorate is a challenge that can in principle be taken up within the Schumpeterian framework, and there is some reason to think that, on average, proportional representation leads to policies that are closer to the preferences of the median voter than does competitive alternation in power (see Rae 1967, 1995, and Powell 2000).

Pressed sufficiently far, however, the emphasis on representativeness turns into a rejection of the competitive ideal. This becomes evident if we suppose that a government could represent all interests optimally,[18] and ask who would the opposition then represent? Perhaps the notion that all views could be fairly represented in decision making is the implicit ideal for those who focus on achieving agreement: if all groups are fairly represented, then they can negotiate an outcome that all can accept, making opposition politics unnecessary. This fallacious reasoning has already been explored in my discussion of Buchanan and Tullock in §1.1.4; it need not detain us here. The consensus model is discussed further in §4.2 when I take up the claim that the divisions in some societies are so intense that majoritarian politics would be explosively dysfunctional. Note, for now, that Schumpeter's view of competition is valuable as a discipline on power-holders independent of its fairness or representativeness when measured by some extrinsic criterion. To be sure, it is integral to the model that politicians have incentives to be at least as responsive as their competitors to the demands of the electorate, and to that extent it is a representative system. But of equal importance is the idea that power monopolies are inherently bad, so that electoral discipline is a valuable constraint on the corrupting effects of power. The value of oppositions, from this perspective, is that they have incentives to shine light in dark corners, exposing corruption, and demanding that governments be held to public account. For electoral competition to facilitate this process, it must be meaningful,

[18] Achieving such optimality is elusive in practice, as the architects of the McGovern-Frazier reforms to achieve pure proportionality within the Democratic party learned when it became apparent that there are more pertinent interests than could be represented proportionately. See Ranney (1975). It may also be elusive in theory. See Rae et al. (1981).

so that creative reforms designed to move the system away from being a functional duopoly or monopoly should be encouraged.

3.3 What Role for Judicial Review?

In §§1.1.1 and 1.1.5 I argued that the conventional liberal constitutionalist case for judicial review, which appeals to the inherent irrationality of legislatures, the Tocquevillian fear of majority tyranny, or both, is unconvincing. Courts are not obviously less rational than legislatures in the specified sense, and the evidence suggests that democratic systems lacking judicial review are no more likely to engage in majority tyranny than those that employ it. Moreover, by usurping the legitimate functions of legislatures, courts can actually hamper democracy's operation. This does not mean, however, that judicial review is necessarily bad. There are other justifications for it, rooted in democracy's logic and geared to enhancing its operation.

One reason to countenance a judiciary that is relatively independent of majoritarian politics is implicit in what has just been said: the players of a game are not well situated to act as their own umpires. This was most dramatically apparent in the aftermath of the 2000 United States presidential election, where the virtual dead heat and the ensuing standoff over the Florida electoral count was ultimately resolved through the courts. To be sure, the heavily partisan behavior of many judges did little to enhance their image, but even those who disagreed strongly with the decision accepted the Supreme Court's appropriate role. Without the existence of some avenue for settling electoral disputes that is widely acknowledged to be both independent and legitimate, the temptation for politicians to engage in naked power grabs would be correspondingly stronger. American politicians feel they cannot openly defy courts with which they strongly disagree, whether their orders involve integrating Southern classrooms, turning over the Watergate tapes, or accepting electoral defeat. Indeed, what was perhaps most remarkable about *Bush v. Gore* was how quickly it became evident that Gore would accept the Supreme Court's ruling despite the partisan division of the justices and widespread criticism of the majority opinion.[19]

The notion that courts should protect democracy from politicians has a venerable history in American jurisprudence, dating at least to Justice

[19] *Bush v. Gore*, 531 U.S. 98 (2000).

Stone's famous fourth footnote in *United States v. Carolene Products* in 1938. Noting that well-functioning democratic processes might disenfranchise "discrete and insular minorities," Stone countenanced the possibility that judicial interference with legislative decisions might in those circumstances be justified and necessary. Stone limited his attention to circumstances that tend "seriously to curtail the operation of those political processes ordinarily to be relied upon to protect minorities."[20] As the paradigmatic case where this is justified, we might think of the response of some Southern legislatures to the enfranchisement of blacks: placing polling stations in locations from which they were barred. This kind of exclusion is so clearly at odds with democracy's operation that Stone felt that a case could be made for courts to step in and say no. The kinds of collusion in restraint of democracy discussed in §3.2.2 might be less blatant than this, but it is not difficult to imagine them passing the threshold where *Carolene*'s logic becomes operable.[21]

Awareness of the combined impact of imperfect decision rules and differential control over political resources has led some commentators to go further, defending "substantive" conceptions of democracy over "procedural" ones, relying on *Carolene*-style reasoning. For instance, Ely (1980) defended much of the judicial activism of the Warren Court by reference to *Carolene*. Ely described his argument as purely procedural, designed to repair defects of democratic process. But as critics have pointed out and the discussion below makes clear, it is obviously a substantive argument (Smith 1985: 89–91, 170–74). Beitz (1988: 155–74) has pressed similar considerations into an argument that the quantitative fairness of equal voting power will never ensure substantively democratic outcomes. In his view, a truly democratic system of "qualitative fairness" requires a prior system of "just legislation," since mere equal voting power can never be relied upon to produce fair outcomes. It should not be thought that *Carolene Products* logic is the exclusive preserve of the political left. For instance, Riker and Weingast (1988: 378–79) employ it to criticize taxation of property, asking, "why is the abridgement of some minority's economic rights less troubling than an abridgement of the political rights of minorities?"

The mere statement of substantively democratic views suffices to make plain their problematic nature. How can Ely know what democratic pro-

---

[20] *United States v. Carolene Products Co.*, 304 U.S. 144 (1938) at 152 n. 4.

[21] One powerful indictment which comes close to making the case that the threshold has been passed is Phillips (2002).

cesses ought to have achieved had they not been corrupted by the *Carolene* problem? Whence the theory of just legislation against which Beitz will evaluate the results of voting procedures? How do Riker and Weingast know which system of property rights is just? These views are reminiscent of Thurgood Marshall's insistence, in *Furman v. Georgia*, that if Americans understood what was actually involved in the administration of the death penalty, they would oppose it.[22] How could he have known? Writers like Ely and Beitz have nothing to say to those who are not attracted by their respective conceptions of "equal concern and respect" and "qualitative fairness," and the Riker-Weingast move underscores the difficulties of turning "protection of minorities" into a substantive conception, already discussed in §2.3. If, as I maintain, there is no criterion for justice that is entirely independent of what democracy generates, this should not be surprising.

To say this is not, however, to respond to the difficulty that motivates *Carolene*-type reasoning. There are no perfect decision rules, and those who are better placed to translate permissive freedoms into political power should be expected, *ceteris paribus*, to get their way. The problem is real, but the proffered solutions overreach, suggesting the desirability of finding a middle ground.[23] "More than process, less than substance" might be an appropriate slogan. It suggests that the role of courts should be limited to preventing subversions of democracy by ensuring that the principle of affected interest is not undermined through disenfranchising legitimate voters, particularly when their basic interests are at stake. But they should generally operate in a reactive, "safety valve," manner—holding legislators' feet to the fire rather than substituting for them.

A number of theorists have sought to develop middle-ground views of this kind. For instance, Burt (1992) contends that democracy involves foundational commitments to both majority rule and nondomination, with the ever present potential for conflict when majorities make decisions that lead to domination. Judicial review is warranted when such conflicts arise, he argues, and courts should not conduct it in ways that assume they know how the conflict should be resolved. Rather, they should declare the domination that has emerged from the democratic process unacceptable, insisting that the parties try anew to find an accommodation. In this sense courts should never act imperially to impose results on recalcitrant legisla-

---

[22] *Furman v. Georgia*, 408 U.S. 238 at 360–69. See also Marshall's dissent in *Gregg v. Georgia*, 428 U.S. 153 (1976).

[23] For discussion of additional weaknesses in the *Carolene Products* approach, see Ackerman (1985).

tures or to protect society from majority rule. Rather, they should use their authority to get legislatures to confront contradictions in their own actions, forcing them to rethink ways of working their majoritarian wills that do not countenance domination.

An example of what should be resisted from this perspective is the approach adopted by Justice Blackmun in his majority opinion in *Roe v. Wade*, the 1973 decision affirming a woman's right to abortion.[24] The Court held in *Roe* that a Texas statute making it a crime to "procure an abortion" unless the life of the mother is threatened by the pregnancy's continuation violated the Due Process Clause of the Fourteenth Amendment.[25] Blackmun's majority opinion dealt with abortion differently during the three trimesters of a normal pregnancy, greatly limiting the power of states to regulate abortion. Before the end of the first trimester abortion could no longer be regulated at all; prior to the point of viability it could be regulated only in the interests of the mother's health; and, after viability, if a state chose to regulate or proscribe abortion acting on its interest "in the potentiality of human life," this could be trumped if the attending physician made an "appropriate" judgment that this was necessary for the "life or health" of the mother. The Court thus acknowledged that the state has an interest in potential human life, but effectively subordinated it to the woman's right to an abortion—even (if with qualification) after the point of viability. Blackmun based his decision on a right to privacy and reproductive freedom that had been recognized in the Court's 1965 decision in *Griswold v. Connecticut*.[26]

Whatever the jurisprudential basis for the right to abortion, it is arguable that it was the manner in which *Roe* was decided—at least as much as the content of the decision—that generated widespread controversy and rendered its legitimacy suspect. After all, in *Roe* the Court did a good deal more than strike down a Texas abortion statute. The majority opinion laid out a detailed test to specify the conditions under which abortion could be expected to pass muster. In effect Justice Blackmun authored a federal abortion statute of his own. Ruth Bader Ginsburg makes a powerful case that decisions of this kind tend to undermine the Court's legitimacy. If courts step "ahead" of the political process, they can produce a backlash, provoking charges that they overreach their appropriate place in a democratic constitutional order (Ginsburg 1993: 30–38).

[24] *Roe v. Wade*, 410 U.S. 113 (1973).
[25] The Due Process Clause states: "No state shall. . . . deprive any person of life, liberty or property, without due process of law."
[26] *Griswold v. Connecticut*, 381 U.S. 479 (1965).

Burt (1992: 344–52) contrasts the Court's handling of the abortion question with its approach in the school desegregation cases of the 1950s. Rejecting what many have seen as its altogether too timid approach in those cases, he argues that the Court took the right stand. In *Brown v. Board of Education*, the justices declared the doctrine of "separate but equal" to be an unconstitutional violation of the Equal Protection Clause,[27] but they did not describe schooling conditions that would be acceptable. Rather, they turned the problem back to Southern state legislatures, requiring them to fashion acceptable remedies themselves.[28] These remedies came before the Court as a result of subsequent litigation, were evaluated when they did, and were often found wanting (Burt 1992: 271–310). But the Court avoided designing the remedy itself, and with it the charge that it was usurping the legislative function. In *Roe*, by contrast, as Ginsburg puts it, the Court "invited no dialogue with legislators. Instead, it seemed entirely to remove the ball from the legislators' court" by wiping out virtually every form of abortion regulation then in existence (Ginsburg 1993: 32).

On the Ginsburg-Burt view, the sweeping holding in *Roe* diminished the Court's democratic legitimacy at the same time as it put paid to various schemes, underway in different states, to liberalize abortion laws. Between 1967 and 1973 statutes were passed in nineteen states liberalizing the permissible grounds for abortion. Many feminists had been dissatisfied with the pace and extent of this reform, and they mounted the campaign that resulted in *Roe*. Burt concedes that in 1973 it was "not clear whether the recently enacted state laws signified the beginning of a national trend toward abolishing all abortion restrictions or even whether in the so-called liberalized states, the new enactments would significantly increase access to abortion for anyone." Nonetheless, he insists that "the abortion issue was openly, avidly, controverted in a substantial number of public forums, and unlike the regime extant as recently as 1967, it was no longer clear who was winning the battle" (Burt 1992: 348). Following the *Brown* model, the Court might have struck down the Texas abortion statute in *Roe* (whether by appeal to Blackmun's privacy argument or to the equality argument favored by Ginsburg, Burt, and others) and remanded the matter for further action at the state level, thereby setting limits on what legislatures might do in the matter of regulating abortion without involving the Court directly in designing that regulation. On the Ginsburg-

[27] *Brown v. Board of Education I*, 347 U.S. 483 (1954).
[28] *Brown v. Board of Education II*, 349 U.S. 294 (1955).

Burt view, this would have left space for democratic resolution of the conflict that would have ensured the survival of the right to abortion while at the same time preserving the legitimacy of the Court's role in a democratic constitutional order (Burt 1992: 349–52).

Perhaps recognizing the lack of legitimacy of its holding in *Roe*, the Court eventually moved to revise its abortion jurisprudence. Its 1992 decision in *Planned Parenthood v. Casey* reaffirmed *Roe*'s basic holding but detached it from Blackmun's trimester-based framework of analysis, reformulating the constitutional right to abortion by reference to an "undue burden" standard rooted in the Due Process Clause of the Fourteenth Amendment.[29]

It is ironic, perhaps, that although *Casey* was decided before Ruth Ginsburg's appointment to the Court, that decision brought the Court's stance into line with the Ginsburg-Burt view of the manner in which it should approach the abortion question. By affirming the existence of a woman's fundamental constitutional right to an abortion, recognizing the legitimacy of the state's interest in potential life, and insisting that states may not pursue the vindication of that interest in a manner that is unduly burdensome to women, the Court set some basic parameters within which legislatures must now fashion regulations that govern abortion.

The dissenters in *Casey* were right to point out that there would be a degree of unpredictability and confusion as different regulatory regimes were enacted in different states and tested through the courts.[30] Particularly given the developmental dimension to the test—which permits increasingly burdensome regulation as pregnancy advances—this was inevitable. On views of adjudication that encourage efficiency and clarity above all else, this may appear as a reprehensible invitation to further litigation.[31]

---

[29] *Planned Parenthood of Southeastern Pennsylvania v. Casey*, 505 U.S. 833 (1992).

[30] In his partly dissenting opinion, Rehnquist—joined by Justices White and Scalia—said of the controlling opinion in *Casey*: "The end result of the joint opinion's paeans for praise of legitimacy is the enunciation of a brand new standard for evaluating state regulation of a woman's right to abortion—the undue burden standard. . . . *Roe v. Wade* adopted a 'fundamental right' standard under which state regulations could survive only if they met the requirement of 'strict scrutiny.' While we disagree with that standard, it at least had a recognized basis in constitutional law at the time *Roe* was decided. The same cannot be said for the 'undue burden' standard, which is created largely out of whole cloth by the authors of the joint opinion. It is a standard which even today does not command the support of a majority of this Court. And it will not, we believe, result in the sort of 'simple implementation,' easily applied, which the joint opinion anticipates." 112 S. Ct. 2791 (1992) at 2866.

[31] See Rehnquist's remarks immediately following those quoted in the preceding footnote. For a more general defense of efficiency in appellate federal adjudication, see Posner (1985b: 169–315). For criticism of Posner's view, see Shapiro (1987: 1009–26).

On the Ginsburg-Burt view, however, that *Casey* invites litigation may be a cost worth paying. It places on democratically elected legislatures the burden of coming up with modes of regulating abortion that are not unduly burdensome, and forces them to do this in the knowledge that the statutes they enact will be tested through the courts and thrown out if they are found wanting. This gives legislators incentives to devise regimes of regulation that minimize the burdens placed on women when they seek to vindicate the states' legitimate interests in protecting potential life. It also assigns the federal courts a legitimate role in a constitutional democracy. "Without taking giant strides and thereby risking a backlash too forceful to contain, the Court, through constitutional adjudication, can reinforce or signal a green light for social change"(Ginsburg 1993: 36).

By adopting the Ginsburg-Burt approach, the Court has arguably begun to belie Alasdair MacIntyre's (1984: 6–8) claim that the different sides in the abortion controversy operate from conceptually incommensurable premises between which it is impossible to adjudicate. On the contrary, as the debate has moved away from metaphysical imponderables—about when life begins and whether a fetus is a person—and toward consideration of what constitutes an undue burden on a woman's constitutionally protected rights in the service of a legitimate governmental interest, it has become plain that there is a good deal of room for rational argument about the legal right to abortion. That abortion can be an unmanageably polarizing issue does not mean that it has to be, and it is certainly an advantage of the *Casey* approach that it pushes the debate away from issues that cannot be resolved in a pluralist culture and toward areas where accommodation is possible.

In this connection it is worth noting that although the Court's decisions in *Casey* and *Webster v. Reproductive Health Services* (the 1989 holding in which *Roe*'s trimester-based test was first abandoned)[32] were widely criticized by pro-choice groups as infringing on abortion rights, the Court's "undue burden" standard offers possibilities for limiting abortion regulations that may be more robust than critics of *Casey* have realized. Certainly it seems to be a plausible interpretive strategy to claim in the wake of *Casey*, as Dworkin (1993: 173) does, that any regulation of abortion decisions should be deemed unnecessarily coercive and therefore "undue" if the same "improvement in responsibility of decisions about abortion could have been achieved in some different way with less coercive consequences." This line of reasoning suggests that if plaintiffs can show

[32] *Webster v. Reproductive Health Services*, 492 U.S. 490 (1989).

that less restrictive regulations can achieve states' stated goals in regulating abortion, existing regulations will have to be struck down. Knowing this, legislatures contemplating the passage of abortion statutes will have incentives not to adopt more stringent regulations than those that can be justified as necessary.[33]

The "undue burden" standard also has the potential to reinvigorate the egalitarian considerations that Blackmun sidestepped when he looked to *Griswold*'s privacy doctrine as a basis for his decision in *Roe*, rather than go the route that some critics suggested, at the time, would have been better constitutional law and political theory—to ground it in the Equal Protection Clause of the Fourteenth Amendment.[34] The reason is that it will likely prove exceedingly difficult to hammer out a jurisprudence of due and undue burdens without reference to egalitarian considerations. This is most obviously true in the area of abortion funding (which, under *Roe*, the Court has consistently held not to be implied by the right to abortion), but one could imagine it arising in other areas as well.[35] As these examples illustrate, by adopting the "undue burden" standard, the Court adopted a test that requires legislatures to enact abortion regulations that minimize the domination of women without telling them what those regulations should be. There remains a good deal of scope for democratic policymaking within its ambit, and the Court is not seen as a legislative imperialist in the way that the *Roe* Court was.

Dissenting Justice Scalia may have a valid point that the idea of undue burden involves philosophical choices about which justices will continue to differ, but he is only partly correct. As the jurisprudence is evolving, it seems clear that it also involves propositions that none of the *Casey* dissenters sought seriously to challenge, such as the claim that a regulation imposes an undue burden if it requires a woman to undergo a less safe abortion procedure when a more safe one is available. Disagreements over which procedures are safest are hotly contested, as was illustrated in *Sten-*

---

[33] See *Maher v. Roe*, 432 U.S. 464 (1977), *Poelker v. Doe*, 432 U.S. 519 (1977), and *Harris v. McRae*, 448 U.S. 297 (1980).

[34] Feminists such as MacKinnon (1987: 93–102) and West (1988: 67–70) saw grounding the right to abortion on the concept of privacy as a retrograde step. Given the ways in which privacy had shielded men from liability for raping their wives and promoted other forms of subjugation, feminists had been opposing it since the 1960s. They would have preferred an equal protection theory, which, as Ginsburg (1993) notes, would in any case have been better constitutional law, rendering the decision less vulnerable to the valid charge that the term "privacy" appears nowhere in the constitution.

[35] For the holdings on abortion funding, see *Maher v. Roe*, 432 U.S. 464 (1977), *Poelker v. Doe*, 432 U.S. 519 (1977), and *Harris v. McRae*, 448 U.S. 297 (1980).

berg v. Carhart. Following *Casey,* a majority on the Court held that "partial birth" abortions could not be proscribed, in circumstances where an abortion is legitimate, on the grounds that the alternative procedures are less safe for the woman.[36]

This claim was disputed by the litigants on the losing side as well as the dissenting justices on the Court, but the United States court system offers ways of dealing with such differences that require appellate justices neither to set themselves up as arbiters of good science nor to defer mindlessly to state legislatures. Questions of fact are not generally revisited in appellate courts. They restrict themselves to legal issues on the theory that the trier of fact heard the witnesses and conflicting claims and was better placed, therefore, to assess their credibility. Appellate courts check that trial courts have followed their own procedures in adjudicating factual disputes, but they generally uphold their factual findings unless the record contains evidence of impropriety in the trial court or the factual findings have no basis at all in the trial record. Knowing that the burdens they place on women will be tested in this way will give legislators incentives to hold the relevant hearings, creating track records that will incline juries and other triers of fact to defer to them rather than their adversaries.

It might be objected that the Court has indeed decided—albeit implicitly—that the state's interest in protecting potential life can never be vindicated under *Casey,* but this is not so. The opinions in *Carhart* made it plain that there would be a majority on the 2000 Court in favor of a less broadly drawn partial birth abortion prohibition statute limiting the procedure to late-term abortions and containing an exception for the life and health of the mother. This reflects the developmental character of the test, which assumes that as the fetus develops (and a fortiori the remaining time during which an unwanted pregnancy must be endured diminishes), it becomes more reasonable to impose the burden of going to term upon the woman. For the "undue burden" does not take a position on the vexed question when life begins. As Judith Thomson (1971) pointed out even before *Roe* was decided, one can agree that a fetus might be a person without acknowledging an obligation to keep it alive.[37] After all, we allow millions in the developing world to starve to death every year who could be saved by our intervention. We do not deny that they are human beings,

---

[36] *Stenberg v. Carhart,* 530 U.S. 914 (2000).

[37] Thomson (1971) famously asks you to suppose you awake one day to discover that a brilliant but sick violinist has been attached by tubes to your kidneys, and that unless the attachment is maintained for nine months, the violinist will die. Without denying that the violinist is a person, you might well insist that you have no obligation to remain attached.

but we do decide—by our actions, at least—that the burden that saving them would place on us is unacceptably high. At issue in the abortion controversy is not whether fetuses are human beings but whether individual pregnant women should be forced to sustain them. The Court's stance—that they should only if it does not burden women unduly—passes the matter back to state legislatures to act within that constraint.

3.4 COURTS AND THE MIDDLE GROUND

The middle-ground views of the role of courts in a democracy illustrated in *Brown* and the post-*Webster* abortion jurisprudence are geared to improving democracy's operation, not substituting for it in the way that conventional liberal constitutionalism does. The middle-ground views flow from two different, though compatible, impulses. One is informed by the *Carolene Products* insight that players in a democracy can undermine its constitutive rules so egregiously as to prevent its operating as a democracy, at least for a significant subset of the population. Disenfranchised minorities continue to be created among permanent "illegal" immigrants who are tolerated for economic reasons, and, more recently, in the move in numerous states permanently to disenfranchise convicted felons. This has led to a situation where an estimated 3.9 million Americans have been disenfranchised, over a million of whom have completed their sentences. They are drawn disproportionately from minority and disadvantaged populations, so that in 1998 13 percent (1.4 million) of African American men were disenfranchised—a group constituting over a third of the disenfranchised population (see Fellner and Mauer 1998, Uggen 2002).

Troubling as these examples are, we saw that the difficulty extends beyond discrete and insular minorities to the monopolistic behavior of political parities. Politicians can no better enforce their own compliance with the rules of the competitive game than can firms enforce theirs. As a result, there is a potentially important remedial and regulatory role for courts. Unfortunately, in the United States they have gone in the wrong direction in the quarter-century since *Buckley,* limiting the regulatory possibilities by equating money with speech. Apart from the inequalities of access this buys for the wealthy that is so often commented upon, it reinforces the anticompetitive dimensions of the system. It increases the entry costs prohibitively for all third-party candidates except millionaires and celebrities, and sustains a world in which the same contributors may be essential to victory for candidates from either political party in a given constituency (see Steen and Shapiro 2002). The dozens of Arthur Anderson and Enron jokes that could be found on the Internet following their collapse in 2002 underscore how routinely it has become accepted for major corporations to contribute to leading politicians of both parties, as well as all influential politicians on committees where they have interests at stake.[38]

That the extent of this problem has generally gone unrecognized is not a failure of Schumpeterian democracy, as we saw; rather, it is a failure to press its logic sufficiently far. The propensity to conflate "agreement," "bipartisanship," and "consensus" with what democracy should be aiming at prevents people from seeing how these values are at odds with the benefits of competition, and why it is so important that competition be sustained. Competition is the engine that provides politicians the reason to be responsive to voters, but for it to work well, they must have the incentive to compete over policies rather than personalities. Competition over policies is likely to diminish if they are in fact responding to contributors on policy matters. If both parties are bound to offer the same message, what remains to attack but the messenger?

It might be objected that if Schumpeterian competition has given up on the Rousseauist project of identifying a general will that embodies the common good, and values competition principally as a means of disciplining politicians, why should we care what they compete over? But this "toss the rascals out" philosophy, while preferable to hereditary monarchs and lifetime dictatorships, misses at least three other dimensions of well-functioning political competition. One is that competition is a major means through which opposition politics is institutionalized. Effective competition requires that there be a potential alternative government whose members have incentives to hold the current government to public account, and offer themselves as vehicles for the interests of those disadvantaged by the prevailing status quo. But if the opposition is as answerable as the government of the day to the Enrons and Arthur Andersons of the world, then their opposition watchdog functions are more likely to revolve around character assassination than shining light in dark corners that might prove uncomfortable for their contributors.

---

[38] As in the observation by one commentator that Enron had "contributed to so many politicians that those who hadn't received any had a general suspicion of unimportance hanging over them." Mark Thomas, "Enron fallout," www.drownedinsound.com/articles/3810.html [9/2/02]. In 2002 it was reported that more than half the then current members of the House of Representatives and 91 senators had been recipients of Arthur Andersen cash since 1989. Over the same period, 71 senators and 186 House members (43 percent)

Second, I noted in §3.2.1 that competition is valuable not merely as a disciplinary constraint on the corrupting effects of power, but also in giving politicians incentives to be more responsive to the majority of voters than are their competitors. When both parties are responsive in the first instance to (perhaps the same) contributors, we get a political market failure on the responsiveness front. For instance, candidates from both parties in a given constituency may have no incentive to disabuse voters of their misperceptions about the probability that they will have to pay the estate tax.[39] It might be in their interest either to avoid talking about the subject or to contribute to the misperception if they are facing heavy pressure from contributors and well-organized lobbyists to repeal it (see Shapiro and Birney 2002). To the extent that competition is the mechanism that gets politicians to be responsive to voters' interests, regulation is needed to prevent this type of political market failure.

Third, the argument here has been that pure proceduralism is not enough. Schumpeterian competition in public institutions is desirable not for its own sake but rather as the best available mechanism to realize middle-ground views geared to limiting domination. To the extent that the disproportionately well endowed and well organized can distort the system's operation, making it less responsive to others, it becomes less effective as a means for achieving that goal. If courts can play a role in limiting those distortions by making the system more genuinely competitive, they contribute to this stripped-down conception of the common good. Because it is a middle-ground view, however, courts overstep their boundaries when they behave imperially—imposing solutions on contending parties. They should always strive to work in democracy-enhancing ways, acting to protect the rules of the game and insisting that elected politicians come up with different solutions when their policies are judged to have crossed the line of fostering domination.

The same is true with courts or other second-guessing agencies that intervene to strengthen deliberative and other oppositional rights, as discussed in §§2.3 and 2.4. Again, the argument is about enhancing the voice

---

reported taking contributions from Enron. See "Enron and Anderson" www.opensecrets.org/news/enron/index.asp [9/2/02].

[39] Although some 2 percent of United States taxpayers pay any estate tax at all, polls reveal that anywhere between 17 and 37 percent of the population believe they or someone in their family will have to pay it. See Gallup Poll (June 22–25, 2000), Wendy Simmons, "Public Has Mixed Feelings about Tax Cuts," Poll Analyses, Gallup News Service (January 24, 2001), and Greenberg Quinlan Rosner Research Poll (June 11, 2002), http://www.ombwatch.org/article/articleview/811/1/125/ [9/2/02]. On the politics surrounding the estate tax repeal, see Shapiro and Birney (2002).

of critically weakened democratic participants, not of declaring in advance what those voices should say. We saw in §1.3 that there are in any case profound difficulties built into theories whose proponents appeal to the idea of deliberation for their legitimacy while at the same time claiming to know how that deliberation—if properly conducted under the right conditions—would come out. In effect these are rationalist theories that seek democratic legitimation by clothing themselves in deliberative garb. Judges in a democracy should always avoid the temptation that Justice Marshall could not resist in *Furman*, of acting on their speculations about what people would decide if they were properly informed. Instead, in their second-guessing roles, they should press for a world in which people can be properly informed and have the wherewithal to participate in collective decisions for themselves.

Some might say that the middle-ground views are in fact implicitly substantive. If courts or other second-guessing agencies intervene in the results of democratic procedures, declaring them to be unacceptable on democratic grounds, there must be a theory of substantive democracy, however implicit, by reference to which such judgments are rendered. This is partly correct, though it is a thin theory of the middle ground, geared to making the system genuinely competitive, preventing disenfranchisement, and protecting those vulnerable to domination by strengthening their opposition rights. And its strongly proceduralist bent, geared always to returning questions to legislatures rather than imposing solutions on them, casts courts in roles that are inherently supportive of democracy rather than antagonistic toward it. Over time, this is the best bet for courts to merit an independent role in a world in which democracy is the font of political legitimacy.

The antivanguardist, nay-saying, dimension of the middle-ground views further distinguishes them from substantive views. People can reasonably find things unacceptable even when they cannot articulate an account of what would be acceptable. During the 1960s and 1970s in South Africa many people had no doubt that apartheid violated essential principles of democratic governance, but few—if any—of them could have spelled out a consistent theory of democratic representation, or even said how they would resolve the various conundrums about democratic representation that have arisen in postapartheid South Africa. They were against domination in Machiavelli's sense mentioned in chapter 1, even if they could not have explained what they favored. This is dramatic but not atypical; in many ways human beings are reactive adaptive creatures. They reject what is unacceptable and shy away from what fails, assuming that it must be possible to come up with something better. Often this is more of a regulative ideal than an implicit theory, and sometimes the hope will prove vain. But not always. The middle-ground views rest on the supposition that often enough human ingenuity can rise to the challenges thrown up by the failures of democratic procedures when they are made manifest, and that loading the dice to facilitate that outcome is a better democratic solution than the going alternatives.

Getting and Keeping Democracy

D<small>ESIRABLE AS SCHUMPETERIAN</small> democracy might be, what are the conditions under which it is attainable and sustainable? After all, most of the world for most of its history has not been democratic. Even today, following the collapse of Soviet communism and the democratization of many authoritarian systems in Africa, Asia, and Latin America, the great majority of the world's population continues to be governed by nondemocratic regimes. Moreover, despite the claims of commentators from Alexis de Tocqueville ([1835] 1969) to Francis Fukuyama (1992) that humankind is marching inexorably in the direction of a democratic end of history, actual events tell a more complex story. In Tocqueville's century the democratic revolutions that swept Europe in 1830 and 1848 both suffered massive setbacks within a few years. The blows dealt democracy by fascism and communism in the twentieth century should temper teleological proclamations that the democratic revolutions since 1989 are yet one more step on the road to a democratic historical terminus. Partisans of democracy may be greatly heartened by its recent victories; they would do well to recognize that these can all too easily be reversed. Many of the fledgling postcommunist democracies are some distance from being secure. Democracy has broken down before in Latin America; it could do so again (see Linz 1978, Linz and Stepan 1978). Complacency about a peculiarly democratic African Renaissance (see Mbeki 1998) trades too heavily on the fragile new regimes in southern Africa; we should remember the Algerian and Rwandan possibilities. By 2002 the United Nations was warning that many of the eighty-one democracies that had come into being since 1980 were in serious jeopardy (United Nations 2000).

Yet those who have insisted that democracy is unattainable in many parts of the world, or predicted its imminent demise, have not fared better than the democracy teleologists. Huntington's (1984) claim that the prospects for the creation of more democracies in the world were slim came at the start of what he was later (1991) to christen the world's "third wave" of democratization. Most of these democracies have entered their second decade and survived numerous elections. A number of them have successfully endured the Huntingtonian test of two turnovers of power via the ballot box. Countries like Russia and South Africa have not yet done that, but they have held several competitive elections at national and local levels, and seem to be functioning better as democracies than many would have predicted in the heady days of their transitions. Robert Kaplan's (1997) suggestion that democracy may be little more than a fleeting moment in the world's political history was a sober corrective to the triumphalism of the early 1990s, but it is far from obviously correct. These questions therefore arise: what does lead to democratic transitions, and what causes democracies, once instituted, to succeed or fail? They are our concern in this chapter.

The early literatures tended to conflate questions about the causes of democracy's arrival with those concerning its survival, but in §4.1, I follow the more recent practice of keeping them distinct because different variables and dynamics are pertinent to the two issues. Indeed, in some circumstances there are tensions between what makes for a successful transition and what makes for a viable democracy in the medium term. These are subjects where the ratio of reliable knowledge to confident assertion is not good in political science. The reliable research that has been done suggests that there are multiple ways of getting to democracy, and that we lack good reasons to endorse the claim that democracy is inherently unsuited to certain types of societies—including so-called divided ones— owing to their ethnic, racial, or religious affiliations and antipathies. This raises the normative questions taken up in §4.2: when should democracy defer to collective commitments and aspirations, and when should its proponents seek to refashion them in democratic ways? Drawing on the arguments about superordinate goods and the principle of affected interests developed in the preceding chapters, I discuss the conditions under which group aspirations merit deference in a democratic polity.

4.1 DEMOCRATIC TRANSITIONS AND CONSOLIDATION

Establishing that Schumpeterian democracy is desirable says nothing about whether it is attainable, or, if attained, how likely it is to endure. It should be evident from what has been said thus far that valid generalizations about these subjects are going to be difficult to come by. The world is not obviously marching toward or away from democracy, and the ways in which democracy arises, or fails to arise, and survives, or fails to survive, may be shot through with contingencies that defy the development of a general theory. Looking for characteristic patterns rather than predictive laws may be the best that can be done in this area. Starting with the literature on transitions to democracy, we find this indeed to be the case.

4.1.1 Paths to Democracy

Generations of scholars have theorized about the conditions that give rise to democracy. Tocqueville ([1835] 1969) alleged it to be the product of egalitarian mores. Seymour Martin Lipsett (1959: 69–105) contends it is a by-product of modernization. For Barrington Moore (1966: 413–32) the critical factor is the emergence of a bourgeoisie, while Rueschemeyer, Stephens, and Stephens (1992) argue that the presence of an organized working class is decisive. It now seems clear that there is no single path to democracy, and, therefore, no generalization is to be had about the conditions that give rise to it. Democracy can result from decades of gradual evolution (Britain and the United States), imitation (India), cascades (much of Eastern Europe in 1989), collapses (Russia after 1991), imposition from above (Chile), revolutions (Portugal), negotiated settlements (Poland, Nicaragua, and South Africa), or external imposition (Japan and West Germany) (see Przeworski 1991: chap. 1, Huntington 1991: chap. 1, Shapiro 1996: chap. 4). Perhaps there are other possibilities.

On reflection this should not be surprising. There is no compelling theoretical reason to suppose that there are not multiple paths to any single destination, or that new paths will not open up once a destination has been identified. After all, once a toaster has been invented, others can imitate it; there is no need for everyone to go through the same invention process. Moreover, indigenous skills and local materials may offer people new ways of making a toaster—even ways of making a better toaster—once they have seen one from elsewhere. True, this does not prevent one from theorizing about the properties an effective toaster must have, and there may be a finite number of ways of making them, so that a more complex theory incorporating the different possibilities could in principle be developed. This may be feasible with respect to democratic transitions, but there is still a considerable distance to go.

This is not to say that the study of democratic transitions has been entirely devoid of theoretical progress. For one thing, one can develop useful classificatory typologies, as does Huntington (1991) when he divides democratic transitions into *transformations* (imposed from above), *interventions* (imposed from without), *replacements* (revolution from below), and *transplacements* (negotiated transitions).[1] Explanatory accounts might also be developed of the conditions that make different types of transitions possible. There may not be much of theoretical interest to say about transformations, interventions, and replacements, because they depend on some sufficiently strong player's deciding to impose democracy unilaterally and doing so. The variety of contingent factors that might lead that to happen seems potentially limitless.[2]

Most of the interest has been in Huntingtonian transplacements, perhaps partly because in them there appears to be more to understand that seems potentially tractable, and partly because negotiated transitions seem desirable for normative reasons. They seem like democratic paths to democracy (see Huntington 1991: 164), and some contend that they make for more viable democracy in the longer term than do the alternatives (see O'Donnell and Schmitter 1986: 39).

In fact, both the normative claims are questionable. In South Africa, for instance, the transition pact was negotiated in secret between the National Party (NP) government and the African National Congress (ANC) after two sets of roundtable negotiations had broken down, since those opposed to the transition—notably right-wing Afrikaner groups and Mangosuthu Buthelezi's ethnic Zulu Inkatha Freedom Party (IFP)—used their position at the roundtable talks to torpedo them. This illustrates the danger, discussed in §2.3, of giving "voice" to everyone, regardless of their interests or agenda. They can use it to procrastinate and stonewall, preventing change. If powerful forces stand to lose from a transition to democracy, unless they are either marginalized (as was the white right), co-opted (as were the radicals in the ANC), or persuaded to change their minds and join the process (as, eventually, with the IFP), democracy may never arrive. There might, indeed, be a trade-off between how democratic negotiated transitions are and how likely they are to be consummated (Jung and Shapiro 1995: 278–92). Certainly there is no case on record of democracy's having been achieved through a strongly inclusive participatory process.

This is one reason for skepticism of the proposition that negotiated transitions are more likely to be viable in the long run, though the small number of cases and the fact that most are in fact hybrids of Huntington's

[1] Transition typologies are something of a growth industry. For other variants see Karl (1990) and Munck and Leff (1997).

[2] It should be said that there is not much scholarship on authoritarianism as it relates to democratization. Perhaps theories could be developed to specify the conditions that make it

types makes confident generalization in this area perilous. But it is far from obvious that Spain, for example, which was a Huntingtonian transformation, is less viable than South Africa, which was a textbook case of a transplacement. Indeed, one of the demerits of negotiated transitions, well illustrated in the South African case, is that the parties to the agreement create institutions that they believe are going to suit them but may not be good for democracy's health. So, for instance, they agreed on a rule to the effect that any member of Parliament who leaves or is expelled from his or her party also loses his or her seat in Parliament and is replaced, by the leadership, by the next person on the party's list. This provision, which has been entrenched in the constitution, creates exceedingly weak backbenchers and one of the most powerful whip systems in the democratic world. Given the overwhelming dominance of the ANC, which might well have a run in South Africa comparable to that of the Congress Party in India or the Liberal Democrats in Japan, the lack of intraparty opposition is especially troubling (Jung and Shapiro 1995: 289–92). Negotiators in transitions look out for what they perceive as their own interests. Whether this is good for democracy in the longer run seems highly contingent and unpredictable, not least because statesmanlike conduct is likely to be idiosyncratically distributed (see Horowitz 2000: 253–84).

This is not to say that we cannot theorize illuminatingly about transition negotiations. Huntington notes, for instance, that transplacements become feasible when reactionaries in the authoritarian government are strong enough to prevent a transformation, revolutionaries in the opposition are too weak to effect a replacement, but government reformers and opposition moderates are strong enough, if they combine, to marginalize the authoritarian reactionaries and revolutionary opposition on their flanks and push through a pacted agreement (see also O'Donnell and Schmitter 1986, Jung and Shapiro 1995).

To be sure, transitions might not occur in such circumstances. Had F. W. de Klerk been shot by a disgruntled right-winger before the 1992 referendum, the South African transition might have fallen apart, and had Yitzhak Rabin not been shot in 1995, a successful agreement between Israelis and Palestinians might have been concluded and implemented. Had these counterfactuals taken place, we might in 2003 be trying to explain Middle East success in contrast to South Africa's being mired in worsening civil strife and racial conflict with no apparent light at the end

---

more or less likely that military juntas will decide unilaterally to democratize; no one to my knowledge has tried to do so.

of the tunnel. Because there are so many more ways for transition negotiations to go wrong than for them to go right, and because they can so easily be upset by unpredictable contingencies, it would be pointless to try to predict when they will succeed. Too many factors have to line up in just the right ways at just the right times, and the key players have to make smart choices at critical moments.[3]

Despite this, at least four considerations suggest that it is nonetheless worthwhile to try to specify characteristic dynamics of, and constraints on, transition negotiations. First, the things that are open to choice are influenced by these dynamics and constraints, affecting the likelihood that players will start negotiations or reach agreements rather than backtrack. For instance, people are more likely to negotiate or conclude agreements if the costs of not doing so increase, or if the available opportunities for success improve. If we can specify what typically alters those costs and opportunities in a given situation, we will be better able to say when people are more or less likely to negotiate and agree, even if we can never know this for sure.

Second, if we can get the relevant dynamics and constraints right, this can help explain why negotiated settlements exhibit certain characteristic forms—why, for example, they predispose the players to agree on institutional rules that limit robust opposition politics in the new order. This, in turn, can be useful in deepening our understanding of the tensions between democratic transitions and the longer-run viability of democratic institutions, and in arguing for changes in the transition from interim to final constitutions (Shapiro and Jung 1996, Luong 2000).

Third, the contingencies and the vicissitudes of human agency may mean that predicting successful outcomes to negotiations is unlikely, but the same is not true for predicting failures. There are necessary conditions for successful agreements. If the conditions are present *and* exogenous shocks do not upset them *and* the players seize the moment when they must, then there can be successful agreements. But if the necessary conditions are lacking, then regardless of what else happens or what the players do, there is not going to be a settlement. For instance, Gerry Adams's emergence on the scene in the late 1980s as a new kind of pragmatic IRA leader "with a human face" led to endless speculation about whether a settlement could now be anticipated. But it seems clear that Adams and his behavior were largely irrelevant until the Blair government came to

---

[3] For a revealing account of the many contingencies that might have derailed the American system in the first two decades after the Revolution, see Ellis (2000).

power in the United Kingdom in 1997. No Tory government in the 1980s or 1990s could conclude an agreement, regardless of who was in charge of the IRA, because they depended on Unionist support in Westminster. They were too weak vis-à-vis their own flank to make the relevant concessions. Labour's victory changed the universe of possibilities, and *then* it became critically important that there be a pragmatic IRA leader capable of compromise and strong enough to make the radical wing of the IRA accept it (Jung, Lust-Okar, and Shapiro 2002). Grasping the necessary conditions for successful transition negotiations makes it plain who the critical players at different junctures are, forestalling misplaced confidence in hopeless scenarios.

Fourth, understanding the characteristic dynamics of successful settlements can reveal opportunities that might otherwise go unnoticed. The windows of opportunity that make them possible rarely open, and they seldom stay open for long. Politicians may often be unwilling to take the considerable risks involved in moving through them, but sometimes it seems that they do not see either the possibilities or how fleeting they may be. A more accurate and widespread understanding of negotiation dynamics might lead them to see the urgency of moving decisively when critical choices present themselves. For instance, had Shimon Peres called a snap election after Rabin's assassination in 1995, polling evidence from that period suggests that he might well have capitalized on Rabin's status as a felled hero—winning a mandate to move the negotiations to a final agreement. (This would have been a move analogous to de Klerk's referendum in March 1992 in South Africa in response to a series of by-election defeats. It delivered the antitransition forces on the white right a decisive defeat from which they never recovered (Jung and Shapiro 1995: 287–89).

Peres, either unwilling to take the risk or unable to understand how quickly his political capital would wane, frittered away his advantage, eventually losing a close election to Benjamin Netanyahu in May 1996. This was at a time when Arafat's move toward what had turned out to be failed negotiations strengthened Hamas and other groups on his radical flank, forcing him to bait and switch—trying to regain his stature and the symbols of resistance. Tragically, by the time Ehud Barak emerged in 2000 as a Labor leader who was willing to alienate coalition partners, go for a deal, and gamble on a referendum if necessary, Arafat was too weak to make the compromises a final agreement would require from the Palestinian Authority. Despite numerous reports in the Western press about his obtuseness at Camp David in 2000, his alleged inability to miss an opportunity to miss an opportunity, and so on, public opinion data strongly suggests that he could never at that time have made an agreement and survived (Jung, Lust-Okar, and Shapiro 2002).

The preceding discussion should suffice to establish that despite inherent limitations in the study of transitions, knowledge about them can usefully advance. Much of the progress is likely to involve disabusing people of wrongheaded faith in misguided possibilities and getting them to focus on the right factors in trying to determine what is feasible in a given situation. Knowledge of this kind is by no means of negligible value, even if its predictions will inevitably be couched in conditionals and hedged in with contingencies.

Moreover, it seems clear that there is no decisive evidence that negotiated transitions are better paths to viable medium-term democracy than other available routes. Indeed, the principals who negotiate settlements may have little reason to create institutions friendly to democracy's health if this conflicts with their immediate political interests. We saw this in the South African example with respect to opposition institutions. If a settlement is ever reached in the Middle East, it, too, may make scant provision for democracy in the new Palestine or for undermining the severe attenuation of the democratic rights of Israeli Arabs. Negotiations are successful when the principals can find common ground and marginalize, co-opt, or convince opponents to accept it. Whether that common ground is good for democracy is either a matter of contingent luck or depends on a statesmanlike ability of the principals to rise above immediate interests. This requires a different kind of luck—also unpredictable.

There is a certain artificiality to the question: which is the most viable route to democracy? Countries are seldom given the choice. There could not have been negotiated transitions in West Germany or Japan after the Second World War. Opposition forces were too weak to achieve replacements in Spain after Franco. Authoritarian governments were too weak to resist them in Portugal in 1974 or in East Germany and Romania in 1989. Transplacements become the only available route out of authoritarianism when a particular balance of forces obtains within and between government and opposition forces, as we have seen. This suggests that the more pertinent question for democratic institutional engineers is not which is the best path, but rather, given the path a country is on, what are the most important things for the principals to achieve so as to increase the chances that democracy, if established, will endure? That is the question I turn to next.

4.1.2 Democracy's Survival

No matter how democracies come into being, it may be that they are more likely to survive and thrive in some circumstances than others. Here the literature takes three tacks: institutional, economic, and cultural. The first two are comparatively straightforward in their claims and, in contrast to the literature on transitions, can be evaluated by reference to a good deal of systematic cross-national data. The cultural literature is more amorphous and empirically slippery, partly because cultural explanations tend to be residual explanations and partly because there are quite different types of cultural explanations in the literature. These issues are taken up following a brief look at the state of the institutional and economic literatures.

The institutional literature grows out of Linz's (1978, 1994) contention that parliamentary systems are more stable than presidential ones. He argued that presidential systems tend toward polarization both in the political culture and between presidents and congresses, which they lack the institutional mechanisms to alleviate. Parliamentary systems, by contrast, were said to be more stable and better able to deal with leadership crises. Linz's view has been challenged by Shugart and Carey (1992: chap. 3), who differentiate among more and less stable presidentialisms, and Mainwaring and Shugart (1997: 12–55), who suggest that weak or "reactive" presidential systems, such as that in the United States, can be as stable as parliamentary ones. Subsequent scholarship suggests that the arrangements that matter most may have less to do with whether-or-not presidentialism, and more with other institutional features. For instance, a substantial presence of the presidential party in the assembly, favorable conditions for coalition politics, and centralized executive authority in the government may contribute more to stability than do parliamentary institutional arrangements. This may account—in Latin America, for example—for the differences between the comparatively more stable and governable countries like Argentina, Chile, and Uruguay and less stable ones such as Ecuador, Peru, and contemporary Venezuela (see Foweraker 1998: 665–70 and Cheibub and Limongi 2000).

The state of the art in the economic literature is Przeworski et al. (2000: chap. 2), who explore the impact of economic development on the stability of democratic regimes. They find that although economic development does not predict the installation of democracy, there is a strong relationship between economic development (in particular the level of per capita income) and the survival of democratic regimes. Democracies appear never to die in wealthy countries, whereas poor democracies are fragile, exceedingly so when annual per capita incomes fall below $2,000 (1975 dollars). When annual per capita income falls below this threshold, democracies have a one-in-ten chance of collapsing within a year. Between annual per capita incomes of $2,001 and $5,000 this ratio falls to one in sixteen. Above $6,055 annual per capita income, democracies, once established, appear to last indefinitely. Moreover, poor democracies are more likely to survive when governments succeed in generating development and avoiding economic crises (Przeworski et al. 2000: 106–17).

Turning to the cultural literature, we find that in some countries governments stage coups rather than give up power when they are voted out of office, yet no defeated American president seriously contemplates sending the tanks down Pennsylvania Avenue. Indeed, we saw in §3.2.2 that, pressed sufficiently hard, Madison's distinction between incentives and constraints survives only if it is buttressed by an inculcated practice of giving up power when elections have been lost—encapsulated in Huntington's two-turnover rule. This may be a good rule of thumb for deciding whether competitive Schumpeterianism has taken root, but it says nothing about what the conditions are that lead the losers in one national setting to give up power whereas those in another decide not to.

Huntington (1991:36–37) contends that commitment to democratic values on the part of political elites is necessary for democracy to endure. This plausible conjecture may help us understand the (otherwise puzzling) endurance of Indian democracy against the odds. Indian elites were often trained in Oxford and Cambridge during the colonial period, and may have imbibed commitments to democracy from the English. This was not true, by contrast, of African political elites, which perhaps has something to do with why democracies did not generally survive in British ex-colonies there. Perhaps institutional variables account for the difference, however. The British engaged in direct rule in India, whereas indirect rule through local surrogates was the African norm (see Mamdani 1996). As the successful installation of democracy in Japan and West Germany after the Second World War might be taken to suggest, democracy can be imposed on countries where it has no successful track record so long as there is direct control until democratic institutions take root. Detracting from this account, and again suggesting the importance of culture and beliefs, is the United States example—where democracy survived despite British reliance on indirect rule. Institutional, cultural, economic, and other variables probably all play their parts. Unfortunately, the available data does not lend itself to the kind of large-n multivariate analysis that would be required to afford a systematic grip on their relative importance.

Commentators in the rational choice tradition have argued that worrying about democratic commitments is either unnecessary or pointless in a democracy. For instance, Przeworski (1991: 19–34) defines democracy as a system of spontaneous or self-reinforcing compliance that operates successfully only when self-interested players who fail to get their way calculate that it is to their advantage to accept defeat and wait for the next chance to prevail within the rules, rather than destroy the system (if they have the power) or cease to participate (if they lack it). When the system works, normative commitments to democracy, while sometimes present, are "not necessary to generate compliance with democratic outcomes." The strategic calculation, by those who have the power to destroy the system, that it is in their interest not to do so is sufficient, and likely necessary as well, for the system to survive. Otherwise the "commitment problem," as game theorists since Thomas Schelling (1960) have labeled it, cannot be solved.

A necessary condition for this outcome is generally assumed to be the uncertainty that results from the existence of crosscutting cleavages in the preferences of the population. Losers in any given round at the ballot box must believe that there is enough uncertainty about the future that they might win next time, perhaps as part of a different coalition, or that they will prevail on enough other issues to warrant continuing participation. This is why such democratic theorists as Di Palma (1990) describe stable democracy as a system of institutionalized uncertainty about the future. The same intuition also informs Miller's observation, discussed in §1.1.2, that the "rational" instability of majority rule is actually a source of political stability in pluralist democratic theory.

If democracies survived only when the conditions for spontaneous self-compliance were met, we would be living in a pure incentives-based world, and Przeworski (1991: 20–22) would be right that trying to induce normative commitments to democracy would be a waste of time. Where they were needed to prevent breakdown, they would probably not produce that result, and where breakdown did not threaten, they would be redundant. Just as incentives matter more than Madisonian constraints in this scheme, they also matter more than culture and beliefs.

Przeworski himself notes the existence of a counterexample to his discussion of necessity, however, and there appear to be other instances where groups whose instrumental interests are harmed by democratic processes have nonetheless supported them (see Shapiro 1996: chap. 4). In subsequent work, Przeworski (1999: 25–31) has acknowledged that to date there has not been a theoretical solution to the commitment problem that relies exclusively on self-interested spontaneous compliance. As an empirical matter, this logic would leave unexplained the fact that politicians often give up power that they have no hope of regaining—as Presidents Reagan and Clinton did in 1988 and 2000, respectively. Even when not prohibited by term limits, they often accept defeat when they know that the chances of regaining power in the future are vanishingly slim. Jimmy Carter and George Bush senior are two recent American illustrations, but this practice goes back two centuries in the United States to John Adams's acquiescence in his defeat by Thomas Jefferson and the Republican party in 1800. Hardin (1999: 136) describes his acceptance as "perhaps the most important single action by anyone under the United States Constitution in its first decades . . . that made the nascent American democracy meaningful in a way that must be at the core of any sensible definition of democracy." That might be an overstatement, but his observation highlights the reality that, while important, the incentives of power-maximizers will never be sufficient to sustain democratic institutions.[4]

Indeed, the idea of spontaneous self-compliance rests on expectations about the conditions for political competition that are unmet in other competitive settings. For instance, in the economy individual firms try to expand their market shares and would become monopolies if they could—assuming they respond only to individual incentives. Yet the survival of competitive markets depends on their accepting rules and norms, enforced by third parties, that prevent this. Stylized definitions of democracy as lacking third-party enforcement suggest that politics differs fundamentally from markets on this dimension, but there are reasons for skepticism at both ends of the alleged disanalogy.

On the one hand, the most powerful economic actors can indeed refuse to play by the rules, as we are reminded by the examples of gangster capitalism in Colombia and Russia and the American robber barons of the nineteenth century. The question therefore remains why they agree to play by the rules in some settings and not others, much as we might ask why the military accepts civilian control in some circumstances and not others. On the other hand, insisting on the disanalogy assumes, implausi-

---

[4] In a different variant of the incentives-based argument, Przeworski (2001) proposes that losers in elections accept the result in rich countries because there is too much at stake in turning against it—there is more to be lost in civil war. If true, this might go some way toward explaining why although democracy is fragile in poor countries, it survives in affluent ones.

bly, that the institutions and practices that constrain economic actors are unavailable to constrain political actors—perhaps because the forces maintaining political stability in a democracy are reduced, in the stylized comparison, to majority-rule democracy operating in a contextual void. In fact, political decision making is always constrained by inherited institutions and practices. Courts, the police and the military, and long-established regulatory bodies all limit what political decision-makers can do—not to mention norms of behavior to which people have become habituated. Political competition operates within these and other constraints just as economic competition does, suggesting that the ideal type of majority-rule democracy as a sui generis spontaneously self-reinforcing system is misleading. Perhaps no system based exclusively on voluntary compliance by utterly instrumental actors would survive, but since democracies are not in fact systems of this kind, it is not clear that anything of practical interest follows from this observation.

The focus on incentives is nonetheless useful; it underscores the importance of avoiding all-or-nothing politics. Ensuring that the stakes in any given contest are comparatively low attenuates the incentive for losers to act on the impulse to defect. If issues can be revisited periodically, if they can be pursued in different forums, if it is never the case that all issues are up for decision at the same time, and if candidates can run for a variety of offices, then they have more reason to remain committed to the system when they lose. To the extent that one wants to create incentives for those who do not prevail in a given contest to keep their opposition to the outcome "loyal," it is important that they perceive future or different avenues for pursuing their goals; otherwise there is no reason for them not to defect—whether this means alienated withdrawal, turning to crime, or becoming a politicized revolutionary. This may not be sufficient for opposition to remain loyal, but it seems reasonable to suppose that it is likely to increase the odds.

It is, in any case, too simple to say that a certain structure of preferences (such as one that the pluralists referred to as a system of crosscutting cleavages) will lead to self-sustaining democratic institutions while others will not. Preferences are not primordial givens; they are shaped, partly by education and acculturation, and partly in response to institutional arrangements, as we have seen. As a result, it seems wise to try to structure things so that people will reflect on their goals from the standpoint of the reasonable demands of others, and be prepared to modify the ways in which they pursue them so as not to undermine democracy. This means that losers must come to accept the legitimacy of present defeats, and sometimes even try to play constructive roles in implementing policies they oppose, while winners should appreciate the wisdom of not exploiting every dimension of their present strategic advantage. They should see the wisdom of tolerating—even valuing—continuing opposition, even if this limits the degree to which their goals can be maximized in a given situation. In short, it is prudent to assume that if democracy is to survive, people will have to be persuaded to value it for more than its short-term instrumental benefits.[5]

Another strand of scholarship on the role of culture in democratic stability focuses on mass rather than elite beliefs. Some research suggests that mass beliefs about democracy may play a role in its durability, but the effect does not seem to be strong and it operates in conjunction with numerous other variables.[6] There is also a literature, centered on Putnam (1993a, 1993b, 2000), that attends to mass political culture in a different way. Here the suggestion is not that mass beliefs *about democracy* are important, but rather that it is membership and, above all, trust in local associations that make democracy durable over the long haul. Putnam's thesis grew out of a study of Italy in which he argued that effective government and institutional success were contingent on the vitality of the civic community. Putnam found that those regions of Italy that had an ongoing tradition of civic engagement also had a higher level of institutional success than those regions without civic participation, despite exhibiting identical institutional structures. For civic engagement to flourish, community members have to trust in the reciprocity of those around them and have the ability and resources to utilize social networks. Putnam deployed the term *generalized reciprocity* to connote a social understanding that one's efforts to participate and protect the common good will be reciprocated by others, known or unknown.

However, Putnam distinguishes two different types of cultural networks: *horizontal*, involving the organization of individuals of equal status and resources, and *vertical*, networks that bring together those of unequal status in relations of dependence or hierarchy. It is horizontal networks,

[5] This suggests that Wollheim's paradox (which turns on the possibility of tension between what an individual wants and how he ought to view that preference in the event that he does not prevail through procedures of democratic decision that he accepts as legitimate) should be thought of more as a problem of political socialization than as a philosophical paradox. Wollheim (1962: 77–87).

[6] An empirical study suggesting that no single cultural variable is decisive in explaining democratic stability is Berg-Schlosser and De Meur (1994: 253–80). For an analysis suggesting that some aspects of political culture matter more than others, see Muller and Seligson (1994: 635–652).

usually resulting from community participation, that he holds to be critical in generating the social capital needed for institutional success. Indeed, vertical networks—for example, the Catholic Church, feudal landholdings, and clientalism—cannot cultivate the social trust deemed essential on his account. The inferior and superior will experience different outcomes from the same moment of cooperation (Putnam 1993a: 173–75). This is in tension with Tocqueville's ([1840] 1969: 450–51) claim that hierarchical civil institutions such as the Catholic Church are good for democracy on the grounds, among others, that in the absence of authoritative allocation of values by the state it is important for social stability that they come from somewhere. On Putnam's account, by contrast, it is horizontal civic participation that, like an upward spiral, brings about the greater trust, networks, and norms that make generalized reciprocity, and hence institutional success, possible.

In a like spirit, Putnam (2000) argues that in the contemporary United States the erosion of local community participation undermines democratic participation—and with it stability and governability. In the first sixty-five years of the twentieth century, participation in political groups, formal social clubs, and informal clubs like bowling leagues or bridge clubs was steadily increasing. After the mid-1960s, however, it began to decline. Putnam charts and then seeks to explain this waning tradition of community socializing and political participation, blaming it on numerous factors ranging from suburbanization to the mass media, particularly television, as well as demographic changes: as the older and involved generation dies out, the younger generations of baby boomers and generation X-ers do not fill in the ranks in social, political, or philanthropic organizations. Nor are they interested in the informal social networks enjoyed by the older generation. The result, on Putnam's telling, is atrophy of the social networks that support the generalized reciprocity essential to effective democratic institutions.

Suggestive as this might be, Putnam's argument has drawn heavy critical fire, from both historians of Italy and students of contemporary American democracy.[7] As a theoretical matter, it is hard to see why strong local attachments and trust within local civic groups should be expected to translate into trust of democratic political institutions. Rousseau ([1762] 1968: 150 ff.) argued long ago that allegiance to "sectional societies" is more likely to undermine than reinforce commitment to collective institu-

[7] See Goldberg (1996), Sabetti (1996), Levi (1996), Gobetti (1996), and Ladd (1999: 25–119).

tions. Levi (1996: 45–56) makes a similar point in relation to Putnam: we at least as plausibly expect intensive trust in local civic associations to breed distrust of government rather than trust—as it does among militia groups, for example. A possible line of response might be that it is large publicly committed civic institutions that are important for democracy, but it is not obvious how to differentiate the Boy Scouts from the Hitler Youth on that count. At present, it is difficult to see a compelling case, conceptual or empirical, that low levels of civic trust are subversive of democracy, or that, if they are, they are more subversive of democracy than of nondemocracy.

4.1.3 Democracy and Cultural Division

One recurring theme in the literature concerns whether the cultural divisions are so deep in certain types of societies that competitive democracy is unworkable; trying to hold competitive elections would amount to pouring gasoline on conflictual fire. Just what "depth" is intended to mean here is often elusive (see the exchange between Koelble and Reynolds 1996: 221–36 and Shapiro and Jung 1996: 237–47). Sometimes it seems to refer to the intensity of attachments to a religious, ethnic, or racial group. (Surprisingly, these are generally used interchangeably in the literature, so that South Africa, the Middle East, and Northern Ireland have all been called divided societies.) At other times *divided society* seems to refer to divisions' being overdetermining in the sense that racial, ethnic, religious, social, economic, and all other differences in the population are mutually reinforcing rather than crosscutting. This is said to obviate the possibility of crosscutting cleavages' producing pluralist stability by ensuring that the same people are not always winners and losers, and by institutionalizing uncertainty about the future as discussed in §4.1.2.[8]

Lurking behind these debates is a series of assumptions about the psychology of human identity and attachment. Usually it is these assumptions that seem to divide those who argue about divided societies from one another. Yet the assumptions are more frequently taken for granted than defended by reference to any kind of compelling evidence or even argued for as sensible default presumptions. It is therefore worthwhile to spell out what is at stake in the two main competing conceptions of identity and attachment, one primordialist, the other postmodern, to make clear just

---

[8] Somewhat confusingly Lijphart (1977) refers to societies where political competition is alleged to be impossible for these reasons as "plural" societies.

how they predispose commentators to particular positions in the debate. We will see that neither is compelling on its own terms or carries the implications that proponents seem to think warranted. This opens the way to a discussion of the default presumptions that seem to make the best sense, given what is actually known in this area.

Starting with the primordialists, if one thinks, as they do, of human identities as unalterable, then the appropriate political stance would be purely instrumental: find ways to prevent people from killing one another by channeling the destructive aspects of their fixed aspirations away from one another. In the divided society literature, such thinking often gives rise to consociationalism. The injunction is to devise systems of minority vetoes or other mechanisms that force leaders of different groups to work out a modus vivendi and govern as a "cartel of elites" (Lijphart 1969: 213–15, 222). Here the appeal to consensus is not based on fairness or a deliberation-inspired view of its inherent desirability; it is intended to avoid civil war. If the primordialists are right, competitive democracy is impossible in such circumstances, and consociational accommodation is the best we can hope for. If they are wrong, however, as I have argued, with Jung, in the South African context that they are, then the primordialists are vulnerable to the charge that their remedy might sustain—or even produce—the malady to which it is alleged to respond (see Jung and Shapiro 1995, Shapiro and Jung 1996). Perhaps consociational arrangements such as those embodied in the 1995 Dayton Accords in the Yugoslavian conflict are required to end ethnic civil wars, but this does not mean they supply a viable basis for democracy. Indeed, Horowitz (1985, 2000) made a compelling empirical case that consociationalism has been singularly unsuccessful as a device for managing ethnic conflict. More recent empirical work on Africa supports this contention (Spears 2000, 2002).

The opposing view stems from the postmodern rejection of primordialism. Postmodernists contend that political identities are "socially constructed," that they are malleable and evolve over time. On this view there is nothing natural or necessary about ethnic, racial, and other group-based allegiances or antipathies. These might have developed differently from the ways they have, and they can change in the present and future (see Vail 1989). Indeed, their fluid character makes it more or less inevitable that they will. Postmodern writers seldom get into the technicalities of how they believe this might be accomplished, but on their view it is reasonable to assume that forms of identity could develop that differ radically from those presently prevailing in the world. In particular, people might come to accept, perhaps even celebrate, differences that today are sources of mutual hatred (see Jung 2000: chap. 9).

Postmodernists can correctly point out that politicized identities evolve with time and circumstance. But to say that they are historically contingent does not imply that they are infinitely malleable; it does not even entail that forms of identity that have been politically mobilized, but might not have been, can subsequently be demobilized. This is more than the problem of getting the toothpaste back into the tube. The degree to which things are alterable may not vary at all with the extent to which they are socially constructed. Many features of the natural world, ranging from the temperature of our bathwater to the genetic structure of our beings, can be altered by conscious human design. Socially constructed phenomena, by contrast, often defy all efforts at conscious human control. Markets are human constructions, yet we may be unable to regulate them so as to operate at full employment with no inflation. Ethnic hatred might concededly be learned behavior, yet we may have no idea how to prevent its being reproduced in the next generation. Proponents of social construction leap too quickly from that idea to alterability; at best the two are contingently related.

An intermediate and more plausible account that avoids the attendant difficulties of both primordialism and postmodernism might run as follows. Human beings are shaped by context and circumstance, but they are also constrained by their inherited constitutions. These constitutions may themselves evolve, but at a given time and place they limit the possibilities of social reconstruction. Human psychology is always malleable but never infinitely so, and certain ways of shaping it are likely to be more effective than others in any given situation. The interesting questions concern what the limits to this malleability are, and which forms of social reconstruction are likely to be more effective than others. The difficulty for democratic institutional designers is that these are empirical questions about which there is not much accumulated knowledge in the social sciences. As a result, it seems wise to work at the margins, and to think about institutional redesign rather than design ex nihilo, as suggested in §3.1. Identities are fixed to some—usually unknown—degree, but they also adapt to circumstances, incentives, and institutional rules. The goal should be to reshape such constraints, where possible, so that at the margins identities evolve in ways that are more, rather than less, hospitable to democratic politics. From this perspective the critique of consociationalism is that, to the degree that politicized identities are malleable, it tends to reproduce the wrong ones.

95

4.1.4 Identities and Electoral Engineering

Electoral systems are potential instruments for undermining group conflict in the service of promoting competitive politics, but, given what has just been said, it is unclear how effective they can be. If we assume group-based affiliations and antipathies to be mobilized at least partly from above, a logical place to start is the incentives facing candidates for office. In a Schumpeterian spirit the minimum goal should be to avoid encouraging aspiring leaders to foment group-based hatred as they seek power. From this perspective we can array electoral systems on an engineering continuum, ranging from *reactive* systems that cater to prevailing commitments, through *reflective* systems that are neutral with respect to existing preferences, to *proactive* systems that seek to alter them in ways that promote competitive democracy.

Secession and partition anchor the reactive pole. Next come apartheid and consociationalism (the former imposed by the stronger party, the latter sanctified by some kind of elite agreement), where the aspiration is to achieve functional partition within a unified polity. Further along are systems that engineer around group differences to produce diversity in legislatures, as is the case with gerrymandering to create majority-minority districts in the American South. These reactive responses all take group-based affiliations as given, hoping to work around them. Toward the center of the continuum we come to reflective responses: those that are sensitive to group-based differences but neutral in the sense of being biased neither for nor against them. The various cumulative voting schemes discussed by Lani Guinier fit this description.[9] Here the principle is to give each voter as many votes as there are seats. If a state is to have eight representatives in the legislature, every voter gets eight votes that can be cast however she wishes—all for one candidate or spread among several. If there are intense minority group–based preferences, members of the group can cast all eight votes for "their" representative; if not, not. Unlike racial gerrymandering and consociationalism, reflective schemes respond to group allegiances without doing anything to produce or reinforce them. As a result, they avoid the critique of reactive systems that they promote balkanization.

[9] For Guinier's proposals, see Guinier (1991: 1077–1154, 1994a: 109–37). On the battle over her confirmation as assistant attorney general for civil rights, which she lost for her advocacy of cumulative voting, see Guinier (1994b). Her fate suggests a criterion, in addition to representative fairness, for evaluating proposed decision rules: whether they can be widely understood and perceived as democratic.

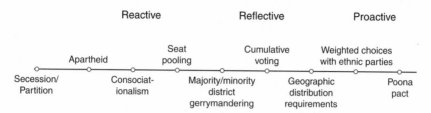

Electoral Engineering Continuum

Although cumulative voting responds to intense group affiliations that might exist in a population without actually producing or reinforcing them, it does not ameliorate or undermine them either. This is why it is inferior, from a democratic point of view, to systems that give aspiring political leaders active incentives to avoid mobilizing forms of identity that exacerbate cultural competition, and to devise, instead, ideologies that can appeal across the group divisions. For these we move to the proactive part of the continuum. Since group-based hatred is often mobilized by political leaders in response to what they see as routes to power, it is important, as Horowitz (1985: 154–55) has argued, to shape the incentives for gaining power in ways that promote a different result. When group antipathies are strong (and assuming partition is not on the agenda), systems are needed that affect the behavior of elites from one group toward the grassroots members of other groups in the right ways. This can be achieved through various mechanisms, all of which require politicians to compete for votes among politicized groups other than their own, and so promote accommodation rather than exclusionary politics.

The most obvious is a combination of coalition politics and heterogeneous constituencies. Horowitz (1991: 154–55) describes a successful example of this kind from Malaysia, in which Malay and Chinese politicians were forced to rely in part on votes delivered by politicians belonging to the other ethnic group. The votes would not have been forthcoming "unless leaders could portray the candidates as moderate on issues of concern to the group that was delivering its votes across ethnic lines." In such situations, which Horowitz identifies as having operated for considerable periods (and then failed) in countries as different as Lebanon, Sri Lanka, and Nigeria, compromises at the top of a coalition are reinforced by electoral incentives at the bottom.

Another possible device is geographical distribution requirements, such as the Nigerian formula for presidential elections employed in 1979 and

1983, in which the winning candidate had to get both the largest number of votes and at least 25 percent of the vote in two-thirds of the then nineteen states of the Nigerian Federation. This type of system would not work in countries like South Africa, however, given the territorial dispersion of politicized groups. In such circumstances, the two most promising candidates are proportional representation utilizing the single transferable vote system, and an alternative vote rule that also lists more than one ordered preference but declares elected only candidates who receive a majority, rather than a plurality, of votes. Both systems require politicians to cater to voters' choices other than their first preferences, so that the politicians' incentives work in the appropriate moderating directions. This will be further accentuated by the alternative vote system, assuming that parties proliferate (Horowitz 1985: 184, 166, 187–96). Such vote-pooling systems are more likely to achieve interethnic political cooperation than are consociational arrangements or systems, whether first-past-the-post or proportional, that merely require seat pooling by politicians in coalition governments; as reactive systems, these do nothing to moderate group antipathies. On the contrary, they give politicians incentives to maximize their ex-ante bargaining position by increasing what economists might describe as their group's reservation price for cooperation.

Despite the intuitive appeal of Horowitz's reasoning, proactive incentives to avoid appealing to intergroup antipathies will not always work. Parties might proliferate within politicized groups in ways that undermine this dimension of the logic behind weighted vote schemes.[10] Moreover, some of the worst of what often (misleadingly) gets labeled interethnic violence is actually intraethnic violence that results when different parties seek to mobilize support from the same ethnic group. Much of the South African violence that erupted in the eastern part of the country after 1984 resulted when the United Democratic Front (representing the then illegal ANC) was formed and challenged IFP support among Zulus there, and some of the worst violence among white nationalists resulted from comparable competition for the white nationalist vote. There are limits to the degree that intraethnic competition of this sort can be ameliorated by weighted vote mechanisms. If parties have incentives to mobilize support in more than one ethnic constituency, they should avoid campaigning as ethnic parties anymore than they have to. In practice, however, parties like the IFP—whose raison d'être is ethnic—may have little scope to cam-

[10] For elaboration of these and related difficulties confronting Horowitz's proposals, see Shapiro (1993: 145–47).

paign on any other basis. Accordingly, they may resist—perhaps vio-lently—any inroads into their "traditional" sources of support. They can only play a zero-sum ethnic game.

Whether this is likely to be is difficult to know. In the early 1990s, the NP transformed itself in a short time into a somewhat viable nonethnic party. More than half of their votes in the 1994 election came from non-whites (mainly Cape Coloureds—it remains to be seen whether their suc-cessor party can make inroads into the black vote). They did this because their leaders came to believe that their alternatives were "adapt or die." In Canada, less apocalyptic thinking appears so far to have been sufficient to cause the leaders of ethnic parties to accept that their aspirations must triumph through a democratic process or not at all. By contrast, Bosnia and the Middle East reveal that sometimes even the likelihood—indeed the certainty—of death is not sufficient to head off the pursuit of mutually incompatible group aspirations. Yet most people do not want to die. The challenge, for democrats, is to devise mechanisms that make it more likely that they will live in conditions of inclusive participation and nondomina-tion. Group aspirations that by their terms cannot be realized within dem-ocratic constraints are to be resisted, but it is better to work for a world in which such aspirations diminish. Getting rid of institutions that press in the opposite direction seems like a logical place to start.

When relying on the logic of cross-group mobilization does not lead to ethnic accommodation, it may be possible to move further along the continuum and become more explicitly proactive, as in the 1931 Poona Pact in India. It required that Untouchables be the representatives in 148 designated constituencies, a number corresponding roughly to their proportion in the population (Van Parijs 1996: 111–12). This both en-sures that the specified number of Untouchables become parliamentary representatives and gives aspirants for office an incentive to seek support from all sectors of heterogeneous constituencies, not merely "their own" ethnic group. (Untouchables are not prohibited from running elsewhere, but, as geographically dispersed minorities in all constituencies, they are seldom elected.)[11]

Attractive as such solutions can sometimes be, they are manifestly pater-nalistic and so unlikely to win legitimacy without widespread acceptance that a minority has been unjustly treated over a long time, and that it will

---

[11] In 1996 they occupied 3 out of a total of 400 (Van Parijs 1996: 112).

not otherwise be represented.[12] Even then, such proposals will likely be attacked on many of the same grounds as are reverse discrimination and affirmative action. They can also be expected to provoke the charge, if from a different ideological quarter, that those competing for the designated minority spots will lack the incentive to represent the relevant minority interests. Rather, the temptation will be to try to outperform the competition as Uncle Toms.

The further institutional designers try to move along the continuum toward explicit proactive systems that force integration in exclusionary and racist societies, the more they will learn about how much redesign of group-based antipathy is feasible in them. At present the only statement that can be made with much confidence is that there is no particular reason to think any society inherently incapable of Schumpeterian electoral competition. As the Indian and Japanese examples underscore, even societies with profoundly inegalitarian cultures and undemocratic histories have adapted to the demands of democratic politics in ways that many would have insisted was impossible before the fact. South Africa might turn out to be another such case in the making, though the jury must remain out until ANC hegemony faces a serious challenge.

4.2 Normative Defenses of Group Rights

Philosophers who argue that political arrangements should mirror group aspirations too often ignore or underplay the reality implied in the preceding discussion, to wit, that groups do not just "have" political aspirations. These aspirations are at least partly mobilized from above by political entrepreneurs who stand to benefit either from maintaining existing systems of group solidarities, or from dismantling them and replacing them with different ones. The temptation to pursue this by fomenting out-group hatred will often be irresistible to leaders and would-be leaders. Notwithstanding the great emphasis on affective ties characteristic of political philosophers such as Sandel (1982, 1996), Walzer (1983, 1987), Taylor (1989), and Kymlicka (1985, 2001), political associations are not families. They consist of multiple overlapping coalitions and potential coalitions whose members' interests are partly complementary and partly competing.

---

[12] According to Nagel (1993: 9–10), a comparable solution operates with respect to four seats reserved for New Zealand's Maoris, who are also geographically dispersed.

It is, indeed, ironic that defenders of the idea that political institutions should embody strongly felt cultural attachments are generally sympathetic to the social construction of reality thesis discussed in §4.1.3, yet they pay so little heed to the ways in which systems of cultural attachment are created, maintained, and evolve in actual politics.[13] Attending to it more would lead them to be a good deal warier than they are of the idea that ethnic, cultural, and religious attachments should be politicized. As I noted in §1.2.1, the thinking behind disestablishing the church after the religious wars of the seventeenth and eighteenth centuries was, after all, not that religious affiliations are unimportant to people but rather that they are intensely important to them, yet potentially conflicting in zero-sum ways. Those who find themselves well disposed to the idea that politics should incorporate powerfully felt group aspirations should reflect on how destructive this idea is in the contemporary Middle East, where almost everyone feels compelled to recognize the political aspirations of both Jews and Palestinians for their own national states. The conflict there would be a lot more tractable if there were the possibility of a single secular state throughout the region in which no government could support or interfere with any religious practice. But when, as there, political aspirations for religious and ethnic conceptions of nationhood are not seriously questioned, it would mean political oblivion for any leader to advocate this possibility. The politicized religious ethnicities in the Middle East may be beyond being depoliticized, at least for the moment. But the example should give pause to those who think that intense forms of group identity should be afforded political recognition elsewhere on the grounds that they are important to people.[14]

This is to say nothing of the possibility of internal domination. The ties that bind can be more or less benign. Claims of the form "The American people believe . . ." or "The Jewish people must stand together . . ." may be attempts to mobilize group support vis-à-vis an out-group, but they can also operate to suppress internal dissent and opposition. Less directly threatening, perhaps, than hauling someone before an un-American activ-

---

[13] For an illuminating discussion of the political mobilization of group identities among Zulus, Afrikaners, and Cape Coloureds in South Africa before, during, and after the transition from apartheid to democracy, see Jung (2000).

[14] In this connection it is heartening that at a conference on democratic transitions and consolidation consisting of some 100 academic experts from 36 countries plus 33 heads and former heads of state held in Madrid in October–November 2001, a final report was adopted in which it was agreed that "rights of citizenship should apply equally to all citizens," and that the majority "must avoid all temptation to define the nation in ethnic terms in the constitutional text or its political practice" (Hidalgo 2002: 34).

ities committee or calling her a self-hating Jew, they may be just as insidi- ous. When political entrepreneurs claim to be articulating the values and aspirations of a group, we should always ask who within the group stands to be harmed by their demands. In debates about the distribution of au- thority in the post-1994 South African constitution, for example, tradi- tional tribal leaders argued for strong regional autonomy, including the retention of marital law within their jurisdictional ambit. Among other things this means the retention of polygamy and related matrimonial and economic practices that subordinate women in the tribal order at least as much as pre-twentieth-century patriarchalism subordinated European and American women.[15] In practice, "respecting traditional communal practice" may amount to validating a system of internal oppression that would be difficult to justify on any independent grounds.[16]

The debate about respecting religious diversity is instructive here. No- tice that virtually no one believes that all religious practices should be tolerated, even if it is easier to agree that limits should be set than to say how it should be done or what they should be. Most people have no qualms about outlawing human and various kinds of animal sacrifices, regardless of what might be their alleged spiritual value or justification.[17] Likewise, we proscribe such practices as witch burning and pedophilia, regardless of whether the practitioners believe that God permits, or for- gives, their behavior. In the gallons of ink that have been spilled over the sex scandals in the Catholic Church in 2001 and 2002, no commentator has made the case that perhaps the secular authorities should keep out on such grounds. One can scarcely imagine a defense attorney's recommend- ing it as a strategy for a priest charged with pedophilia.

Moreover, we routinely distinguish religions from cults, denying the latter the protections afforded to the former. The reasons for making such distinctions surely cannot be defended by reference to the plausibility of the religious beliefs themselves: what Moonies, practitioners of voodoo, or Heaven's Gaters believe is no more intrinsically bizarre than what Christians, Jews, or Muslims believe. Rather, our everyday practice reflects what I would recommend: that we treat the beliefs themselves as part of

[15] For helpful discussions of the tensions between the egalitarian aspects of South Africa's postapartheid constitution and the ways in which Zulu customary law operates to the disad- vantage of Zulu women, see Chambers (2000), Bennett (1995), and the Human Rights Watch report "South Africa: The State Response to Domestic Violence and Rape," available at http://www.hrw.org/reports/1995/Safricawm-02.htm [9/2/02].

[16] For discussion of many of the forms this can take, see Barry (2000: 155–93).

[17] Though the Supreme Court held that animal sacrifice is protected by the First Amend- ment in *Church of Lukumi Babalu Aye v. City of Hialeah*, 508 U.S. 520 (1993).

the superordinate goods about which outsiders have nothing to say, and focus instead on the behavior. Where the behavior includes domination, a polity geared to minimizing domination appropriately steps in. This is true whether the domination is direct, as with sacrifice or sexual exploitation of minors, or indirect, as when huge barriers to exit are created through brainwashing, appropriation of assets, and the like. No doubt there will be disagreements concerning when the relevant threshold permitting domination has been crossed, but these are disagreements over the application of the principle, not the principle itself. In this they are comparable to issues raised by the "undue burden" standard in abortion litigation discussed in §3.3.

But how should that line be drawn? Once we get beyond obvious prohibitions on killing, maiming, and enslaving, the further suggestion that flows from the discussion of insiders' wisdom in §2.2 is that it is generally better to try to get people to vindicate their group affiliations in ways that are compatible with democracy than to impose democracy on them. Particularly in the case of religion, historical experience with types of conflict engendered by established churches suggests that direct interference should be a solution of last resort to deal with the worst abuses. But indirect measures can be fruitful. For instance, society can make the tax exemption for religious institutions conditional on their avoidance of objectionable practices, as the Supreme Court agreed in 1983 when it held that the federal government may deny tax-exempt status to religions that would otherwise qualify but which engage in racial discrimination.[18] This leaves it up to the religious organization in question to decide whether to forgo the tax advantage and continue their discriminatory practice, or alter their behavior. Government should not pass judgment about any beliefs people have, or claim to have, concerning superordinate goods, deferring instead to insiders' wisdom. The focus should always be on what people do, not what they believe. When their behavior facilitates domination, then democrats reasonably become concerned. The challenge then becomes to devise that combination of incentives and constraints which maximizes the odds that the cure will not be worse than the disease.

---

[18] In *Bob Jones University v. United States*, 461 U.S. 574 (1983). For discussion of the issues that arise if the *Bob Jones* reasoning is extended to religions that engage in gender discrimination (as in the Catholic Church's proscription on the ordination of women), see the debate between Shapiro (1986: 242–45, 2002a), who argues that the same logic should apply, and Barry (2000: 148–49, 168–74), who argues that it should not.

Democracy and Distribution

No CONCEPTION OF DEMOCRACY as geared toward reducing domination can ignore the relations between the political system and the distribution of income and wealth. In §4.1.2 I dealt with the effects of the economy on democracy; here I take up the complementary subject of the effects of democracy on economic distribution. I discuss not the much debated question whether democracy promotes or detracts from economic growth, but rather the question whether it leads to downward redistribution of income and wealth.[1] My particular concern is whether, and under what conditions, democracy redistributes to the bottom quintile of the population—in the United States those who are living, or are in danger of living, in poverty. One might have various justice-related or prudential reasons for being interested in the distributional effects of democracy on this sector of the population. Its members' basic interests, as discussed in §2.3, are in serious jeopardy, and as a result they are vulnerable to domination. This gives us democratic reasons for being interested in their condition in addition to any other reasons we might have, and it suggests that we should be interested in types of democratic reform that would improve it.

We have become accustomed to the coexistence of democracy with substantial inequality, but this is surprising when considered in a larger historical and theoretical perspective. Nineteenth-century elites who resisted expansion of the franchise and socialists who endorsed the "parliamentary road to socialism" agreed that if majority rule is imposed on a massively unequal status quo, then most voters will favor taxing the rich and transferring the proceeds downward. This was formalized in political science via the median voter theorem, which predicts majority support for downward redistribution, given a distributive status quo like that in the advanced capitalist democracies.

In fact, there is no demonstrable relationship between expanding the democratic franchise and downward redistribution. Indeed, universal

---

[1] The most recent and comprehensive empirical study suggests that democracy likely has no overall effect on economic growth, but that per capita incomes grow more quickly in democracies than dictatorships, probably because they have lower rates of population growth. Women fare especially poorly in dictatorships: they are paid less, have more children, and see more of them die (see Przeworski et al. 2000: 161–63, 216–18, 269–77).

franchise democracies have sometimes coexisted with regressive redistribution. In the United States this was dramatically the case with the sharp rise in inequality between the early 1970s and the mid-1990s, despite the 1965 Voting Rights Act and the reduction of the voting age to eighteen in 1971. Real incomes of many toward the lower end of the income distribution declined (or were maintained only through the replacement of single-earner with two-earner households) during this period, and the gap between the poor and the wealthy widened significantly (Winnick 1989, Wolff 1994, Shammas 1993). Similar, if less extreme, patterns can be observed in other advanced industrial democracies (Alesina, Glaeser, and Sacerdote 2001: 189–203). Although democracies spend somewhat more than nondemocracies on the poor, this spending has no systematic impact on inequality and leaves significant proportions of the populations in poverty (Nickerson 2000).[2] Even Marxists like G. A. Cohen (2000) no longer claim that egalitarianism must inevitably triumph.

It is unlikely that there is any single explanation for the relative dearth of downward redistribution in modern democracies, or any single prescription to increase it. Persistent and increasing inequality results from numerous factors, some of which operate more or less independent of the political system. In thinking about which factors should command our attention, we should thus distinguish two senses in which a factor is important: causal and subject to beneficial change. That is, we should be concerned not only to understand what explains most of the variation in accounting for the relative dearth of redistribution to the poor, but also which factors are likely to be alterable by democratic political reform. It is unlikely that these will be the same. The creative challenges involve devising feasible innovations that can improve the condition of the bottom quintile and undermine the tendency of inequalities to compound themselves so as to facilitate domination.

My procedure will be to approach this problem first from what we might think of as the supply side, in §5.1, asking why politicians and political elites do not try to put more redistributive policies on the table, and then, in §5.2, from the demand side, asking why there is not more pressure from the poor for redistributive policies. Distinguishing these dimensions is to some degree artificial because they may interact: the failure of both major parties in the United States to offer policies that benefit the poor

---

[2] For data on the changing absolute and relative shares of income and wealth for the bottom quintile of the population in the United States over the past half-century, see Mishel, Bernstein, and Schmitt (2000: 48–51, 261–64).

compounds their political alienation, which in turn strengthens politicians' incentives to ignore them. This difficulty comes with the territory when we are dealing with a phenomenon that has numerous interacting causes. Approaching it in this way nonetheless provides a useful heuristic for thinking about how various factors influence one another, and it supplies focus for considering different points of intervention and their likely effects. In §5.3 I turn to the question whether the structure of inequality itself should be expected to have an effect on the propensity of a democratic polity to engage in downward redistribution. Intuitively one might think that, the greater the inequality, the more likely there will be effective demand for downward redistribution. Decisive evidence on this topic has yet to be adduced, but I suggest several reasons for thinking that the opposite may be true—that as inequality rises and passes certain thresholds, downward redistribution becomes less likely. In §5.4, I return to the subject of institutional reform in light of the intervening discussion.

5.1 The Supply Side

I start by assuming what will be questioned later—that there is demand, which we might think of as a potential winning coalition, for more downwardly redistributive policies than we see—and ask why they are not supplied through the political process. What stops politicians from competing for the votes of the less well-to-do by offering policies that would redistribute income from wealthier groups to them?

Some explanations for this have to do with obstacles to taxing. Among the usual suspects are the agendas of campaign contributors who influence party platforms, politicians' fear of capital flight, countermajoritarian institutions such as courts and others with veto powers, and various structural and institutional limits on the capacity to raise revenue. Other explanations focused on the supply side look to expenditures, emphasizing the power of interest groups other than the poor to influence government spending, and the limited effectiveness of ameliorative policies in an economy that is continuously producing new sources of inequality, a factor that is said to be of growing importance in this era of skill-biased technological change, increasing openness to trade, and winner-take-all markets.[3] I begin with a closer look at these various supply-side explanations.

---

[3] As the term suggests, winner-take-all markets arise when the winning competitor achieves a preeminent position in a market, vastly increasing inequality of rewards within it.

5.1.1 Raising Revenue

Since Marx and Engels coined the phrase "the executive committee of the bourgeoisie," the argument has been made that governments in democratic market economies bow down before the power of capital. The classic point of departure on this in the contemporary literature is Przeworski and Wallerstein (1988), who do indeed show that anticipation of capital strikes limits the willingness of politicians to tax. It seems reasonable to expect this to get more pronounced with globalization and the decline of capital controls around the world. These developments increase the leverage of capital vis-à-vis national governments, who must increasingly worry that capital strikes will take the form of capital flight—both internationally and within federal and other decentralized systems. The effects of this are difficult to establish decisively, partly because it is the possibility, not the reality, of capital flight that is at issue. As a result there is inevitably a speculative element to arguments about it. It seems reasonable to conjecture, however, that even if the pace at which national governments are losing control has been exaggerated (see Garrett 1998), the limits on their ability to raise revenue may be increasing.[4]

Raising the subject of institutional capacity suggests another limitation to the Weberian conception of the state as a monopoly of legitimate coercive force in a given territory, discussed at the start of chapter 3. Enforcement is always costly, sometimes to the point of not being worthwhile. For instance, certain taxes might be so costly to raise that the net gain to the treasury is negligible—this is sometimes said of the estate tax in the

---

For instance, prior to the advent of the gramophone record, there may have been an opera singer in every town who could make a living by giving live performances, and the differences in remuneration between the competent singers and the best ones may not have been substantial. Once recordings of Pavarotti are cheaply available on a mass scale, however, he can dominate the market for opera music—vastly increasing his income at the expense of less accomplished performers. Frank and Cook (1996) contend that one important source of the increased inequality in the last quarter of the twentieth century was the growth of such winner-take-all markets.

[4] Globally the distributive results may be more complex than one might expect. Garrett (2001) finds, for example, that although there are mild distributive costs to trade openness for the poor in developed economies, most of the benefits accrue to populations in middle-income economies and the wealthy elites in poor countries, with no benefits to their poor populations. This casts a dubious light on the claim that protectionist workers in the developed world are in fact contributing to starvation wages in Malaysia. It is also unclear how much the growth of wage inequality in the developed world is due to trade rather than technology. In the United States there is some evidence of a race-to-the-bottom phenomenon, though there is some stickiness (Peterson and Rom 1989, Tweedie 1994, Figlio, Koplin, and Reid 1999).

United States. How the cost is perceived, vis-à-vis other actions the government might take, is more pertinent for an understanding of what governments actually do than the mere fact that in principle they command a monopoly of the legitimate exercise of force. In the United States, where people compute their own taxes and there are resources to audit fewer than 1 percent of tax returns, the IRS must constantly make choices concerning the kinds of enforcement to pursue. It seems likely that there is an inverse relationship between progressivity and ease of raising taxes (consumption taxes vs. property taxes vs. income taxes vs. estate taxes). Certainly it is no secret that proponents of optimal tax theory generally reject progressive taxation (Avi-Yonah 2002: 1401–2). Other things equal, the efficiency costs of progressive taxation limit the redistributive instruments at the state's disposal.

It seems clear, from my discussion in §3.2.2, that a second major factor on the supply side is campaign contributions, since politicians need large sums of money to be viable candidates. Particularly if the wealthy give to both parties, we might reasonably anticipate bipartisan support for distributive policies to the right of the median voter (such as abolishing the estate tax). However, like the capital strike/flight problem, this is difficult to study empirically, because there are so many ways in which contributors can help or hinder candidates that will not show up in the data (e.g., by threatening to fund a challenger if the desired policies are not supplied, by engaging in independent "expenditures" that cannot be regulated at all by Congress under *Buckley*, and so on). Various proposals for campaign-finance reform are on offer (such as the constraint on soft money championed by Senators McCain and Feingold and Congressmen Shays and Meehan enacted in 2002),[5] but it is not clear that any of them would make much difference to how well the bottom quintile of the population fares.

Among the more desirable reforms would be those aimed at undermining the quasi-monopolistic dimensions of the system discussed in §3.2.2, making it more genuinely competitive for votes. A good start would be to limit, as the political equivalent of price-fixing, contributions to more than one candidate in the same contest, or members of both parties on the same legislative committee. Another interesting proposal is Ayres's (2000) suggestion that the donation booth should be like the polling booth—secret. Donors could give what they liked to whom they liked, but it would be filtered through a mechanism that hid the identity of the

---

[5] The Bipartisan Campaign Finance Reform Act of 2002 (BRCA), available at http://www.fecwatch.org/law/statutes/hr2356enrolled.pdf [9/2/02].

donor from the recipient, so that when the donor said, "I contributed five thousand dollars to your campaign," the politician would have no way of knowing whether this was true—driving a wedge between the logics of giving and extracting a quid pro quo. Ayres's proposal is ingenious in being consistent with *Buckley*, since it neither challenges the Court's equation of money with speech nor limits what people can spend or contribute. In a subsequent formulation he and Ackerman propose supplementing this with a system in which every voter would be given a credit card with fifty "patriot dollars." Upon entering the donation booth voters would swipe the card through an automatic reader, allowing them to contribute to any party, candidate, or organization of their choice (Ackerman and Ayres 2002: 12–44). Like any proposal that would truly curtail the role of money in undermining political competition, if pressed, such suggestions are likely to encounter ferocious opposition.

A third supply-side factor concerns institutional structure. We should expect redistribution to be more difficult to achieve in some institutional contexts than others. Generally, the greater the number of institutional veto points, the more difficult it is to innovate. If, as is the case, the status quo is highly unequal and the economy is continuously producing new inequalities, then political systems in which the institutional dice are loaded against government innovation will be less able to ameliorate inequalities. From this perspective the United States is particularly hamstrung. It has federalism, which contains more veto points than unitary systems; bicameralism, which contains more veto points than unicameral systems; and separation of powers, which contains more veto points than parliamentary systems (Tsebelis 1995, 2002, Treisman 2000).

Bicameralism and the separation of powers are the classic veto points built into the constitution to promote institutional sclerosis, as discussed in §3.2.1, but federalism can be no less insidious from the standpoint of redistribution to the poor, or even preventing redistribution from them. A dramatic example in the United States was the deinstitutionalization of mental patients that accelerated in the 1970s and 1980s following the discovery of Thorazine and other psychotropic drugs. The resulting reduction in inpatient beds represented an enormous savings for state budgets. However, as the deinstitutionalized patients swelled the ranks of the urban homeless, there was no mechanism to ensure that these savings were passed on to the fiscally strapped cities in which white flight and escalating local property taxes were perpetuating one another (see Blau 1992: 77–90, Shorter 1997: 255–80). Indeed, the growth of suburbanization in this period led to the reality, discussed further in §5.3, that state legislatures are disproportionately controlled by suburban voters. They have few incentives not to turn a deaf ear to the needs of the urban poor, who slip through the cracks of fiscal federalism as a result.[6]

The separation-of-powers system is of particular importance in American politics, given the interventionist role of the federal courts, most notably in the *Lochner* era but also in our own, in limiting attempts at downward redistribution by the federal government. Increasingly it seems that the Warren era was an outlier that gave the left imprudent faith in the courts as engines of progressive reform (see Alesina, Glaeser, and Sacerdote 2001: 221–22). Comparative evidence seems to corroborate this claim (Hirschl 1999, 2000). The recent trend in democracies toward ceding authority for monetary policy to independent banks may be another institutional limitation on downward redistribution. Bankers are likely to perceive fiscal policies designed to achieve downward redistribution to be inflationary, and counteract them with the monetary instruments they control. There is some evidence that democratic governments increasingly tie their own hands by ceding such authority to such veto players, and to other veto players such as international financial institutions, to insulate themselves from populist demands (Stokes 1996, Vreeland 2003).

These considerations about the role of veto players in limiting institutional capacity to redistribute cast a less-than-sanguine light on claims that are often made for political decentralization, "strong" civil society, and the transfer of government functions to civic groups. Claims of this kind emanate from the political left (Cohen and Rogers 1995, Bardhan 1999: 93–111), center (Putnam 2000), and right (as in George Bush senior's appeal to "a thousand points of light," framed as policy in George W. Bush's "faith-based initiatives"), but all may be classified together as deleterious from this point of view. Whatever their other advantages, they pose the double danger of further reducing the institutional capacities of the state by dismantling them, and of creating additional veto points further to constrain governmental action in the future.

Another facet of this problem concerns institutional arrangements in the legislature. Party leaderships are comparatively weak in the United States Congress owing to a combination of the constituency-based electoral system and weak political parties. In contrast to list-system proportional representation (PR), for example, where party leaderships control both who is on the party list and the campaign and legislative agendas, in

---

[6] On the consequences of fiscal federalism for the poor, see Rich (1991) and Peterson (1995).

the American system aspiring politicians must first win a primary or caucus and then be elected in a local constituency. The result, not surprisingly, is that they are more beholden to small segments of voters and to the lobbyists, contributors, and others who have the capacity to influence their electoral prospects within a single constituency than they are to party leaderships. This may have advantages from some points of view, but from the perspective of redistribution to the bottom quintile, the greater the "herding cats" problem that legislative leaders face, the less likely they are to be able to line legislators up behind redistributive agendas that cut across constituency boundaries and are at odds with the interests of strategically well placed local players. The redistribution that does occur is more likely to serve powerful local interests, as the result of logrolling that their congressman or senator is able to engage in, than the interests of the poor across the national polity.

We should also ask whether two-party systems are less willing to redistribute to the bottom quintile than are multiparty systems associated with PR electoral arrangements.[7] Although the sense in which these systems are fairer and more representative can be overstated, as I noted in §3.2.2, there is some reason to think that they would be more downwardly redistributive if we believe that this would be favored by the median voter. That is, there is some evidence that PR systems enact policies that are closer to the preferences of the median voter (Powell 2000), and that they are more downwardly redistributive (Alesina, Glaeser, and Sacerdote 2001: 216–21).[8] Because multiparty systems enjoy less robust opposition politics than two-party systems, there may be trade-offs to think about

[7] Duverger's (1954) law tells us that plurality voting electoral systems lead to two-party systems, whereas PR is associated with multiparty systems.

[8] Britain's post–World War II Labour governments, which were strongly redistributive toward the bottom quintile, stand as a counterexample to this proposition about PR—as does the New Deal in the United States. Perhaps these are outliers, but another possibility—which, to my knowledge, has not been studied in a systematic empirical way—is that the strength of leadership control of political parties may be an important factor, confounding the apparent effects of PR reported by Powell (2000) and Alesina, Glaeser, and Sacerdote (2001). PR systems also have strong party leaderships, in virtue of their control of party lists. This is somewhat weaker in open-list PR systems such as Greece, Brazil, and Italy (until the reforms of the 1990s), where voters are entitled to name individual candidates—though even there the leadership still controls who gets onto the party list from which voters select. In the United States the strength of leadership control has declined owing to the rise of primaries and other factors, such that one wonders whether a redistributive legislative program on the scale of the New Deal could be enacted today. If, indeed, such programs could not be enacted today, this would carry the implication that people who favor decentralized control of political parties are misguided if they would also like to see greater downward redistribution.

between favoring them on the grounds that they would be more downwardly redistributive, for the reasons just adduced, and pressing for a system that promotes strong opposition politics, for the meritorious reasons discussed in §3.2.2.

Since it is rare that countries change their electoral systems and highly unlikely that PR will be adopted in the United States in the foreseeable future, perhaps more pertinent than worrying about this trade-off is to consider what other types of reforms to the electoral system would increase responsiveness to the median voter. As well as reforms geared to limiting the influence of money already mentioned, it might make more sense to pursue political antitrust measures along the lines suggested in §3.2.2. These would be geared to limiting the "market share" of any party's votes, as well as the various types of collusion that are fostered when bipartisan, rather than nonpartisan, entities are allowed to be responsible for enforcement of campaign-finance laws, the rules of political debates, and other aspects of electoral law enforcement such as overseeing vote tabulation. Appealing to competition offers two advantages: it is difficult to argue against in the American context, and it is not an area where the good is the enemy of the best. Even if major reforms could not be achieved in the short term, some of the more minor ones possibly could be, making the system less uncompetitive at the margin at the same time as it encouraged people to think about the system's shortcomings from an antitrust perspective.

A final supply-side factor to think about concerns the macroeconomic context. Perhaps certain contexts are more propitious than others for revenue raising, particularly on the rich. The evidence seems to suggest that this is so. In the United States at any rate it appears to be possible significantly to increase taxes on the wealthy only during wars and other times of great crisis. Otherwise there is little change in the structure of progressivity over time regardless of which political party is in office (Witte 1985, Steinmo 1993). Related contextual questions concern whether it is more difficult to raise taxes in expansions than in recessions, and when deficits are larger or smaller. Perhaps counterintuitively, the answer in both cases seems to be yes (Witte 1985). As was underscored dramatically in 2001, when times are good and budgets are in surplus, the pressure is to cut taxes. During and after the 2000 election campaign, the only real difference between the parties concerned how much they would be cut—with the differences between them not that great. The Republicans wanted a $1.6 trillion tax cut over ten years, while the Democrats pushed to keep it at around a trillion, leading to the $1.35 trillion "compromise" that was signed into law.[9]

5.1.2 Expenditures

One possible conclusion to what has been said thus far for those who would like to see more downward redistribution is that they should forget about increasing progressivity in tax raising. Given the difficulties, structural and contextual, of making the system more progressive than it is, perhaps it would be better to abandon progressivity in revenue raising, and instead go for the most effective method in a given context and worry about distributive agendas on the expenditure side. Particularly if one's interest is in increasing what those at the bottom get, rather than decreasing what those at the top get, this may be the way to go. This argument tends to be made in developing countries, where the limits of state capacity are more dramatically evident, but arguably it makes sense more generally. Disadvantages to this approach surface in §5.3, but here I consider it without reference to whether we should be concerned, from a democratic perspective, about the reduction in relative inequalities in addition to the absolute condition of the bottom quintile.

One question is whether the type of expenditure influences the likelihood that policies enforcing redistribution to the bottom quintile will actually be enacted. It seems that the answer is yes. In the United States, outlays are more difficult to enact than so-called tax expenditures such as deductions and exemptions, which have to go through fewer institutional veto points and often are not perceived as government spending. Charitable deductions, home-interest mortgage deductions, and the like might be on a conceptual par with subsidies and transfer payments, but they are not perceived as the government writing checks. They may be components of Howard's (1997) *Hidden Welfare State*, but people do not think of them as welfare. From this perspective it is not surprising that ideas like a social wage or universal basic income (Van Parijs 1995) get so little traction in the United States. This hostility to identifiable tax expenditures is presumably why it is so difficult to have discussion of them. Even when elements of these proposals are enacted, it seems they must be euphemistically termed "refundable tax credits" or a "negative income tax." This

[9] See "2001 Legislative Summary: Tax Cut Reconciliation," *Congressional Quarterly Weekly*, December 22, 2001, p. 3049, and Kelly Wallace, "$1.35 Trillion Tax Cut Becomes Law," June 7, 2001, http://www.cnn.com/2001/ALLPOLITICS/06/07/bush.taxes/ [9/2/02].

seems a significant cultural difference between the United States, on the one hand, and Europe and Japan on the other.

The moral of Howard's United States story is arguably this: get your foot in the door in the dark, given that most tax expenditures begin as obscure loopholes, growing over time into vast programs. Yet if incrementalism and camouflaged policies are better bets than bold innovations to improve the condition of the poor, what are the costs of these policies? Such approaches run counter to arguments for publicity and transparency that often go with defenses of democracy (e.g., Fishkin 1995, Gutmann and Thompson 1996). This is an underattended-to subject in the literature on deliberation, whose proponents tend to make optimistic assumptions that informed discussion will lead to enlightened policies; as we saw in §1.2.2, there is no reason to suppose that this is true. Normative considerations to one side, however, the danger of politics by stealth is that those with regressive agendas and more political resources at their disposal are likely to be better at it, suggesting that, on balance, pragmatic considerations may favor openness and efforts to expose the hypocrisies attending the hidden welfare state rather than trying to emulate it.[10]

Are there fixed components of the budget, such as interest payments or certain types of military expenditures, that limit the possibilities for transfer payments? Some literature suggests there is a "crowding out" effect on redistributive policies when deficits are large. An example is Skocpol's (1997) argument in *Boomerang* that the failure of the Clinton health care reform was made more or less inevitable by the deficits Reagan left behind—though this is in some tension with the argument already discussed that lack of budgetary pressure makes it harder to increase taxes. Perhaps there are upper ceilings on taxes that will be tolerated in noncrisis times, and the *Boomerang* logic prevails once this threshold has been passed. No systematic work has been done on this. Some literature suggests that there are limits to the proportion of the budget available for transfer payments, so that increasing the numbers who benefit from transfer payments leads to reductions in the size of the payments themselves (Peterson and Rom 1989). If this is so, it would be a consideration favoring the tax-expenditure rather than the transfer route—at least insofar as it is politically feasible.

---

[10] Some literature suggests that it is easier to enact universal programs such as Social Security than those targeted at groups, such as AFDC—the theory being that the targeting brings demonization with it. However, there is some contrary evidence too. There are intermediate possibilities. See Skocpol (1991: 411–36, 1995: 250–74). This is better tackled under the

Some literature suggests that transfer payments are more palatable when they are limited and linked to work (Ribar and Wilhelm 1996, 1999; Moffit, Ribar, and Wilhelm 1998). It stands to reason that such transfers are more likely to survive when they command support from interest groups on the left and the right, for which such requirements seem to be important. Thus Aid to Families with Dependent Children, containing no work requirement, was wiped out by President Clinton's 1996 welfare reform bill with considerable bipartisan support, replaced by Temporary Assistance to Needy Families, which has a lifetime five-year cap. By contrast, the work-dependent Earned Income Tax Credit, which was sharply expanded in 1990 and increased again in 1993, survived welfare reform (Hotz, Mullin, and Scholz 2000).

5.1.3 Redistribution and Smaller Government

Given the difficulties on the expenditure side, an important challenge for those who want to see more downward redistribution is to think about policies that do not operate through the fisc, or do so only minimally in the sense that tax expenditures do. This suggests the wisdom of trying to structure tax incentives to encourage redistribution of the kind one wants to see, which may involve tax write-offs for specified transfers, hiring unemployed workers, and so on. The only ongoing role for government here is for the IRS.

One could go even further and work for redistributive policies that do not operate through the fisc at all, such as Senator Bill Bradley's proposal in the 2000 Democratic presidential primaries to index the minimum wage to the median income—a kind of unfunded mandate on the economy. There are some advantages to this. Economists will say it will "distort" labor markets, but this is true of any minimum wage. A disadvantage is that it will not get to those completely outside the labor market, at least not directly, and this includes many in the bottom quintile. Since levels of welfare payments are usually linked to the minimum wage, however, there may be an indirect benefit even to them. And to the degree that those not employed in the labor market are dependents of minimum wage workers, they will benefit as well.

The possibilities for redistribution that need not flow through the state become greater if we consider not only cash transfers but also the redistri-

---

demand side (below) since the logic is about the amounts and kinds of opposition different policies should be expected to provoke.

bution of opportunities for economic advancement, of which the most important is education. Ruling out discrimination in admissions against groups that tend to be disproportionately poor (such as blacks) is an obvious bottom line, but more proactive policies are feasible and worth exploring. The Hope Scholarships Program in Georgia, which guarantees every high school graduate who achieves a B average a place in one of the state's public universities, is a case in point.[11] The campaign to get Ivy League schools to adopt need-blind admissions policies is another.[12] Indeed, to the extent that new sources of inequality are technology- rather than trade-dependent, redistributing educational opportunity may be one of the more effective responses to them. It enables those who have the capacity but not the resources to move upward. To be sure, it will not do much for those who lack the capacity, and for this reason—if no other—it should be thought of as a complementary rather than an alternative strategy. Like the antitrust arguments for political reform, it has the added advantage of appealing to values that are widely accepted in American culture. This brings us to the demand side of the problem.

5.2 THE DEMAND SIDE

Having held the demand side constant up to this point, we must now recognize that it is not. There are numerous reasons why demand for the type of redistribution predicted by the median voter theorem fails to eventuate. Before we get to them, two prefatory points should be noted. One concerns the scope of the inquiry; the other concerns the appropriate methods for prosecuting it.

Notice, first, that we are not concerned here with that old chestnut: why is there no socialism in the United States? Nor are we concerned to

---

[11] Since the Hope Scholarship Program is funded out of the Georgia State Lottery, it is an example of a potentially progressive program funded by a regressive tax. See http://www.dtae.org/hope.html [9/2/02]. As the program has evolved, however, it has become less progressive and more of a middle-class benefit whose effect is to subsidize and keep in-state students who would otherwise have gone elsewhere to college. See Luke Boggs, "State Should Shelve Lottery, HOPE," *Atlanta Journal and Constitution*, June 26, 2002, Wednesday Home Edition Editorial Section, p. 14A, and "B's Not Need Are Enough for Some State Scholarships," in the edition of the *New York Times*, October 29, 2002, available at http://www.nytimes.com/2002/10/31/education/31MERI.html [9/29/02]. To the degree that Hope is deployed as a model for the redistribution of educational opportunity, care has to be taken to ensure that its purposes are not compromised in these ways.

[12] Private universities began adopting need-blind admissions policies in the 1960s; in 2002, Brown became the last Ivy League school to institute such a policy.

explain why the poor do not rebel, unionize at higher rates than they do, or engage in other forms of collective action outside of democratic institutions. Whatever its limitations, universal suffrage democracy solves one major collective action problem for the dispossessed: it provides a mechanism, which they need neither create nor sustain, through which they can harness the power of the state to redress their disadvantages—absolute or relative. The question is why they do not seek to make more use of it than they do. Intrinsically interesting as other forms of quiescence might be, they will concern us only to the extent that they illuminate this problem.

With respect to method, it is worth noting at the outset that the economics and rational-choice-influenced literatures are less helpful here than in thinking about the supply side, because the assumptions behind rational choice do less well with mass behavior than with the behavior of politicians and other self-consciously strategic actors. Just as in economics these models do better at explaining the behavior of firms than of consumers, so in politics they do better with parties than with voters (see Green and Shapiro 1994: 47–71, 1996: 235–76). We will see that some suggestively illuminating hypotheses have come out of economics literature in this area, but for the most part the literatures in sociology and social psychology take us further.

5.2.1 Logics of Distributive Reference

In 1984 Ronald Reagan ran for reelection trumpeting the brutally effective slogan "Are you better-off than you were four years ago?" It directed people to think about a bundle of goods represented by their disposable income, and to ask whether their stock of it had increased. This is self-referential comparison: it requires no attention to what others have. In the world of self-referential comparisons everyone is seen as trying to get on a higher indifference curve than they were before, and reference to the well-being of others is purely incidental. This is the logic of the Pareto system.

Now consider this: you are department chair, and colleague Brown walks in declaring, "I don't care what my raise is, so long as it's larger than Walker's." Brown's well-being is inescapably reliant on what Walker gets; it rests on an other-referential standard. Notice that other-referential comparisons need not be selfish. An egalitarian colleague might insist on a raise that is no larger than anyone else's, and a parent might improve her well-being by securing opportunities for her child. The point is that the referent for one's own well-being is inescapably bound up with the well-being of others.

A more extreme type of other-referential comparison trades on internal relationships among people's experiences, as in the claim that income inequality makes the poor unhappy because they envy the rich, or the rich unhappy because they pity or fear the poor. Economists call these interdependent utilities (see Yunker 1983: 132–55). The sadist gets his jollies from the suffering of his victim. Schadenfreude is activated, comparably, in bitter divorces when a dollar is transferred from the pocket of one spouse to a lawyer, causing the other spouse's utility to go up. The joy arises from another's suffering (see Feather 1994, Smith et al. 1996). Interdependent comparisons can also be altruistic rather than malevolent, as when a parent's happiness is critically reliant on the happiness of his child. Hatred and love involve internal relationships of this kind almost by definition; they anchor one polar extreme on the continuum from self- to other-referential comparisons. Chronic autism stands at its opposite end.

Some types of motivation will be difficult to classify by reference to this distinction. If I want a better computer than I now have, that is self-referential, and if I want a better computer than you have, that is other-referential. But there is a difference between my wanting at least as good a computer as you own and my wanting the fastest possible computer, purely for my own time-management reasons, and seeing that your computer meets that test better than mine. By the same token, if, on becoming aware of a new limited-edition car, I want it because it performs better than my present car, then I remain in the world of self-referential comparisons. If, however, my reason for wanting it is that it is a limited edition, then (like all status-based desires) it is inherently other-referential.[13]

This range of examples indicates that classifying motivation as self- or other-referential leaves many questions unanswered. It tells us nothing about the extent to which people are selfish or altruistic, what their views about redistribution and government's appropriate role in it are likely to be, or whether and to what extent people are generally alike in the comparisons that they make. Nonetheless, we learn some things about distributive politics by finding out more about whether and to what extent people are self- or other-referential in thinking about distribution, and, if other-

---

[13] Admittedly, it will sometimes be unclear whether motivation is self- or other-referential. I might pretend, perhaps even to myself, to have self-referential reasons for wanting the faster computer or the limited-edition car because the other-referential truth would embarrass me. But this very formulation underwrites the distinction as valid—even if it might take ten years of therapy to get at the truth of the matter in the case at hand.

referential, who the relevant others are. A simple example will drive this home. Suppose that the market wage for a certain type of production line worker is $40,000 per year. There are ten such workers in a corporation owned by one individual, paid the going rate. The owner discovers that by renting five machines for $40,000 per year each and laying off half the workforce, he can increase the productivity of the remaining five workers by 400 percent. These workers are able to negotiate a 25 percent raise, owing to the higher market wage for the skills they develop to operate the new machinery. Are they better-off than before? By reference to self-referential comparisons, certainly. By reference to other-referential comparisons, it depends on who the relevant other is. If they compare themselves to the owner (as Marx hoped they would), they will conclude that his relative share of the surplus has increased more than theirs, and they will regard themselves as worse-off—hence more exploited. If, however, their comparative point of reference is the five fired employees, then they will see themselves as better-off. Likewise if the reference group is workers in similar firms where there has been no technological innovation and wages are still $40,000.

Does the thesis that the poor will press for downward redistribution in a democracy—call it the redistributive thesis—require them to make other-referential comparisons? Not necessarily. Absolute improvements in someone's circumstances might be seen as beneficial regardless of what happens to others, but that does not mean he will not try to get more. The conventional assumption is, after all, not that people merely want to get onto a higher indifference curve but rather that they want to get onto the highest possible indifference curve. So, notwithstanding the judgment that their circumstances have improved, at the margin they would always want to be better-off still. To explain why self-referentially motivated people might not push for downward redistribution, we must attend to the other factors taken up below.

In its Marxist variants the redistributive thesis depends exclusively on other-referential comparisons. The capitalist employer's increasing relative share of the surplus value produced by the worker is the source of the latter's escalating alienation, galvanizing him eventually to revolutionary action.[14] In reality, although other-referential comparisons motivate people a good deal of the time, they are not made with the comparators Marx had in mind. People make more local comparisons, measured by class, status, and physical proximity, when evaluating their circumstances. The

---

[14] For elucidation of various ways in which this is unpersuasive, see Roemer (1995).

empirical research shows that workers do not compare themselves to their employers in assessing their circumstances. They do not even compare themselves to other wealthy individuals, but rather to similarly situated workers. This is true up and down the occupational scale. A professor will be much more troubled to learn that his salary is $10,000 less than that of a peer down the corridor than that it is $200,000 less than that of the cardiologist down the street (Frank 1985: 39–107).[15]

The reasons for this are much debated; no doubt more than one dynamic is often in play. Cognitive limitations, the need for recognition from peers, what Tversky and Kahneman have described as "availability heuristics," and physical proximity are all implicated in perceptions of relative well-being.[16] In different ways they all lend credence to W. G. Runciman's view that deprivation relative to a salient group of comparatively local others is more important than global economic position in influencing the demands people are likely to make—though there is more than one way of being local, as I note below.[17] Although Runciman's relative-deprivation thesis has a mixed empirical record in predicting collective mobilization for political change, it does better than objective class position, and in any case its failures may have more to do with lack of organizational resources or with the requirements of spatial proximity than with the thesis itself (Kelley and Evans 1995: 174–75). As an account of how people see their entitlements in relation to others, it seems to do reasonably well a good deal of the time. It may also help account for the phenomenon that in contemporary Western countries the overwhelming majority conceives of itself as middle-class. People tend to see the world as an enlarged version of their—comparatively homogenous—local reference groups, pushing those very different from themselves into the background (Evans, Kelley, and Kolosi 1996: 461–82, Hodge and Trieman 1968: 535–47).[18]

[15] Generally, see Kelley and Evans (1995).

[16] On availability heuristics, see Tversky and Kahneman (1981) and Kahneman, Stovic, and Tversky (1982).

[17] For the classic statement, see Runciman (1966: 3–52). For a recent discussion of the evidence, arguing that physical proximity is an important variable in mobilizing, see Canache (1996: 547–71).

[18] See also Canache's (1996: 556–66) argument that poor people are more prone to violence when they find themselves in comparatively homogeneous rich neighborhoods, where "the contextual evidence of deprivation is most explicit," than when they live in more diverse neighborhoods, even if the neighborhoods are equally wealthy overall. See also Powers (2001: 84–86), who argues based on evidence from Argentina that greatly heterogeneous housing conditions among the poor hinder their collective mobilization, as the residents of

5.2.2 Knowledge and Beliefs

The sense on the part of people toward the bottom of the income distribution that they are better-off than they actually are is buttressed by their beliefs about the shape of the income distribution and their place in it. Long ago Weber (1997: 183–84) suggested that organized collective action to achieve social change depends on the existence of transparent power arrangements against which to react. In 1971 Frank Parkin developed this into the "transparency thesis" to explain why people are generally less well informed about the distribution of income and wealth in market systems (believing them more egalitarian than they are), and about their place in them (believing themselves better paid than they are), than in nonmarket systems (Parkin 1971: 160–64). Parkin contended that market systems are comparatively opaque because the allocation of economic rewards is not in the hands of a visible social group. On the Weber-Parkin account, part of why people look to local reference groups in market systems is that others are shrouded in fog. We need visible benchmarks to perceive inequality. The formal egalitarianism of market systems obscures it.

No less consequential than people's beliefs about the nature of inequality are their beliefs about its causal dynamics and what these mean for them. Most obviously, there are trickle-down arguments—invariably contentious but never vanquished. Don't squabble over the cake; let's get a bigger one for all. The rich will burn their crops before giving them to the poor. South Africa needs the white man. In this spirit people might embrace a version of Bentham's distinction between actual and practical equality, which led him to advocate redistribution only to the (concededly elusive) point at which it began to reduce the overall stock of wealth (Bentham 1954: 442). To the extent that people believe versions of this claim, they might temper their redistributive demands, with the result that governments need not resist redistributive pressure from below. Rather, voters—whether rational or ideologically dupes—do not create the pressure predicted by the redistributive thesis in the first place.

That one might be the passive recipient of others' largesse, as in trickle-down theories, is one possibility. Another is the belief that one will become those fortunate others.[19] Here, formal egalitarianism seems to be essential.

---

abandoned buildings, squatters, and people living in hotels fail to acknowledge common problems requiring common solutions.

[19] See Bénabou and Ok (2001), who argue that it is possible for a majority of the population simultaneously to be poorer than average in terms of current income and rationally to

Formally closed systems galvanize collective opposition, but formal openness forestalls it. Hence Parkin's (1971: 161) observation that with systems of racial exclusion "the social visibility of the dominant group is especially marked and the dividing line between exploiters and exploited can be represented in a fairly unambiguous way." Inequalities that stem purely from the market, however, "rarely have this degree of transparency, so that perceptions and identities of a class character are less easily formed" than those of a racial character.[20] This suggests an explanation as to why American blacks could be mobilized against legal racial exclusion from full civic participation, whereas comparably effective mobilization against economic exclusion has failed to materialize. Likewise with the recent South African experience: apartheid's transparent racial exclusions bred massive—eventually irresistible—organized opposition, yet since 1994 many commentators have been surprised at the dearth of significant pressure on the ANC government for downward redistribution. Like Parkin, Alexis de Tocqueville might have predicted it. Of the rich in democratic societies he said, "They have no conspicuous privileges, and even their wealth, being no longer incorporated and bound up with the soil, is impalpable and, as it were, invisible." They no longer form "a distinct class, easily identified and plundered."[21]

This result is less surprising in light of research in social psychology which supports the notion that in formally egalitarian systems people opt for individual advancement rather than collective action to improve their circumstances.[22] Thus Wright, Taylor, and Moghaddam (1990: 994–1003) argue that perceived "group permeability" is critical in accounting for collective opposition. In their experimental research, subjects took tests, which they failed, to enter a more "elite" group. However, the relative "openness" of the elite group was varied over the course of the experiment. The result: subjects opted overwhelmingly to pursue individual

---

oppose downward redistribution, provided future income is anticipated to be increasing and a concave function of present income. For an account that links views about redistributive taxation to beliefs about social mobility, see Piketty (1995).

[20] This may not be true in nonmarket systems, however. For an account of the origins of the Solidarity movement in Poland in the high levels of economic awareness of Polish workers, see Laba (1986: 47–67).

[21] As he elaborates, "I am not suggesting that they [the middle class] are themselves satisfied with their actual position or that they would feel any natural abhorrence toward a revolution if they could share the plunder without suffering the calamities; on the contrary, their eagerness to get rich is unparalleled, but their trouble is to know whom to despoil." Tocqueville ([1835] 1969: 635–66).

[22] Here, bearing the South African reality in mind, we should perhaps include crime in the category of individual advancement.

action when faced with rejection by an elite group that was said to be open to all who were qualified. In contrast, individuals opted for socially disruptive collective action when faced with rejection by a closed elite group. Perhaps more interesting is how little openness is needed to forestall collective action. Even when faced with a stringent restriction (such as a 2 percent quota of admission), most subjects still opted for individual action. In a subsequent study Lalonde and Silverman (1994: 78–85) also found a greater preference for collective action when groups are closed than when they are open, and that even when groups are closed, the preference is no stronger than for individual action. This underscores how powerful the preference for individual advancement is, at least in the United States. These results are in line with a 1993 study by Lalonde and Cameron in which subjects were asked how they would respond to unambiguous discrimination in housing or employment. The overwhelming preference was for individual rather than collective redress. Only in circumstances of total exclusion—as when people lose fundamental rights, such as the right to vote—do they consider collective action (Lalonde and Cameron 1993: 257–88).[23]

The research on boundary permeability thus suggests that modest tokenism may be sufficient to defuse pressure for collective redistribution, even when the status quo is seen as unjust. As Wright (1997: 1286) sums up another experimental study: "The success of a very small number of disadvantaged group members can undermine endorsement of collective action by focusing attention on personal rather than collective injustice and by reducing confidence about the illegitimacy and instability of the intergroup context." No doubt some of the reasons for this have to do with the same irrational optimism that leads people in their millions to buy lottery tickets every day. And some of these reasons have to do with the well-documented human reluctance to identify with disadvantaged groups.[24] Whatever the causes, it seems that people opt for individual mobility over collective action unless its hopelessness is flatly undeniable. If

[23] This individual response may make a degree of pragmatic sense. For instance, Martin (1986: 217–40) proposes a "sequential contingent model," according to which people consider a sequence of behaviors to alleviate perceived injustice, starting with those that involve the least personal effort. Thus someone who feels relatively deprived will seek first to improve her individual economic situation before sparking a class rebellion, out of practical considerations of time, energy, and risk trade-offs.

[24] There is considerable evidence, for instance, that even when people perceive discrimination as directed toward the group with which they identify, they perceive less discrimination to be directed at themselves as individuals. See Crosby (1984: 371–86), and Taylor et al. (1990: 256–62).

they perceive even the remotest possibilities for upward mobility, they are much less likely to favor collective redistribution through collective action (Alesina and La Ferrara 2001).

This research might well explain why we do not see junior faculty unions at Harvard and Yale, but the type of collective action predicted by the redistributive thesis differs. As I have noted, with the advent of a universal franchise, perhaps the most serious obstacle to collective action has been overcome. The mechanism for achieving redistribution exists. It is this reality, after all, that motivates the redistributive thesis. It is testimony to how powerful beliefs in individual efficacy are if tokenism and minimal boundary permeability can forestall support for collective redistribution in this context as well.

5.2.3 Ideology

James Tobin (1988: 161) has noted that people often oppose increases in particular taxes to which they will not themselves be subject, even when they know this. That they take this stand may be due to the way the issue is dealt with (or not) in the media, but it may be more deeply rooted in their beliefs for other reasons. Whatever the cause, an inquiry into the veracity of the redistributive thesis must come to grips with what people believe is just, since this is likely to influence their propensity to press for redistribution through collective institutions. Unsurprisingly, disadvantaged people who believe they live in a just world show less propensity for group discontent than those who believe their world is not just (Hafer and Olson 1993: 30–38). The question arises, therefore, how widespread is the belief that the inequalities generated by market systems are just?

In the United States, at least, although people might be egalitarian in many facets of social life, the great majority accept the market's economic differentiation (Hochschild 1981: 55–71). Distributive outcomes are accepted as legitimate unless they are seen to be both procedurally and substantively unfair, and this seldom happens, because the market is widely believed to be a fair distributive instrument.[25] Hochschild's 1995 study of American beliefs reveals remarkably widespread endorsement of the ideology of the American Dream, understood to include the ideas "that skill rather than need should determine wages," and that "America should pro-

[25] See Martin (1986), Taylor et al. (1987: 259–72) and Smith and Tyler (1996: 171–200).

mote equal opportunity for all" rather than "equal outcomes."[26] Over-whelming majorities from different occupational, racial, and political groups endorse this view. Eight out of ten whites and nine out of ten blacks agree that "the American Dream is alive today," and although blacks tend to believe there is more racial discrimination in the system than do whites, as a group they are actually more confident than whites of their own prospects (Hochschild 1995: 55–69; see also Elster 1995: 305–8).

To be sure, not everyone believes in the justness of capitalism or in the American Dream. Hochschild herself notes (1995: 184–213) that a subset of the population is estranged from it. Other scholarship displays a differ-ent side of poverty, involving notably less optimism about upward mobil-ity. Jonathan Kozol's *Amazing Grace* (1995) portrays the South Bronx as a center of hopeless despair, where many of the poor are going nowhere and do not seem to care. William Julius Wilson (1996) records a sense of desolation and inefficacy in inner-city neighborhoods in *When Work Disappears*, and Elijah Anderson's (1990) ethnographic study *Streetwise* documents a similar lack of concern for upward mobility among inner-city teenagers.

Because desolation and apathy are unlikely to coexist with ambition and determination for success, it seems clear that differently situated poor people have different beliefs and aspirations. It also seems clear that any general distinction between an "underclass" (whose members might be alienated from the system) and the rest of the poor (who believe in upward mobility and the American Dream) is untenable. For instance, in an eth-nographic study of two groups of teenagers in the same housing project, one white, one black, Macleod (1987) found that most of the blacks thought of themselves as upwardly mobile and were working to advance themselves, while the white teenagers simply wasted their time smoking pot and skipping school. In another ethnographic study, Fine and Weis (1998) found high degrees of aimlessness and apathy among the working poor in Buffalo. This suggests that aspirations for advancement may not be limited to the working poor, and that apathy may not be monopolized by those who are often stigmatized as the "underclass."

A more promising candidate for distinguishing those who buy into the American Dream from those who are alienated from it may be experience of, and prospects for, rewarding employment. In Macleod's study the par-ents of the alienated white teenagers were predominantly not high school

---

[26] See also Olson (1986: 57–78), who finds that having appropriate qualifications is per-ceived as part of procedural fairness that legitimates inegalitarian outcomes.

graduates, they had other children who were dropping out of school, they had lived in the projects for up to three generations, and, if employed, they worked in temporary menial jobs. By contrast, parents of the ambitious black teenagers were new residents in the projects and had steady employment (Macleod 1987: 55). In Fine and Weis's study, too, it seems to have been the disappearance of heavy industry jobs that had paid a "family wage," and their replacement by low-paying fast-food and other service jobs, that explained the apathy and disillusionment (Fine and Weis 1998: 29–39). Other ethnographic studies provide indirect support for this. Anderson draws a sharp distinction between the older generation, with their traditional Protestant work ethic values, and their offspring who reject those values, and in *Slim's Table* Duneier highlights a similar value gulf between older and younger generations of inner-city blacks (Anderson 1990: 69–73, Duneier 1994). What is the main difference between the generations? As Wilson emphasizes, steady employment in manufacturing jobs that the older generation enjoyed is unavailable to the younger inner-city generation. They subsist either on welfare or in dead-end service-sector minimum wage jobs. This, he speculates, erodes their sense of efficacy and ambition (Wilson 1996: 76).

If experience of, and prospects for, rewarding employment account for the distinction between the apathetic and the upwardly mobile, what are the implications for the redistributive thesis? Macleod contends that the disaffected are mobilizable for redistributive politics on the grounds that those "who see their chances for upward mobility as remote are more likely to involve themselves in collective political action than will their counterparts who see considerable opportunity for significant individual mobility" (Macleod 1987: 158–59). But those who do not seek individual advancement may not be mobilizable for collective action either. It is well known that participation increases with both education and income (Verba, Schlozman, and Brady 1995: 5, 19, 188–91, 228–68; Sobin 1973: 83–101, 121–22).

There are additional reasons for thinking that those most disaffected from the system may also be those who are least inclined to try to change it. Robert Lane argues that low status and a sense of deprivation tend to be associated with the belief that one is ineffective. Unlike anger, unhappiness (which is negatively associated with anger) is immobilizing; depressed people do not engage in politics (Lane 1991, 2001). This is intuitively plausible. It is difficult to imagine the South Bronx communities described by Kozol as suddenly galvanized into petition drives and town hall meetings to demand better services, housing, and police protection, let alone to organize to put pressure on politicians to fight for redistributive transfers. There is too much despair and not enough anger.[27] Political disengagement, perhaps interspersed with occasional riots of the kind we saw in Los Angeles in 1992, seems like a more plausible prognosis. Perhaps the reality is that those who could organize for redistributive politics are insufficiently disaffected to embrace the role, while those who are sufficiently disaffected are incapable of organizing.

Another feature of ideology concerns the place people ascribe to economic inequality among other priorities. People who are aware of the full dimensions of economic inequality might nonetheless deem other things more important than trying to redress it, such as the redistribution of status and dignity. This seems particularly likely in new democracies, where rights of participation might be valued for their own sake in comparison with recent exclusion. In South Africa, for instance, the abolition of second-class citizenship, acquisition of the dignity that comes with the act of voting, and the right to speak one's own language in court are tangible gains. Those who have never been subject to second-class citizenship may discount them. Those who have might value them, however, and perceive them as tangible noneconomic gains from democracy.

Perhaps new democracies are not so distinctive in this regard. Presumably part of the appeal of ethnic and other forms of identity politics in countries like the United States comes from the persistence of status inequalities. The rage Louis Farrakhan articulates reflects this.[28] Much of the women's movement over the past four decades has been about the reduction of status inequality. Some of it has also been redistributive, as in the demand for equal pay for equal work (though this may have no effect on the reduction of class inequality in the society—see Rae et al. 1981: 82–128). But much of it has to do with matters that are not distributive in the conventional sense at all, such as abolition of the marital rape exception and intraspousal tort immunity. To the degree that redistribution of status and dignity motivates people, their propensity to press for reductions in economic inequality may take a backseat.

---

[27] In response to the question whether the poor in the South Bronx might rise up in organized political resistance, one of Kozol's interviewees replies, "No. People protest specific actions of the city. They protested the waste burner. But there's a sense of powerlessness that makes it hard to keep up momentum." Another: "Everything breaks down in a place like this. The pipes break down. The phone breaks down. The electricity and heat breaks down. The spirit breaks down." Kozol (1995: 81, 181).

[28] "Some of us are here because it's a march through which we can express anger and rage with America for what she has and is doing to us." *Time*, October 16, 1995. http://cgi.pathfinder.com/time/special/million/minister2.html [9/2/02].

This is related to, but distinct from, the literature suggesting that if political competition occurs in multiple dimensions, then voters who prefer downward redistribution might not end up voting for it. If the distributive dimension is crosscut by a "values" dimension, for example, where preferences are differently arrayed, then the median voter may no longer favor redistribution (see Roemer 1998: 399–424, 1999). In subsequent work Roemer and Lee (2002) suggest that the level of racism in a society should be expected to influence the demand for redistribution for analogous reasons, so that countries in which it is high, such as the United States, will be comparatively inegalitarian in the redistributive demands that are expressed through a competitive democratic process. That demand for downward redistribution is dampened by racism is also supported by the research of Alesina, Glaeser, and Sacerdote (2001: 226–46).

5.2.4 Framing Effects

Closely related to knowledge, beliefs, and ideologies concerning redistribution, but distinct from them, are the framing effects that shape what people see as pertinent alternatives (Tversky and Kahneman 1981). Here the concern is less with what people might in principle, or on reflection, believe or know, but rather with what they actually focus on when making a particular decision. Because we all have cognitive limitations, framing effects are not simply forms of incomplete information; they deal with what people regard as pertinent reference points in a given situation. Accordingly, studies and surveys of what people believe about the distributive consequences of different policies might not get us close to how they will behave in concrete situations when confronted with choices about voting for redistributive policies. Consider some possibilities.

One reason people might not make demand-after-demand that ceases only in death stems from the reactive and backward-looking character of much human behavior. After all, the query "Are you better-off than you were four years ago?" directs attention to a worse status quo ante—with the implication that the alternative to the present might be not further advance but backsliding into the old world. Once a marginal advance has occurred, there is always the possibility of losing it. Reagan's 1984 slogan sought partly to trade on that fear, suggesting that a Mondale victory would mean a return to 1970s stagflation and erosion of the gains made since. People who are surprised that there is not more demand for downward redistribution tend to work on the assumption that those near the bottom of the economic distribution think they have nothing to lose but their chains. This is true of a handful of the population only, and certainly not of the median voter. In many circumstances voters might indeed make the judgment that things could get worse—particularly if they have been worse in the recent past.[29]

Rallying grassroots supporters for the Million Man March in October 1995, Louis Farrakhan insisted that the time had come for the dispossessed in the black community to draw on their own resources and bootstrap themselves out of poverty. "Clean up, black man, and the world will respect and honor you. But you have fallen down like the prodigal son and you're husking corn and feeding swine. . . . Black man, you don't have to bash white people. All we've got to do is go back home and turn our communities into productive places."[30] The message is unequivocal: forget the inequality out there and focus on yourself. When people internalize ideologies of this kind, they will not demand redistribution through public institutions. Instead they will blame themselves for their distributive circumstances and accept that they should look inward when trying to improve them. We might think of these as inward-looking framing effects.

Inward-looking framing effects are likely significant in accounting for the dearth of redistributive demands in the United States, given the power of bootstrapping ideologies there. Whether the inward-looking focus is on the individual or on a comparatively dispossessed identity group, it is significantly *not* on the distribution of goods and opportunities in the larger society. Hence the literature questioning the wisdom of identity politics from a progressively distributive point of view (Fraser 1997: 11–39, Barry 2000).

In addition to looking backward and inward when considering their distributive condition, people also look downward. Commentators on capitalism from the left and the right may have underestimated the importance of this in dampening demand for redistribution to the poor. Several interacting dynamics focus working- and middle-class attention on the people below them in the social order, rather than on those who are better-off. The poor can seem threatening in at least three ways: they will rise up and kill us, they will bankrupt us with their welfare benefits, or we will fall down into their ranks.

---

[29] Presumably there would be links here to the literature on retrospective voting. See Fiorina (1981).

[30] *Time*, October 16, 1995. http://cgi.pathfinder.com/time/special/million/minister2.html [9/2/02].

Fear of the marauding rabble of dispossessed poor long predates democratic capitalism. Christopher Hill (1965: 300–302) points out that a recurrent theme in early Stuart literature was a strong upper-class mixture of fear and contempt for the "many-headed monster" (Sidney's phrase in *Arcadia*) of dispossessed poor. The same sentiment is repeated in many of the political tracts of the propertied classes, as summed up in Deloney's quip in 1597 that "the poor hate the rich because they will not set them on work; and the rich hate the poor because they seem burdensome." Ruling-class fear of the masses seems to have intensified in response to visible social consequences of economic and demographic changes that got underway in the mid–seventeenth century: urbanization and the growth of a wage-laboring class (Hill 1961, 1965: 306–14, 1972: 39–56). The propertied classes often expressed comparable fears in the eighteenth century, not least in their enactment of vast numbers of new capital crimes for minor offenses against property (Hay 1975: 17–63). And Adam Smith is famous for the steely-eyed declaration that it is only the power of the civil magistrate that prevents the poor from expropriating the rich.[31]

Rather than disappear under democratic capitalism, however, fear of and contempt for the poor seem to take on distinctive forms. For one thing they have a petit bourgeois flavor, since they revolve importantly around middle-class, especially lower-middle-class, antipathy for those below them. For another, there seems to be a tendency for elite strata within disadvantaged groups in formally egalitarian systems to distance themselves from the group in question—identifying instead with the norms in the dominant culture.[32] This may reflect partly a need to have some group to look down on, and partly individual-regarding social mobility, already discussed. Perhaps more significant is that a good deal of democratic electoral politics seems to revolve around stoking middle-class fears of the underclass in ways that reinforce downward-looking framing effects. Much of the trench warfare around affirmative action, for instance, is about promotions in the police department, the post office, and the fire

[31] "The affluence of the rich excites the indignation of the poor, who are often both driven by want, and prompted by envy, to invade his possessions. It is only under the shelter of the civil magistrate that the owner of that valuable property, which is acquired by the labour of many years, or perhaps many successive generations, can sleep a single night in security. He is at all times surrounded by unknown enemies, whom, though he never provoked, he can never appease, and from whose injustice he can be protected only by the powerful arm of the civil magistrate continually held up to chastise it." Smith ([1776] 1937: 670).

[32] See Cohen (1999: chap. 2) on the phenomenon of middle-class blacks' internalizing the norms of the dominant culture and distancing themselves from those of dispossessed black communities.

department; it has little impact on people who live in Scarsdale or Beverly Hills. It also has little impact on the structure of the income distribution, moving people around within it instead. This is why Michael Lind (1995: 150) can write of a white overclass, whose members support racial preferences and multiculturalism from which they are largely immune, that they "live right and think left." They look askance at lower-middle-class opposition to these policies, seeing it as "not so much immoral as simply *vulgar*."[33] Whether one would want to go as far as he does in portraying affirmative action as the result of a divide-and-rule conspiracy to keep the lower orders squabbling among themselves, it may often have that effect: feeding racism and fracturing what might otherwise be coalitions for redistributive change (Lind 1995: 139–80).[34]

Downward-looking framing effects are sustained by the demonizing of those toward the bottom of the social order. Gilens (1999: 3, 6–7) shows that hostility to welfare in the United States is often not the result of opposition to the welfare state, or even to targeted welfare programs when they are seen as "helping the deserving poor help themselves."[35] Rather, hatred of welfare stems from the perception that most recipients are the undeserving poor. Media portrayals of welfare recipients as disproportionately black, and blacks as disproportionately lazy, reinforce this hostility, if they do not produce it, sustaining the picture of an extractive underclass that must be contained or otherwise warded off.[36] This is to say nothing of crime. No account of downward-looking framing effects in the United

[33] In this connection it is perhaps of interest that Alesina, Di Tella, and MacCulloch (2002) find that although inequality is reported to be correlated with higher levels of unhappiness in Europe, in the United States the happiness of the poor and those who think of themselves as on the left is uncorrelated with inequality, but the rich are bothered by inequality.

[34] For a general treatment of the importance of race in American politics, see Smith (1997). On the tensions between racism and progressive redistributive politics, see Leiman (1993) and McMath (1993: 171–75), who contends that the culturally ingrained racism of Southern and Midwestern Populists was largely responsible for their failure to achieve class solidarity and significant redistributive reform. He notes in particular how initial attempts at black/white solidarity among the Populists eventually crumbled in the face of relentless race baiting by the Democratic party in the South.

[35] This stands in contrast to the conventional wisdom, which holds that Americans generally support universalist programs but are hostile to targeted ones. See Skocpol (1991: 414). Consistent with Gilens and in opposition to this conventional orthodoxy is a study by Bobo (1998: 996), which finds, perhaps surprisingly, that "[t]he more whites are committed to notions of reward for hard work, the less likely they are to hold negative beliefs about the effects of affirmative action for blacks."

[36] For a review of the evidence indicating that in the United States the poor are more hostilely perceived and more widely regarded as responsible for their own plight than in Europe, see Alesina, Glaeser, and Sacerdote (2001: 237–46).

States can be complete without attending to it. The vast numbers of people we now incarcerate constitute a manifestly demonized threatening group, even if, despite public perceptions to the contrary, most of them have not committed violent crimes.[37] Criminalizing the poor provides a convenient target—even a magnet—for downward-looking framing effects.

Something that is perhaps a second cousin of a framing effect but may well influence demands for redistribution is best characterized by the term *anecdotal distraction*. In *Albion's Fatal Tree* Douglas Hay tells the story of an eighteenth-century criminal law that operated almost exclusively in the interests of propertied elites, but as a result of which the occasional noble-man was publicly subjected to extreme forms of punishment, even the death penalty, for relatively minor offenses against property mentioned earlier (Hay 1975: 32–39). Part of the explanation for this has, no doubt, to do with the logic of deterrence when enforcement institutions are weak.[38] Hay argues powerfully, however, that much of it had to do with instilling awe for the legal order that protected the propertied classes. What better way to get the poor to think that the law is not the instrument of the rich than to have it so visibly enforced against a member of the nobility? Comparable stories could perhaps be told about Michael Milken and Leona Helmsley in our time: that they were endlessly portrayed in the media as getting their comeuppance provides anecdotal legitimation for the system, regardless of how representative they might actually be.

Anecdotal distractions need not be directed at the rich only: lurid stories about "welfare queens" driving Cadillacs direct attention away from the behavior of most welfare recipients to freeloaders. Stories about the venal behavior of public officials can serve a similar purpose, reinforcing the perception that redistributive taxation is less a Robin Hood enterprise than rent-seeking by bureaucrats—less "from the rich to the poor" and more "from us to the government." Horatio Alger stories are also effective anecdotal distractions, as Reagan understood all too well when declaring in 1983, "[W]hat I want to see above all is that this country remains a country where someone can always get rich."[39] When politicians visibly

---

[37] For data on the explosive growth of incarceration in the United States (which has transformed the United States from a country that incarcerated around 100 per 100,000 between World War II and 1970 to one that incarcerated over 400 per 100,000 by the mid-1990s), see Irwin and Austin (1997: 1–61). They note that almost three-quarters of those incarcerated have not committed violent offenses of any kind, convictions for drug possession or trafficking accounting for the preponderance of the increase.

[38] In particular, there are reasons to anticipate an inverse relationship between the severity of punishment and the probability of apprehension. See Posner (1985a: 1193–1231).

[39] Quoted in Hochschild (1988: 168).

single out individuals who have moved from welfare to work or otherwise triumphed over adversity—standard fare in State of the Union presidential addresses since Reagan—they exhibit their understanding of the power of anecdotal distractions. The man in the street does not ask questions about random sampling or selecting on the dependent variable.

5.3 EFFECTS OF DISTRIBUTIONAL SHAPE

The expectation that democracies will redistribute downward is often motivated by the observation of poverty amid opulence. It seems reasonable to anticipate that the greater the manifest wealth of the few, the stronger will be the redistributive pressure from below. Paradoxically, however, something closer to the opposite might actually be the case.

Aspirations do not form in vacuums. People must be able to conjure up in imagination the objects and lifestyles for which they will strive. For this, psychic distance matters. You can imagine yourself stepping unaided over a puddle, perhaps swimming a lake, but not across the Atlantic. At some point the gap between where you are and where you might hope to get will seem so huge that certain goals will be abandoned from your field of aspirations. We might think of this as an empathy gulf. It suggests that exceedingly high levels of inequality might actually dampen redistributive demands from the very poor. An extreme example will make this point. In contemporary Cape Town it is common for domestic cleaners who live in squatters' camps to work for five dollars a day cleaning half-million-dollar houses, where the cars in the garages cost many multiples of their expected lifetime earnings. It may just be impossible for them to imagine themselves in their employers' shoes.[40]

Empathy gulfs can operate in the opposite direction as well. To the degree that willingness to tolerate downward redistribution is part of a prudential calculation "There but for fortune go I," it has to be believable. If the gap between you and the poor you see around you is so massive that no calamity you can imagine befalling you will put you into their circumstances, then any prudential reasons you might have for improving their lot disappear. Presumably this is one reason why most people can tune out panhandlers and street people, and acquiesce in the demoniza-

---

[40] Note that this can be true whether people are self- or other-referential.

tion of the underclass. The mighty may be tumbled in Zola's novels, but no one who reads them really expects it to happen to them.[41]

This may be particularly relevant in the postcommunist era. During the period between the Great Depression and the collapse of the Soviet Empire, elites in democratic capitalist systems had reason to worry that capitalism could collapse, and that socialist and communist ideologies might seduce the disadvantaged populations in their own countries. This gave them prudential reasons to be concerned about the people at the bottom. In an era when the idea that capitalism might collapse is no longer taken seriously, and there is no competitor ideology that could vie for the allegiance of the poor, these prudential reasons inevitably wane. It becomes that much easier to adopt a Malthusian attitude toward the poor, treating their fortunes as divorced from ours.

It might be said that Islamic fundamentalism has replaced communism as the main ideology that defines itself against, and as an alternative to, democratic capitalism, and that it could begin to command the allegiance of the dispossessed in the advanced countries. There is perhaps some truth to this, but Islamic fundamentalism differs from communism in that it lacks a political economy and is not, therefore, at bottom a competitor to capitalism. When Islamic fundamentalists have gained control of a national polity, as in Iran, they are forced to try to make capitalism work— even if the consequences are disastrous. This suggests that despite the havoc that terrorist groups might be able to wreak through episodic violence, Huntington (1996) is mistaken in projecting a "clash of civilizations" between democratic capitalism and Islamic fundamentalism, and that Kepel (2002) is perhaps closer to the mark in arguing that Islamic fundamentalism is in decline. In any event, this reality suggests that economic elites in countries like the United States are likely to continue to perceive the Islamic fundamentalist threat as a terrorist and national security problem, rather than a potential competitor for the hearts and minds of dispossessed local populations.

In the past elite support for downward redistribution was reinforced by Keynesian assumptions about the need to stimulate demand in the economy, but we need to confront the disquieting possibility that there are

---

[41] There is in any case some reason to think it misleading to draw a sharp distinction between relative and absolute inequalities. In the health area, for example, increases in relative inequality have been shown to have an adverse effect on the health of poor populations (see Wilkinson 2001). Generally Alesina, Di Tella, and MacCulloch (2002) have found that higher levels of inequality are associated with higher levels of reported unhappiness, though this is less pronounced in the United States than in Europe.

many ways to stimulate demand that do not involve redistribution to the poor. In recent years in the United States these have ranged from multibillion-dollar subsidies to farmers, to comparably vast investments in prisons, high-tech weapons research, and space exploration, to name some high-visibility examples.[42] To them we must now add the potentially bottomless pit of a "war" on terrorism that can never officially be declared to be over, and for which spending will easily be justifiable. The economy's perceived need for deficit spending might have helped the poor in the past, but there is no necessary reason to suppose that it will do so in the future.

The more extreme the income inequality, then, the greater the psychic distance between the have-nots and the haves. Beyond certain thresholds that would have to be determined empirically, it may be expected to spawn empathy gulfs that reduce demands from below and harden attitudes above. Vast empathy gulfs may breed resentment, crime, and, in the limiting case, revolution. But if the resources for that are lacking, or the political order is not seen as fundamentally illegitimate, then empathy gulfs will reinforce the inegalitarian status quo. This may fuel characteristic types of conflict among different groups and classes toward the lower end of the socioeconomic spectrum, but it is unlikely to have much effect on the overall distribution of income and wealth (Lind 1995: 139–80).

Geography produces another kind of distance that attenuates redistributive demands, one based on physical gulfs between people. We might think of this as another kind of framing effect: out of sight, out of mind. But it is both more and less than this.

It is more than a framing effect in that physical segregation of the have-nots from the haves in capitalist democracies is real and increasing. The starkest illustration of this in the United States is the middle-class dash from cities to suburbs that took off a generation ago and is now culminating in enclave living. As recently as 1960 "gated communities" numbered in the hundreds and were for the elderly and the superrich. By 1997 there were as many as twenty thousand gated communities in the country comprising more than three million housing units, at least a third of which were middle-class and a growing number even working-class in

---

[42] On government subsidies to farmers, which have doubled since the early 1990s and have exceeded $20 billion per year for the past several years, see Edwards and DeHaven (2001); on prisons, see U.S. General Accounting Office, "Private and Public Prisons: Studies Comparing Operational Costs and/or Quality of Service," August 1996, GAO/GGD-96-158, and Bender (2000); on spending for defense and weapons research, see "National Defense Budget Estimates for FY 2001" available at http://www.dtic.mil/comptroller/fy2001budget/fy2001grbk.pdf [9/2/02]; on space exploration, see http://www.brook.edu/dybdocroot/gs/cps/50ge/endeavors/space.htm [9/2/02].

orientation (Blakely and Snyder 1997: 6–7). These numbers greatly understate the reality of enclave living, since many country towns (often functional suburbs) can for all practical purposes be inaccessible to inner-city residents.[43]

The net effect is the development of what Douglas Rae has described as "segmented democracy," in which the only true public spaces (i.e., no charge for admission) are the inner cities (Rae 1999: 165–92, Sugrue 1993). Freedom of movement lives cheek by jowl with effective segregation by race and class that is in many respects as extreme as apartheid South Africa (Blakely and Snyder 1997: 152–56). Movement by poor black and brown people from the inner cities into middle- and upper-class neighborhoods is not a realistic option, given the realities of transportation and local policing practices. This was underscored with poignancy in the 1992 Los Angeles riots following the acquittal of four white police officers in the videotaped beating of a black man, Rodney King, that was shown endlessly on television for months before the trial. Although inner-city blacks rioted, they turned the vast bulk of their aggression on other local ethnic groups, notably Koreans. None of them headed for Brentwood or Beverly Hills.

Spatial segregation also means that the middle and upper classes restrict their urban life to business districts and daylight hours, a trend that is greatly enhanced by the flexibility to work from home afforded by the Internet. And those who live in refurbished parts of inner cities have enclaves of their own. Their daily paths from guarded apartment buildings to work, to gyms and Yuppie restaurants, enable them to keep contact with people disturbingly different from themselves to a minimum. In this way the physical gulfs of Rae's segmented democracy reinforce the empathy gulfs already discussed.

Yet physical gulfs amount to less than a framing effect, in the television age, in that out of sight is not—strictly speaking—out of mind. The paradox is that despite the geographic reality of physical segmentation, the have-nots are not ignorant of what the haves have. Tocqueville said that the poor knuckle under in aristocracies because they are ignorant of comfort: "[T]hey despair of getting it and they do not know enough about it to want it" (Tocqueville [1835] 1969: 531). The implied suggestion is that, were it available, such knowledge would become the engine of redistributive demands. Yet despite the fact that people are bombarded with

---

[43] It is thus possible to live on the shoreline of Branford, Connecticut, a fifteen-minute drive from New Haven, and not need to own a key to one's house.

images of how the other half (or, more accurately, the other 2 percent) live, the demand does not eventuate. Knowledge by acquaintance is more important, it seems, than knowledge through television.[44]

This conclusion is consistent with the research suggesting that what people learn through the media is not a substitute for everyday proximity in shaping their aspirations (Frank 1985: 8–9, Canache 1996). It also suggests that something like the group permeability dynamic discussed in relation to occupational inequalities may be at work here. On this view, official segregation, such as the Group Areas Act that launched South Africa's residential segregation in 1950, should be expected to breed collective resistance, but removing the legal prohibitions will take the wind out of its sails. People will respond, rather, by aspiring toward individual physical mobility—even if the odds of success are negligible. The contemporary United States provides anecdotal evidence in support of this contention, and postapartheid South Africa offers a natural experiment to test it. Nine years into the new regime there is negligible erosion of residential segregation in cities like Cape Town, though there has been an even more explosive growth of gated communities than in the United States in response to the proliferation of squatters' camps that encircle the enclave suburbs. Time will tell whether the demand for collective policies to produce integration will remain as muted as it has been to date.

A different set of effects of distributional shape has to do with the steepness of inegalitarian distributive arrangements and the resources of the wealthy. Nineteenth-century formulations of the redistributive thesis depended on a crude Marxian picture of capitalism evolving into a two-class system: a tiny bloated ruling class and a vast working class whose members were scraping by at subsistence. A small subset of the bourgeoisie might make it into the ruling class, but most would fall down into the proletariat—all the more easily mobilized because of the seething resentments they would bring with them.

Part of Marx's failure here was conceptual. His theory of exploitation moves illicitly between the claim that the relative immiseration of the proletariat will increase (which follows analytically from his theory of exploitation) and the claim that their absolute immiseration will (which does not). As already noted, the rate of Marxian exploitation can increase while wages remain constant or even rise. Part of Marx's failure was empirical:

---

[44] Hence the research suggesting that poor young men who live in middle- or high-status communities are more likely to be delinquent than those living in poor communities. See Johnstone (1978: 49–72).

in all capitalist democracies an enduring middle class includes many people Marx would have classified as workers: they must sell their labor-power to others in order to survive. Yet they live nowhere near subsistence (even defined to include a "historical and moral element" (see Marx [1867] 1976: 275, 701–6); nor are they going to. For them the proverbial state of affairs in which chains are the only things to be lost is not in the cards, as Cohen (2000), among others, has noted.

Marxian political economists have sometimes claimed that this is a transient state of affairs: working-class discontent is bought off through welfare states that will eventually succumb to fiscal crises, after which the inexorable contradictions will surface, leading to two-class polarization (see Miliband 1969, O'Connor 1973). In fact, a three-class dynamic might be quite stable for reasons that are distinct from the considerations about reference groups, knowledge, beliefs, framing effects, and empathy and physical gulfs already adduced. Even in a highly inegalitarian world of full-information self-referential maximizers, it is far from clear that a one-dimensional median voter who cares only about economic well-being will vote to redistribute downward. An illustration is suggestive of the possibilities. One reason there is not significant pressure for downward redistribution from the grass roots of the ANC in South Africa flows from the extreme character of the maldistribution of income and wealth there. An increase in taxes on even the top 20 percent of the population would be an increase on much of the black working class, so they have self-interested reasons to oppose it. And, if they did support redistribution, it would scarcely be to those at the bottom of the economic order in a country where 40 percent of the black population is unemployed (Nattrass and Seekings 2001). This suggests the importance of looking seriously into the counterintuitive possibility that the more unequal the distribution, the harder it may be to mobilize lower-middle- and working-class support for redistribution downward—certainly for redistribution to those at the bottom.

In one attempt to model this type of logic Breyer and Ursprung (1998: 135–56) show formally that economically powerful (i.e., above average) income earners are indeed in a position to bribe the small segment of voters with incomes between the median and the mean to resist the temptation of confiscatory taxation. Snyder and Kramer (1988: 197–230) develop another model which suggests that a majority of middle- and upper-income taxpayers might support a relatively progressive income tax to reduce their tax burden at the expense of the poor. Breyer and Ursprung note that although these kinds of outcomes can be theoretical equilibria, they are unstable, for the well-known reason that all taxation schemes are vulnerable to overturn by some majority coalition. This can be seen from the divide-a-dollar game invoked in chapter 1: if three voters must divide a dollar by majority rule, there is no distribution that is not vulnerable to upset by some majority coalition (see Mueller 1989: 19–31).

Despite this potential for instability, indeed because of it, one cannot but be struck by the remarkable stability of taxation arrangements in most democracies over time (see Witte 1985, Steinmo 1993). Perhaps, therefore, results like those just discussed can be shown to be retentive in practice, and more strongly retentive the more inegalitarian the status quo. Intuitively: the more the wealthy minority has, the more affordable it will be for them to continue bribing the voters between the median and the mean, as Breyer and Ursprung suggest, whether through marginal tax cuts, middle-class tax benefits such as home-interest mortgage deductions, or subsidies for their children's higher education.[45] And this middle group's members may well be more concerned about what they stand to lose in an aggressive system of progressive taxation than attracted to the uncertain benefits of allying with those below them in order to soak the rich.

5.4 IMPLICATIONS FOR DEMOCRACY AND DISTRIBUTION

My examination of the effects of democracy on the distribution of income and wealth suggests that we should not be surprised that nineteenth-century expectations concerning the redistributive thesis have not been borne out by history. There are numerous features of democratic systems that limit downward redistribution and, indeed, even facilitate upward redistribution. Several of these features are particularly pronounced in the United States—part of the reason, perhaps, that it exhibits higher levels of poverty and inequality than the other advanced capitalist democracies.[46]

On the supply side we saw that democratic governments find themselves constrained in revenue raising by the potential for capital strikes, which are increasingly likely to manifest themselves as capital flight. It is true that

[45] This is compatible with Frank's (1985: 9–10) contention that, to the degree that people want status recognition, high-status people will be willing to pay low-status people to stay in the pond and afford them recognition rather than move to a smaller pond where the low-status people might become high-status people.

[46] For data on income inequality in the United States, see Williamson and Lindert (1980: 62–68), Wolff (1994), Winnick (1989), and Shammas (1993).

decisive evidence on these points is difficult to come by, and history is filled with examples where, contra Bentham, the rich did not burn their crops rather than part with them, and various factors can and do impede the race to the bottom. Nonetheless, the mobility of capital vis-à-vis both labor and the state is increasing, even if at a slower pace than some breathless commentators would have us believe, strengthening its position relative to theirs. The collective action problems here might seem insurmountable, but the same could once have been said of proposals to eliminate slavery—yet it was achieved. Pressure for multilateral action to increase regional and international labor standards is an important place to start, as is pressure on national governments to act bilaterally in trade agreements and unilaterally in contracting with suppliers, which has been effective in the past and could be so again (Shapiro 1999a: 190–95). Since the logic of capital flight is driven by international minimums, the best way to limit its effects is through pressure to move them upward.

We saw that in addition to the relative power of investors vis-à-vis governments, there are issues of institutional capacity arising from enforcement costs that are inadequately addressed in the Weberian picture of the state as enjoying a monopoly of legitimate coercive force within a given territory. Focusing on them raised the possibility of abandoning aspirations toward progressivity on the tax side (the more progressive taxes being also more difficult to raise) and dealing with distributive concerns on the expenditure side instead. Other considerations speak decisively against this approach, however. For one thing, we saw that there are few good reasons to suppose that the bottom quintile is well positioned in terms of resources, organization, or political muscle to avoid being crowded out of the expenditure side of the budget by more effective interest groups and coalitions. To be sure, much redistributive politics does indeed occur on the expenditure side.[47] However, it is unlikely that the bottom quintile will fare well in it unless they are allied with others who are strategically well placed to extract their pound of flesh when so many others are struggling to do likewise.

Another consideration is the importance of relative inequalities. If they matter—as my discussion of empathy gulfs, physical gulfs, and the impact

[47] One anecdotal illustration of this came in an off-the-record interview I conducted with a leading liberal Democratic member of the House of Representatives in 2002 concerning the politics surrounding the repeal of the estate tax the preceding summer. When asked why labor and other traditional Democratic coalitions and interest groups had not come out more forcefully against the repeal, he replied that it is impossible to get them to invest resources on tax issues. "When you call them and tell them to get out there, they tell you that tax issues

of the structure of inequality itself all suggest—then improving the condition of the bottom quintile in a democratic system is likely conditional on also reducing relative inequalities. Recent scholarship suggests that the expansion of modern welfare states in the United States and northern Europe was more importantly dependent on support from business elites than historians and social scientists had previously realized (Swenson 1991, 2002). My discussion suggests that this kind of support is less likely to be forthcoming as relative inequalities increase, which in turn suggests that abandoning the pursuit of progressivity on the revenue-raising side would be self-defeating even from the perspective of improving the absolute condition of the bottom quintile.

A third sense in which we saw that relative institutional capacity might be significant arose out of my discussion of the finding in the veto points literature that political innovation becomes more difficult as the number of veto points increases. It might be said that, *ceteris paribus*, this would apply equally to innovation to undermine the position of those at the bottom and to that aimed at augmenting it. Indeed, as Pierson (1996) has argued, projects of welfare state retrenchment can confront opposition that thwarts even the most determined partisan governments. But the difficulty is that the status quo is not static. Market economies continually manufacture new sources of inequality, as the period between the mid-1970s and the late 1990s illustrated so dramatically in the United States. Institutionally weak and hamstrung governments will be less able to respond to this than those that are more capable of decisive action. Accordingly, the multiplication of veto points and the forces of fiscal federalism should be resisted, as should the impulse to further weaken the institutional capacities of the state by transferring its functions to religious and other civic organizations.

We saw that the logic behind the median voter theorem as an engine for predicting more downward redistribution than we actually see runs into a variety of difficulties. To the extent that it is frustrated on the supply side, this is likely a partial result of the role of money in politics, as well as other institutional factors, notably the electoral system, that make it more difficult for the preferences of the median voter to be enacted. We also noted Powell's (2000) finding that PR systems tend to produce policies more closely aligned with the median voter's preferences than do first-past-the-post systems. This creates a potential trade-off between favoring

---

divide their membership. They only campaign to protect the spending and regulatory programs that they want," he said.

PR on the grounds that it is more likely to issue in downwardly redistributive policies and favoring the strong opposition of two-party systems, which, as we know from Duverger (1954), is associated with first-past-the-post systems. In fact, Rae (1995) has shown there may be ways to make PR systems operate more like two-party systems on the competitiveness front by manipulating minimum vote thresholds and district magnitude, so that it might in principle be possible to get the best of both worlds—or at least to compute an optimal trade-off.

In any case I noted that there are numerous other ways in which the American system is chronically uncompetitive that could be addressed within a political antitrust framework. Doing so could reasonably be expected to make the system more responsive to whatever demand for downward redistribution might be expressed by the median voter, even if, as seems likely, this has to await a propitious macroeconomic environment. In the interim it seems prudent to press for forms of redistribution to the bottom quintile that must operate minimally, if at all, through the fisc, and for other types of redistribution—most notably of educational opportunity—that could improve the condition of many in the bottom quintile. Valuable as these strategies might be, they will not benefit all those who are vulnerable to domination for distributive reasons; accordingly, they should not be seen as alternatives to trying to make the political system more responsive to the poor.

But not all of the problems concerning the median voter theorem's redistributive predictions stem from the supply side. People care about things in addition to, or instead of, economic distribution. In some ways this is unobjectionable from the perspective of a democratic conception that prizes minimizing domination. Some of the other things people try to pursue through democratic politics may have to do with reducing other forms of domination, such as those based on gender or race. Others may involve preferences people seek to achieve collectively that have nothing to do with domination—they may concern the pursuit of superordinate goods. Although there is no reason to oppose the latter, the goal of minimizing domination should take precedence, and we saw that the danger of defining it by reference to multiple dimensions is that it can lead to divide-and-rule results even where these are not consciously planned. Racism and sexism are independently objectionable sources of domination. When they operate to dampen demand for redistribution to the poor, they become doubly so.

More illuminating than the median voter theorem, in this area, is the divide-a-dollar logic. It tells us that the decisive questions on the demand side concern which coalitions will actually form, and that the creative challenges for those who would like to see more redistribution to the bottom quintile involve finding ways in which their interests can be pursued consistently with those of groups whose support they need. To fix intuitions, consider again the example of affirmative action. If this involves set-asides of college admissions spots or quotas for scarce promotions in the police and fire departments, it is not difficult to see why it becomes a zero-sum phenomenon that divides what might otherwise be part of a coalition in support of policies that would benefit the bottom quintile. The creative challenge is to find ways that reframe the agenda in positive-sum terms for the potential coalition. For instance, rather than set-asides, affirmative action proposals could create additional admissions spots funded out of a tax on the wealthy, or at least out of general revenues. People who, for affirmative action reasons, are denied promotions they would otherwise have received could be compensated with funds levied in a similar fashion. The logic here is to externalize the costs of the policy onto potential coalition outsiders, while reinforcing support among potential coalition members.

Nor need the coalition be restricted to those toward the bottom of the socioeconomic order. Divide-a-dollar alerts us to the theoretical possibility of the kinds of cross-class coalitions identified in Swenson's work. Although business elites might be less open to worrying about the needs of the poor than was the case during the New Deal and the Great Society for the reasons I discussed in §5.3, a serious economic crisis could change that. In any event, business has self-interested reasons for supporting some redistributive policies that would have a positive impact on the welfare of the bottom quintile—most obviously in the area of health care insurance. National health care insurance would be to the advantage of business, particularly small-business owners, for whom carrying the health insurance costs of employees can be cripplingly expensive. I have suggested elsewhere that the failure of business to support it is better thought of as a collective action problem among firms than a conflict between capital and labor (Shapiro 1999a: 184–95). Providing health insurance through employment is a major encumbrance on wage bargaining, and the advantages of competing with other employers by providing better health benefits come at a significant cost over time. There is potential here for a Swenson-type cross-class coalition in support of national health insurance when the contextual macroeconomic variables are right, and if interest groups and politicians who are strategically well placed to organize in support of it see the possibility and act on it.[48]

An instructive example of creative coalition building is the Family Business Estate Tax Repeal Coalition that was put together in the mid-1990s to secure repeal of the estate tax. Although this tax is paid only by the exceedingly wealthy top 2 percent of taxpayers, and half of it by the top 0.5 percent, the coalition managed to win support in key constituencies from environmentalists concerned about the effects of breaking up large estates; gay and lesbian groups concerned by the possible interaction of the estate tax with their exclusion from the laws of marital transfers; minority groups (including the Congressional Black Caucus) concerned about its effect on undermining capital formation in the black community; women's business groups with comparable concerns about the first generation of successful businesswomen; and family-owned newspapers, farmers, and small-business groups concerned about the buying up of their members' assets by conglomerates. To be sure, there was much misinformation about who would pay the tax, but many who would not pay it were thus given other reasons to favor abolishing it, and the empathy gulf between those who would and those who would not pay it was bridged by its reframing as a nondistributive issue—an unfair "death tax" levied on the families of people who had just suffered life's worst calamity (Shapiro and Birney 2002).

The coalition's success in achieving the repeal as a $138 billion component of the 2001 ten-year Bush tax cut is a good illustration of how successful redistributive politics in a democracy may indeed need to rely on coalitions among strange bedfellows. My concern here is with the bottom quintile, not the top 2 percent. No doubt the larger group lacks the connections, organizational resources, and political knowledge of the smaller one, suggesting that involving it in effective political coalitions is more difficult. Perhaps so, but history provides examples of coalition building that improved their lot in the past, and there is no necessary reason why it cannot happen in the future. But even when the structural variables line up in propitious ways, it will still take ingenuity and political will to achieve the desired result. Democracy offers the possi-

---

[48] Indeed, Swenson and Greer (2002) make a compelling case that one of the major factors that undermined the Clinton administration's national health insurance proposal was lost business support for this idea that businesspeople had backed in 1992. By 1994 they had found other ways of reducing health care inflation and abandoned the administration as a result.

bility of downwardly redistributive politics, but there are no guarantees that it will happen, and many cards are stacked against it, particularly in the American system. One of the more important challenges now facing democratic theorists is to explore the creative possibilities that do exist within this structure, as well as the feasible reforms to it that might make it more genuinely democratic.

Reconsidering the State of Democratic Theory

I BEGAN THIS INQUIRY into the state of democratic theory with the observation that, for all the difficulties that have been identified in the theory of democracy, its political legitimacy is seldom seriously challenged in the contemporary world. Democracy's nonnegotiable political status stems, no doubt, from many sources. Part of it derives from the economic and military successes of twentieth-century democracies when compared with their major competitors. Part of it derives from agitation by weak and dispossessed groups in undemocratic countries to better their circumstances, and their hope (perhaps often naive) that democratization will help bring this about. And part of it derives from claims for more democratic governance of international institutions. The pressure that emanates from the leaders of many poor countries to democratize the United Nations and other international bodies implicitly affirms democracy's legitimacy. One can scarcely insist on democracy in international institutions without thereby conceding the validity of democratic principles; these then are enhanced willy-nilly in domestic political contexts.

Democracy means many things to many people, but I argued in chapter 1 that much academic analysis in both the aggregative and deliberative traditions trades on some version of Rousseau's identification of it with the search for a common good that reflects society's general will. Despite their other differences, this way of framing the problem leads theorists in both traditions to harbor rationalist expectations of democracy on which it is impossible to deliver. However, I also argued that this impossibility should not be judged a failure. Rather than think of democracy as a mechanism for institutionalizing the general will, we should recognize its claim to our allegiance as the best available system for managing power relations among people who disagree about the nature of the common good, among many other things, but who nonetheless are bound to live together. To be sure, this view rests on a conception of the common good. But it is a comparatively thin one, best captured by the formulation that it embodies what those with an interest in avoiding domination share.

Indeed, the possibility of diminishing—if not eradicating—domination is often what draws people to democracy. Confronted with the injustices of apartheid or totalitarian communism, they turn to democracy as the instrument of their emancipation because of its constitutive commitment to nondomination. One major reason to try to press for reforms in democratic systems to make them more responsive to the interests of those who are vulnerable to domination is thus to supply the vulnerable with reasons to remain allied to it—to keep their disagreements and disappointments within the zone of "loyal" opposition to the government of the day rather than to democracy itself. Despite the considerable optimism attending the third wave of democracies that came into being in the last decades of the twentieth century, indeed because of it, there is reason for concern on this front. A United Nations study in 2002 revealed that persistent poverty, disease, and rampant corruption were breeding political disillusionment in many of the new democracies, increasing the danger that they might collapse, as Pakistan did in 1999, into authoritarianism of one form or another (United Nations 2002).

There is no guarantee that democracy will reduce domination. Partly because there are no perfect decision rules, partly because of the many factors influencing the economic and social contexts in which democracies operate, and partly because of the interactions between political institutions and socioeconomic contexts, democracy's characteristic instruments of governance can often fail to reduce domination in particular settings and might, on occasion, even increase it. There are no silver bullets to fix the problem. The conventional appeals to deliberation, to liberal constitutionalism, to consensus of one kind or another, to weakening the state, and to group rights all turn out on close inspection to be problematic. Democratic systems are most likely to reduce domination to the extent that they bring decision making into better conformity with the principle of affected interest and strengthen the hands of those whose basic interests are vulnerable in particular settings. What this means in practice varies with particularities of context, with the limits imposed—and opportunities offered—by inherited political practices and institutions, and with creative appreciation of the many ways in which power structures human interaction.

My discussion of the considerable literature that has developed on the subject of deliberation in chapters 1 and 2 reflected and reinforced this outlook. The advantages of deliberation, if it can be pressed into the service of minimizing domination, are obvious. People with insiders' wisdom in a given setting are more likely to know how to do this effectively. Solutions that they devise and embrace are more likely to command their allegiance than those imposed on them by outsiders, and their choices may be more sophisticated and better informed as a result of deliberation about them with others. But deliberative processes can be manipulated by people with ulterior motives, they can marginalize the inarticulate (who may well also be those most vulnerable to domination), and they can result in stonewalling by the powerful in the face of needed changes. Accordingly, rather than advising a straightforward endorsement or rejection of deliberation, I suggested that the right to insist on it is best placed in the hands of those whose basic interests are at stake in a given setting. This by no means guarantees that deliberation's benefits will be realized, but it limits the potential for its abuse, while creating incentives for people to try to find deliberative solutions when they are available.

My examination of the debate about competitive democracy in political institutions narrowly conceived was also intended to both embody and advance the idea that democracy should be geared to limiting domination. I argued that we should reject all versions of the claim that politics is limited to what goes on in these institutions on the grounds that power relations are ubiquitous to human interaction, but that we should recognize, nonetheless, that political institutions present distinctive challenges for democratic theory. Elsewhere in collective life it makes sense to distinguish the superordinate goods people pursue—production of goods and services, education of children, advancement of knowledge, pursuit of excellence at sport, and so on—from the power relations that infuse those activities. The trick is to come up with ways to minimize domination with respect to the power dimensions of the activities while keeping interference with the superordinate goods to a minimum. Political institutions differ in that their raison d'être is to manage power relations. There may be particular superordinate goods concerning how best to run courts, the executive branch, or legislative committees within governmental institutions as discussed in §2.2, but at the end of the day there is no superordinate good beyond managing power relations so as to reduce domination to which institutional designers should aspire to defer. In this circumstance, the imperative to minimize domination is best realized by competitive democracy of the sort proposed by Schumpeter. We saw that structured competition for power is a better way to limit political domination than is deliberation or liberal constitutionalism. In a world in which power is ubiquitous, structured competition beats the going alternatives. This is not to say that it is perfect, even when it operates as it should. Churchill's more sober assessment that it is "the worst form of government except all those other forms that have been tried from time to time" is a more accurate way to put it.[1]

Structured competition for power is desirable also because it is geared to institutionalizing argument rather than agreement. None of the appeals to agreement as a political ideal prevalent in the literature held up under scrutiny. Whether postulated as the endpoint of deliberation, the starting point of a stylized constitutional convention, or the antidote to conflict in "divided" societies, the arguments for the superiority of agreement over competition were found wanting. The competitive model recognizes and seeks to institutionalize Mill's ([1859] 1978: 9–32) insight that the competition of ideas contributes to illumination in public life, something he thought threatened by the growth of consensus—which he saw as breeding slavish conformity. It is a measure of the degree to which the consensus model has eroded the competitive one in the public mind that people generally do not recognize bipartisan agreement for the collusion in restraint of democracy that it actually is.

We saw that the major flaws with Schumpeterianism in American political institutions concern how incompletely realized it is. The excessive number of veto points that result from federalism, bicameralism, and the separation of powers; the role of money in displacing competition for votes with competition for campaign contributions and expenditures—often from the same well-heeled contributors for both sides; the huge incumbency advantages that produce exceedingly low rates of turnover among political officeholders; and the domination of the system of electoral regulation by bipartisan rather than nonpartisan institutions all render the American democracy remarkably uncompetitive by any comparative standard—let alone an ideal type. The problem here is not with competitive democracy but with its absence, and the answer is surely not to replace it with institutions that are less competitive still. Rather, we should be pressing in the opposite direction—deploying the logic of political antitrust to develop theories about how the system can be made more competitive.

To be sure, Schumpeterianism is no panacea. Although I argued that the "countermajoritarian problem" is often overstated, as a pure procedural device majoritarian political competition can generate perverse results. Obvious instances are when majorities vote to undermine democracy along lines suggested in *Carolene Products,* or otherwise to foster

---

[1] Winston Churchill, Speech to the House of Commons, November 1947. See http://adamsharp.com/RAVES/QUOTES/index.asp [9/2/02].

domination. But responding to the weakness of pure proceduralism with theories of "substantive" democracy creates difficulties of its own, the most striking being the need to choose among them without resort once more to proceduralism. Yet we saw that there is room for a middle ground here, where courts and other second-guessing agencies operate in democracy-reinforcing ways to limit democracy's propensity to produce outcomes at variance with its constitutive ethos. The informing intuition here is that the goal should be to respond to the political equivalent of market failure rather than replace the political market with something else.

As I noted in chapter 4, there is no good reason to suppose competitive democracy unachievable in some parts of the world, but this does not mean it can always be established. Entrenched antipathies might be difficult to overcome in the relevant ways, dictators might have vicelike grips on power, or other factors might operate to make democratic innovation unlikely. Yet we do know something about the necessary conditions for at least some types of democratic transitions, and we also know that democracy can be instituted in improbable settings. More consequential is whether democracy, no matter how instituted, is likely to survive. On this there is surprisingly little accumulated knowledge in political science. The absence of severe poverty and the presence of economic growth seem to help, and parliamentary systems do seem to be more stable than presidential ones—even if the reasons for this are unclear. Beyond this, the literatures on which institutional and cultural factors are more and less conducive to democratic political stability remain very much works in progress. Building support for democracy, particularly among elites, is surely not a bad bet, though it is difficult to say how much difference it can make in the face of destabilizing factors.

In chapter 5, my focus shifted to an examination of the effect of democracy on the distribution of income and wealth. There are both prudential and normative reasons to focus on this subject, given the role of the absence of poverty in democratic survival and the fact that its presence renders people vulnerable to the kinds of domination by others that they reasonably expect to be alleviated by democracy. Yet we saw that, despite what nineteenth-century expectations and the median voter theorem would suggest, there is no strong relationship between democracy and downward redistribution, and quite possibly no relationship at all. No single explanation for this will do; a host of interacting factors are relevant, some structural, some contextual, some psychological, some embedded in the logic of decision rules, and some geographic. I suggested various ways of thinking about how to make democracy in general and American democracy in particular more responsive to the needs of the poor and near poor, but this is an area in which we have just begun to scratch the surface. More research, and even more creative political thinking, remain to be done.

Ackerman, Bruce. 1980. *Social Justice in the Liberal State*. New Haven: Yale University Press.

———. 1985. "Beyond *Carolene Products*." *Harvard Law Review* 98: 713–46.

———. 1993a. "Crediting the Voters: A New Beginning for Campaign Finance." *American Prospect* 13: 71–80.

———. 1993b. *We The People: Foundations*. Harvard University Press.

Ackerman, Bruce, and Ian Ayres. 2002. *Voting with Dollars: A New Paradigm in Campaign Finance*. New Haven: Yale University Press.

Ackerman, Bruce, and James Fishkin. 2002. "Deliberation Day." *Journal of Political Philosophy* 10: 129–52.

Alesina, Alberto, Rafael Di Tella, and Robert MacCulloch. 2002. "Inequality and Happiness: Are Europeans and Americans Different?" Mimeo. Harvard University. Available at: post.economics.harvard.edu/faculty/alesina/pdf-papers/AHineqJune30.pdf [9/2/02].

Alesina, Alberto, Edward Glaeser, and Bruce Sacerdote. 2001. "Why Doesn't the United States Have a European-Style Welfare State?" *Brookings Papers on Economic Activity* 2: 187–254. Washington, D.C.: The Brookings Institution. Available at: post.economics.harvard.edu/faculty/alesina/pdf-papers/0332-Alesina2.pdf [9/4/02].

Alesina, Alberto, and Eliana La Ferrara. 2001. "Preferences for Redistribution in the Land of Opportunities." Mimeo. Harvard University. Available at: post.economics.harvard.edu/faculty/alesina/pdf-papers/landopp1.pdf [9/4/02].

Anderson, Elijah. 1990. *Streetwise: Race, Class, and Change in an Urban Community*. Chicago: University of Chicago Press.

Antholis, William. 1993. "Liberal Democratic Theory and the Transformation of Sovereignty." Ph.D. diss., Yale University.

Aristotle. [ca. 330 B.C.] 1977. *The Nicomachean Ethics*. Harmondsworth: Penguin.

Arneson, Richard, and Ian Shapiro. 1996. "Democracy and Religious Freedom: A Critique of *Wisconsin v. Yoder*." In *NOMOS XXXVIII: Political Order*, edited by Ian Shapiro and Russell Hardin. New York: New York University Press.

Arrow, Kenneth J. 1951. *Social Choice and Individual Values*. New York: Wiley.

Avi-Yonah, Reuven. 2002. "Why Tax the Rich? Efficiency, Equity, and Progressive Taxation." *Yale Law Journal* 111: 1391–1416.

Ayres, Ian. 2000. "Disclosure versus Anonymity in Campaign Finance." In *NOMOS XLII: Designing Democratic Institutions*, edited by Ian Shapiro and Stephen Macedo. New York: New York University Press.

Bachrach, Peter, and Morton S. Baratz. 1962. "The Two Faces of Power." *American Political Science Review* 56: 947–52.

Bachrach, Peter, and Morton S. Baratz. 1970. *Power and Poverty: Theory and Practice.* New York: Oxford University Press.

Barbieri, W. 1998. *Ethics of Citizenship: Immigration and Group Rights in Germany.* Durham, N.C.: Duke University Press.

Bardhan, Pranab. 1999. "Democracy and Development: A Complex Relationship." In *Democracy's Value,* edited by Ian Shapiro and Casiano Hacker-Cordón. Cambridge: Cambridge University Press.

Barry, Brian. [1965] 1990. *Political Argument.* 2d ed. Herefordshire: Harvester Wheatsheaf.

————. 2000. *Culture and Equality: An Egalitarian Critique of Multiculturalism.* Cambridge: Polity.

Beitz, Charles. 1988. "Equal Opportunity in Political Representation." In *Equal Opportunity,* edited by Norman E. Bowie. Boulder, Colo.: Westview.

Bénabou, Roland, and Efe A. Ok. 2001. "Social Mobility and the Demand for Redistribution: The POUM Hypothesis." *Quarterly Journal of Economics* 116, no. 2: 447–87.

Bender, Edwin. 2000. "Private Prisons, Politics, and Profits." National Institute on Money in State Politics (July). Available at http://followthemoney.org/issues/private_prison/private_prison.html [9/3/02].

Benhabib, Seyla. 2001. *Transformations of Citizenship: Dilemmas of the Nation State in an Era of Globalization.* Amsterdam: Koninklijke van Gorcum.

Bennett, T. W. 1995. *Human Rights and African Customary Law.* Johannesburg: Jutas.

Bentham, Jeremy. 1954. "The Psychology of Economic Man." In *Jeremy Bentham's Economic Writings,* edited by W. Stark, vol. 3. George Allen & Unwin.

Berg-Schlosser, Dirk, and Gisèle De Meur. 1994. "Conditions of Democracy in Interwar Europe: A Boolean Test of Major Hypotheses." *Comparative Politics* 26: 253–80.

Blakely, Edward, and Mary Snyder. 1997. *Fortress America: Gated Communities in the United States.* New York: The Brookings Institution.

Blau, Joel. 1992. *The Visible Poor: Homelessness in the United States.* New York: Oxford University Press.

Bobo, Lawrence. 1998. "Race, Interests, and Beliefs about Affirmative Action." *American Behavioral Scientist* 41: 985–1003.

Bowden, Michael M. 2001. "Is a Two-Hundred-Year-Old Pirate Law the Next Wave in Tort Suits? Lawyers Find Way to Bring Foreign Workers into U.S. Courts." *Lawyers Weekly.* http://www.lawyersweekly.com/pirate.cfm [9/4/02].

Breyer, Friedrich, and Heinrich W. Ursprung. 1998. "Are the Rich Too Rich to Be Expropriated? Economic Power and Feasibility of Constitutional Limits to Redistribution." *Public Choice* 94: 135–56.

Buchanan, James M., and Gordon Tullock. 1962. *The Calculus of Consent: Logical Foundations of Constitutional Democracy.* Ann Arbor: University of Michigan Press.

Burke, Edmund. [1790] 1968. *Reflections on the Revolution in France*. Harmondsworth: Penguin.

Burt, Robert A. 1992. *The Constitution in Conflict*. Cambridge: Harvard University Press, Belknap Press.

Canache, Damarys. 1996. "Looking Out My Back Door: The Neighborhood Context and the Perceptions of Relative Deprivation." *Political Research Quarterly* 493: 547–71.

Chambers, Davis. 2000. "Civilizing the Natives: Marriage in Post-Apartheid South Africa." *Daedalus* 129: 101–24.

Cheibub, José, and Fernando Limongi. 2000. "Parliamentarism, Presidentialism, Is There a Difference?" Mimeo. Yale University.

Coase, R. H. 1960. "The Problem of Social Cost." *Journal of Law and Economics* 3: 1–44.

Cohen, Cathy J. 1999. *The Boundaries of Blackness: AIDS and the Breakdown of Black Politics*. Chicago: University of Chicago Press.

Cohen, G. A. 1989. "On the Currency of Egalitarian Justice." *Ethics* 99: 906–44.

———. 1995. *Self-Ownership, Freedom, and Equality*. Cambridge University Press.

———. 2000. *If You're an Egalitarian, How Come You're So Rich?* Cambridge: Harvard University Press.

Cohen, Joshua, and Joel Rogers. 1995. *Associations and Democracy*. New York and London: Verso.

Coleman, Jules, and John Ferejohn. 1986. "Democracy and Social Choice." *Ethics* 97: 11–22.

Condorcet, Marquis de. [1785] 1972. *Essai sur l'application de l'analyse à la probabilité des décisions rendues à la pluralité des voix*. New York: Chelsea Pub. Co.

Crosby, Faye. 1984. "The Denial of Personal Discrimination," *American Behavioral Scientist* 27: 371–86.

Crosby, Ned. 1995. "Citizen Juries: One Solution for Difficult Environmental Questions." In *Fairness and Competence in Citizen Participation: Evaluating Models for Environmental Discourse*, edited by Ortwin Renn, Thomas Webler, and Peter Wiedemann. Boston: Kluwer Academic Publishers.

Crosby, Ned, Janet Kelly, and Paul Schzefer. 1986. "Citizen Panels: A New Approach to Citizen Participation." *Public Administration Review* 46: 170–78.

Dahl, Robert A. 1956. *A Preface to Democratic Theory*. Chicago: University of Chicago Press.

———. 1961. *Who Governs? Democracy and Power in an American City*. New Haven: Yale University Press.

———. 1971. *Polarchy: Participation and Opposition*. New Haven: Yale University Press.

———. 1979. "Procedural Democracy." In *Philosophy, Politics and Society*, edited by Peter Laslett and James Fishkin. 5th ser. New Haven: Yale University Press.

———. 1989. *Democracy and Its Critics*. New Haven: Yale University Press.

Dahl, Robert A. 1997. "Decisionmaking in a Democracy: The Supreme Court as National Policymaker." *Journal of Public Law* 6: 279–95.

———. 1999. "Can International Organizations Be Democratic?" In *Democracy's Edges*, edited by Ian Shapiro and Casiano Hacker-Cordón. Cambridge: Cambridge University Press.

———. 2002. *A Democratic Critique of the American Constitution*. New Haven: Yale University Press.

Daniels, Norman. 1991. "Is the Oregon Rationing Plan Fair?" *Journal of the American Medical Association* 265: 2232–35.

Di Palma, Giuseppe. 1990. *To Craft Democracies: An Essay on Democratic Transitions*. Berkeley and Los Angeles: University of California Press.

Downs, Anthony. 1957. *An Economic Theory of Democracy*. New York: Harper.

Duneier, Mitchell. 1994. *Slim's Table*. Chicago: University of Chicago Press.

Dunn, John. 1979. *Western Political Theory in the Face of the Future*. Cambridge: Cambridge University Press.

Duverger, Maurice. 1954. *Political Parties: Their Organization and Activity in the Modern State*. New York: Wiley.

Dworkin, Ronald. 1981. "What Is Equality? Part II: Equality of Resources," *Philosophy and Public Affairs* 10, no. 4: 283–345.

———. 1986. *Law's Empire*. Cambridge: Harvard University Press.

———. 1993. *Life's Dominion*. New York: Knopf.

Easterbrook, Frank H. 1982. "Ways of Criticizing the Court." *Harvard Law Review* 95: 802–32.

Edwards, Chris, and Tad DeHaven. 2001. "Farm Subsidies at Record Levels as Congress Considers New Farm Bill." Cato Institute Briefing Paper no. 70 (October 18). Available at http://www.cato.org/pubs/briefs/bp70.pdf [9/3/02].

Ellis, Joseph J. 2000. *Founding Brothers: The Revolutionary Generation*. New York: Random House.

Elster, Jon. 1995. "Local Justice and American Values." In *Local Justice in America*, edited by Jon Elster. New York: Russell Sage.

Ely, John Hart. 1980. *Democracy and Distrust: A Theory of Judicial Review*. Cambridge: Harvard University Press.

Engels, Frederick. [1878] 1959. *Anti-Dühring*. Moscow: Foreign Language Publishing House.

Epstein, Leon D. 1986. *Political Parties in the American Mold*. Madison: University of Wisconsin Press.

Evans, M.D.R. Jonathan Kelley, and Tamas Kolosi. 1996. "Images of Class: Public Perceptions in Hungary and Australia." *American Sociological Review* 57: 461–82.

Feather, Norman. 1994. "Attitudes toward High Achievers and Reactions to Their Fall: Theory and Research concerning Tall Poppies." In *Advances in Experimental Social Psychology*, edited by Mark P. Zanna, 26: 1–73. San Diego, Calif.: Academic Press.

Fellner, Jamie, and Marc Mauer. 1998. "Losing the Vote: The Impact of Felony Disenfranchisement Laws in the United States." Sentencing Project and Human Rights Watch. Available at http://www.hrw.org/reports98/vote/ [9/3/02].

Ferejohn, John. 2000. "Instituting Deliberative Democracy." In *NOMOS XLII: Designing Democratic Institutions*, edited by Ian Shapiro and Stephen Macedo, 75–104. New York: New York University Press.

Ferejohn, John, and Pasquale Pasquino. 1999. "Deliberative Institutions." Paper presented at the Institute of Governmental Studies at U.C. Berkeley, http://www.igs.berkeley.edu:8880/research_programs/ppt_papers/deliberative_institutions.pdf [9/3/02].

Figlio, Koplin, and William E. Reid. 1999. "Do States Play Welfare Games?" *Journal of Urban Economics* 46: 437–54.

Fine, Michelle, and Lois Weis. 1998. *The Unknown City.* Boston: Beacon.

Fiorina, Morris P. 1981. *Voting in American National Elections.* New Haven: Yale University Press.

Fishkin, James. 1979. *Tyranny and Legitimacy: A Critique of Political Theories.* Baltimore: Johns Hopkins University Press.

———. 1991. *Democracy and Deliberation: New Directions for Democratic Reform.* New Haven: Yale University Press.

———. 1995. *The Voice of the People: Public Opinion and Democracy.* New Haven. Yale University Press.

Foucault, Michel. 1972. *The Archeology of Knowledge.* New York: Pantheon.

———. 1977. *Discipline and Punish: The Birth of the Prison.* New York: Pantheon.

———. 1980. *Power/Knowledge: Selected Interviews and Other Writings 1972–1977.* Edited by Colin Gordon. Translated by Colin Gordon, Leo Marshall, John Mepham, and Kate Soper. New York: Pantheon.

———. 1982. "The Subject and Power." *Critical Inquiry* 8: 777–95.

Foweraker, Joe. 1998. "Institutional Design, Party Systems and Governability—Differentiating the Presidential Regimes of Latin America." *British Journal of Political Science* 28: 651–76.

Frank, Robert. 1985. *Choosing the Right Pond: Human Behavior and the Quest for Status.* New York: Oxford University Press.

Frank, Robert, and Philip Cook. 1996. *The Winner-Take-All Society: Why the Few at the Top Get So Much More Than the Rest of Us.* Harmondsworth: Penguin.

Fraser, Nancy. 1997. *Justice Interruptus: Critical Reflections on the "Postsocialist" Condition.* New York: Routledge.

Fukuyama, Francis. 1992. *The End of History and the Last Man.* New York: Free Press.

Garrett, Geoffrey. 1998. *Partisan Politics in the Global Economy.* Cambridge: Cambridge University Press.

———. 2001. "The Distributive Consequences of Globalization." Mimeo. Yale University.

Gaventa, John. 1980. *Power and Powerlessness: Quiescence and Rebellion in an Appalachian Valley.* Urbana: University of Illinois Press.

Gilens, Martin. 1999. *Why Americans Hate Welfare.* Chicago: University of Chicago Press.

Ginsburg, Ruth Bader. 1993. "Speaking in a Judicial Voice." Madison Lecture, New York University Law School. Mimeo.

Gobetti, Daniela. 1996. "Regularities and Innovation in Italian Politics." *Politics and Society* 24: 57–70.

Goldberg, Ellis. 1996. "Thinking about How Democracy Works." *Politics and Society* 24: 7–18.

Green, Donald P., and Ian Shapiro. 1994. *Pathologies of Rational Choice Theory: A Critique of Applications in Political Science.* New Haven: Yale University Press.

———. 1996. "Pathologies Revisited: Reflections on Our Critics." In *The Rational Choice Controversy: Economic Models of Politics Reconsidered,* edited by Jeffrey Friedman. New Haven: Yale University Press.

Guinier, Lani. 1991. "The Triumph of Tokenism: The Voting Rights Act and the Theory of Black Educational Success." *Michigan Law Review* 89: 1077–1154.

———. 1994a. "(E)racing Democracy: The Voting Rights Cases." *Harvard Law Review* 108: 109–37.

———. 1994b. *The Tyranny of the Majority: Fundamental Fairness in Representative Democracy.* New York: Free Press.

Gutmann, Amy, and Dennis Thompson. 1996. *Democracy and Disagreement.* Cambridge: Harvard University Press, Belknap Press.

Habermas, Jürgen. 1975. *Legitimation Crises.* Boston: Beacon Press.

———. 1979. *Communication and the Evolution of Society.* Boston: Beacon Press.

———. 1984. *The Theory of Communicative Action, Reason and Rationalization of Society.* Vol. 1. Boston: Beacon Press.

———. 1994. "Three Normative Models of Democracy." *Constellations* 1: 1–10.

———. 1995. "Reconciliation through the Public Use of Reason: Remarks on John Rawls's *Political Liberalism.*" *Journal of Philosophy* 92: 109–31.

———. 1996. *Between Facts and Norms.* Cambridge: Polity.

Hacker, Jacob. 1997. *The Road to Nowhere: The Genesis of President Clinton's Plan for Health Security.* Princeton: Princeton University Press.

Hadorn, David C. 1991. "Setting Health Care Priorities in Oregon: Cost-Effectiveness Meets the Rule of Rescue." *Journal of the American Medical Association* 26: 2218–25.

Hafer, Carolyn, and James Olson. 1993. "Beliefs in a Just World, Discontent and Assertive Actions by Working Women." *Personality and Social Psychology Bulletin* 19: 30–38.

Hamburger, Tom, and Theodore Marmor. 1993. "Dead on Arrival: Why Washington's Power Elites Won't Consider Single Payer Health Reform." *Washington Monthly,* September, 27–32.

Hamilton, Alexander, James Madison, and John Jay. [1788] 1966. *The Federalist Papers.* Harmondsworth: Penguin.

Hansmann, Henry. 2000. *The Ownership of Enterprise.* Cambridge: Harvard University Press, Belknap Press.

Hardin, Russell. 1999. *Liberalism, Constitutionalism, and Democracy.* Oxford: Oxford University Press.

Hartz, Louis. 1955. *The Liberal Tradition in America: An Interpretation of American Political Thought since the Revolution.* New York: Harcourt, Brace & World.

Hay, Douglas. 1975. "Property, Authority and the Criminal Law." In *Albion's Fatal Tree: Crime and Society in Eighteenth-Century England,* edited by Douglas Hay, Peter Linebaugh, John Rule, E. P. Thompson, and Cal Winslow. New York: Pantheon.

Hayward, Clarissa Rile. 2000. *De-Facing Power.* Cambridge: Cambridge University Press.

Hegel, G.W.F. [1807] 1949. *The Phenomenology of Mind.* 2d ed. rev. London: G. Allen & Unwin.

Held, David. 1995. *Democracy and the Global Order.* Stanford: Stanford University Press.

———. 1999. "The Transformation of Political Community: Rethinking Democracy in the Context of Globalization." In *Democracy's Edges,* edited by Ian Shapiro and Casiano Hacker-Cordón. Cambridge: Cambridge University Press.

Hidalgo, Diego, ed. 2002. *Conference on Democratic Transition and Consolidation.* Madrid, Spain: Siddharth Mehta Ediciones.

Hill, Christopher. 1961. *The Century of Revolution 1603–1714.* New York: W. W. Norton.

———. 1965. "The Many-Headed Monster in Later Tudor and Early Stuart Political Thinking." In *From the Renaissance to the Counter-Reformation: Essays in Honor of Garrett Mattingly,* edited by Charles H. Carter. New York: Random House.

———. 1972. *The World Turned Upside Down.* New York: Pelican.

Hirschl, Ran. 1999. "Towards Juristocracy: A Comparative Inquiry into the Origins and Consequences of the New Constitutionalism." Ph.D. diss., Yale University.

———. 2000. "The Political Origins of Judicial Empowerment through Constitutionalization: Lessons from Four Constitutional Revolutions." *Law and Social Inquiry* 25: 91–147.

Hirschman, Albert O. 1970. *Exit, Voice, and Loyalty.* Cambridge: Harvard University Press.

Hobbes, Thomas. [1968] 1985. *Leviathan.* Edited with an introduction by C. B. Macpherson. Harmondsworth: Penguin.

Hochschild, Jennifer. 1981. *What's Fair? American Beliefs about Distributive Justice.* Cambridge: Harvard University Press.

Hochschild, Jennifer. 1984. *The New American Dilemma: Liberal Democracy and School Desegregation.* New Haven: Yale University Press.

———. 1988. "The Double-Edged Sword of Equal Opportunity." In *Power, Inequality, and Democratic Politics,* edited by Ian Shapiro and Grant Reeher. New York: Westview.

———. 1995. *Facing up to the American Dream: Race, Class, and the Soul of the Nation.* Princeton: Princeton University Press.

Hodge, Robert, and Donald Trieman. 1968. "Class Identification in the United States." *American Journal of Sociology* 73: 535–47.

Holmes, Stephen. 1995. *Passions and Constraint: On the Theory of Liberal Democracy.* Chicago: University of Chicago Press.

Holmes, Stephen, and Cass Sunstein. 1999. *The Costs of Rights: Why Liberty Depends on Taxes.* New York: W. W. Norton.

Horowitz, Donald L. 1985. *Ethnic Groups in Conflict.* Berkeley and Los Angeles: University of California Press.

———. 1991. *A Democratic South Africa? Constitutional Engineering in a Divided Society.* Berkeley and Los Angeles: University of California Press.

———. 2000. "Constitutional Design: An Oxymoron?" In *NOMOS XLII; Designing Democratic Institutions,* edited by Ian Shapiro and Stephen Macedo. New York: New York University Press.

Hotelling, Harold. 1929. "Stability in Competition." *Economic Journal* 39: 41–57.

Hotz, V. Joseph, Charles Mullin, and John Scholz. 2000. "The Earned Income Tax Credit and Labor Market Participation of Families on Welfare." In *The Incentives of Government Programs and the Well-Being of Families,* edited by Bruce Meyer and Greg Duncan. Washington, D.C. Joint Center for Poverty Research. Available at http://www.jcpr.org/book/pdf/IncentivesHotzChap3.pdf [9/3/02].

Howard, Christopher. 1997. *The Hidden Welfare State.* Princeton: Princeton University Press.

Huntington, Samuel P. 1984. "Will More Countries Become Democratic?" *Political Science Quarterly* 99: 193–218.

———. 1991. *The Third Wave: Democratization in the Late Twentieth Century.* Norman: University of Oklahoma Press.

———. 1996. *The Clash of Civilizations and the Remaking of World Order.* New York: Simon and Schuster.

Irwin, John, and James Austin. 1997. *It's about Time: America's Imprisonment Binge.* New York: Wadsworth.

Isaac, Jeffrey. 1987a. "Beyond the Three Faces of Power." *Polity* 20: 4–30.

———. 1987b. *Power and Marxist Theory: A Realist View.* Ithaca: Cornell University Press.

Johnstone, John. 1978. "Social Class, Social Areas, and Delinquency." *Sociology and Social Research* 63: 49–72.

Jung, Courtney. 2000. "The Myth of the Divided Society and the Case of South Africa." Mimeo. New School for Social Research.

Jung, Courtney, Ellen Lust-Okar, and Ian Shapiro. 2002. "Problems and Prospects for Democratic Transitions: South Africa as a Model for the Middle East and Northern Ireland?" Mimeo. Yale University.

Jung, Courtney, and Ian Shapiro. 1995. "South Africa's Negotiated Transition: Democracy, Opposition, and the New Constitutional Order." *Politics and Society* 23: 269–308.

Kahneman, Daniel, Paul Stovic, and Amos Tversky. 1982. *Judgment under Uncertainty.* Cambridge: Cambridge University Press.

Kaplan, Robert. 1997. "Was Democracy Just a Moment?" *Atlantic Monthly.* Available at www.theatlantic.com/issues/97dec/democ.htm [9/2/02].

Karl, Terry. 1990. "Dilemmas of Democratization in Latin America." *Comparative Politics* 23, no. 1: 1–21.

Kelley, Jonathan, and M.D.R. Evans. 1995. "Class and Class Conflict in Six Western Nations." *American Sociological Review* 60: 157–78.

Kepel, Gilles. 2002. *Jihad: The Trail of Political Islam.* Cambridge: Harvard University Press.

Koelble, Thomas, and Andrew Reynolds. 1996 "Power-Sharing Democracy in the New South Africa." *Politics and Society* 24: 221–36.

Kozol, Jonathan. 1995. *Amazing Grace: The Lives of Children and the Conscience of a Nation.* New York: Crown.

Kymlicka, Will. 1985. *Multicultural Citizenship: A Liberal Theory of Minority Rights.* Oxford: Oxford University Press.

———. 1999. "Citizenship in an Era of Globalization: Commentary on Held." In *Democracy's Edges,* edited by Ian Shapiro and Casiano Hacker-Cordón. Cambridge: Cambridge University Press.

———. 2001. *Politics in the Vernacular: Nationalism, Multiculturalism, and Citizenship.* Oxford: Oxford University Press.

Laba, Roman. 1986. "Worker Roots of Solidarity." *Problems of Communism* 35: 47–67.

Laclau, Ernesto, and Chantal Mouffe. 1985. *Hegemony and Socialist Strategy: Towards a Radical Democratic Politics.* London: Verso.

Ladd, Everett Carl. 1999. *The Ladd Report.* New York: Free Press.

Lalonde, Richard, and J. E. Cameron. 1993. "Behavioral Responses to Discrimination: A Focus on Action." In *The Psychology of Prejudice: The Ontario Symposium,* edited by M. P. Zanna and J. M. Olson, vol. 7. Hillsdale, N.J.: Lawrence Erlbaum Associates.

Lalonde, Richard, and Randy Silverman. 1994. "Behavioral Preferences in Response to Social Injustice: The Effects of Group Permeability and Social Identity Salience." *Journal of Personality and Social Psychology* 66: 78–85.

Lane, Robert. 1991. *The Market Experience.* Cambridge: Cambridge University Press.

Lane, Robert. 2001. *The Loss of Happiness in Market Democracies*. New Haven: Yale University Press.

Leiman, Melvin M. 1993. *Political Economy of Racism*. London: Pluto.

Levi, Margaret. 1996. "Social and Unsocial Capital: A Review Essay of Robert Putnam's *Making Democracy Work*." *Politics and Society* 24: 45–56.

Lijphart, Arend. 1969. "Consociational Democracy." *World Politics* 21: 207–25.

———. 1977. *Democracy in Plural Societies*. New Haven: Yale University Press.

Lind, Michael. 1995. *The Next American Nation*. New York: Free Press.

Linz, Juan J. 1978. *The Breakdown of Democratic Regimes: Crises, Breakdown and Reequilibration*. Baltimore: Johns Hopkins University Press.

———. 1994. "Presidential or Parliamentary Democracy: Does It Make a Difference?" In *The Failure of Presidential Democracy*, edited by Juan J. Linz and Arturo Valenzuela. Baltimore: Johns Hopkins University Press.

Linz, Juan, and Alfred Stepan, eds. 1978. *The Breakdown of Democratic Regimes: Latin America*. Baltimore: Johns Hopkins University Press.

Lipsett, Seymour Martin. 1959. "Some Social Requisites of Democracy: Economic Development and Political Legitimacy." *American Political Science Review* 53: 69–105.

Lowenstein, Daniel. 1995. *Election Law: Cases and Materials*. Durham, N.C.: Carolina Academic Press.

Lukes, Steven. 1974. *Power: A Radical View*. London: Macmillan.

Luong, Pauline Jones. 2000. "After the Break-Up." *Comparative Political Studies* 33: 563–92.

Macedo, Stephen, ed. 1999. *Deliberative Politics: Essays on Democracy and Disagreement*. New York: Oxford University Press.

Machiavelli, Niccolò. [ca. 1517] 1979. *The Discourses*. Translated by Leslie J. Walker, with revisions by Brian Richardson. Harmondsworth: Penguin.

MacIntyre, Alasdair. 1984. *After Virtue: A Study in Moral Theory*. 2d ed. Notre Dame, Ind.: University of Notre Dame Press.

Mackie, Gerry. 2003. *Democracy Defended*. Cambridge: Cambridge University Press.

MacKinnon, Catharine. 1987. *Feminism Unmodified: Discourses on Life and Law*. Cambridge: Harvard University Press.

Macleod, Jay. 1987. *Ain't No Makin' It: Leveled Aspirations in a Low-Income Neighborhood*. Boulder, Colo.: Westview.

Mainwaring, Scott, and Matthew Soberg Shugart, eds. 1997. *Presidentialism and Democracy in Latin America*. Cambridge: Cambridge University Press.

Mamdani, Mahmood. 1986. *Citizen and Subject: Contemporary Africa and the Legacy of Late Colonialism*. Princeton: Princeton University Press.

Mandel, Harlan. 1989. "In Pursuit of the Missing Link: International Worker Rights and International Trade?" *Columbia Journal of Transnational Law* 27: 443–82.

Mandela, Nelson. 1979. "Address to the Court before Sentencing." In *Ideologies of Liberation in Black Africa, 1856–1970*, edited by J. Ayo Langley. London: Rex Collins.

Mansbridge, Jane J. 1980. *Beyond Adversary Democracy*. New York: Basic Books.

Marcuse, Herbert. 1965. "Repressive Tolerance." In *A Critique of Pure Tolerance*, edited by Robert Paul Wolff, Barrington Moore, Jr., and Herbert Marcuse. Boston: Beacon Press.

Marmor, Theodore, ed. 1994. *Understanding Health Care Reform*. New Haven: Yale University Press.

Marshall, Terrence H. 1965. *Class, Citizenship, and Social Development*. New York: Doubleday.

Martin, Joanne. 1986. "Tolerance of Injustice." In *Relative Deprivation and Social Comparison*, edited by James Olson, C. Peter Herman, and Mark Zanna. Hillsdale, N.J.: Lawrence Erlbaum Associates.

Marx, Karl. [1844] 1972. "On the Jewish Question." In *The Marx-Engels Reader*, edited by Robert C. Tucker, 26–52. New York: W. W. Norton.

———. [1867] 1976. *Capital: A Critique of Political Economy*. Vol. 1. Harmondsworth: Penguin.

Mbeki, Thabo. "Africa Will Surprise the World Again." Speech made at the United Nations in Tokyo as reported in *Business Day* (Johannesburg, South Africa), on April 14, 1998.

McDermott, Kathryn. *Controlling Public Education: Localism versus Equity*. Kansas City: University Press of Kansas, 1999.

McMath, Robert C. 1993. *American Populism*. New York: Hill and Wang.

Menand, Louis. 2001. *The Metaphysical Club: A Story of Ideas in America*. New York: Farrar, Straus, & Giroux.

Michels, Robert. 1962. *Political Parties: A Sociological Study of the Oligarchical Tendencies of Modern Democracy*. Translated by Eden and Cedar Paul. New York: Free Press.

Miliband, Ralph. 1969. *The State in Capitalist Society*. New York: Basic Books.

Mill, John Stuart. [1859] 1978. *On Liberty*. Indianapolis: Hackett.

Miller, Nicholas R. 1983. "Pluralism and Social Choice." *American Political Science Review* 77: 735–43.

Mills, C. Wright. 1956. *The Power Elite*. Oxford: Oxford University Press.

Minow, Martha. 1990. *Making All the Difference*. Ithaca: Cornell University Press.

Mishel, Lawrence, Jared Bernstein, and John Schmitt. 2000. *The State of Working America 1998–9*. Ithaca: Economic Policy Institute/Cornell University Press.

Moffitt, Robert, David Ribar, and Mark Wilhelm. 1998. "The Decline of Welfare Benefits in the US: The Role of Wage Inequality." *Journal of Public Economics* 68: 421–52.

Montague, Jim. 1997. "Why Rationing Was Right for Oregon." *Hospitals and Health Networks*, February 5, 64–66.

Moore, Barrington. 1966. *The Social Origins of Dictatorship and Democracy: Lord and Peasant in the Making of the Modern World.* Boston: Beacon Press.

Mosca, Gaetano. 1939. *The Ruling Class.* New York: MaGraw-Hill.

Mouffe, Chantal. 1992. *Dimensions of Radical Democracy.* New York: Verso.

Mueller, Dennis C. 1989. *Public Choice II.* Cambridge: Cambridge University Press.

Muller, Edward N., and Mitchell A. Seligson. 1994. "Civic Culture and Democracy: The Question of Causal Relationships." *American Political Science Review* 88: 635–52.

Munck, Geraldo, and Carol Leff. 1997. "Modes of Transition and Democratization." *Comparative Politics* 29, no. 3: 343–62.

Murphy, Walter. 1964. *Elements of Judicial Strategy.* Chicago: University of Chicago Press.

Nagel, Jack. 1993. "Lessons of the Impending Electoral Reform in New Zealand." *PEGS Newsletter* 3: 9–10.

Nattrass, Nicoli, and Jeremy Seekings. 2001. "Two Nations? Race and Economic Inequality in South Africa Today." *Daedalus* 130, no. 1 (Winter): 45–70.

Neblo, Michael. 1998. "Deliberate Actions: Identifying Communicative Rationality Empirically." Available at http://www.spc.uchicago.edu/politicaltheory/neblo98.pdf [9/3/02].

———. 2000. "Counting Voices in an Echo Chamber: Cognition, Complexity, and the Prospects for Deliberative Democracy." Presented at the University of Chicago Political Theory Workshop, Paper Archive http://www.spc.uchicago.edu/politicaltheory/neblo00.pdf [9/3/02].

Nickerson, David. 2000 "Do Autocracies Obey Wagner's Law?" Mimeo. Yale University.

Nozick, Robert. 1974. *Anarchy, State, and Utopia.* New York: Basic Books.

O'Connor, James R. 1973. *Fiscal Crisis of the State.* New York: St. Martin's Press.

O'Donnell, Guillermo, and Philippe Schmitter. 1986. *Transitions from Authoritarian Rule.* Baltimore: Johns Hopkins University Press.

Okin, Susan Moller. 1989. *Justice, Gender, and the Family.* New York: Basic Books.

Olson, James. 1986. "Resentment about Deprivation." In *Relative Deprivation and Social Comparison*, edited by James Olson, C. Peter Herman, and Mark Zanna. Hillsdale, N.J.: Lawrence Erlbaum Associates.

Parker, R. B. 1979. "The Jurisprudential Uses of John Rawls." In *NOMOS XX: Constitutionalism*, edited by Roland Pennock and John Chapman. New York: New York University Press.

Parkin, Frank. 1971. *Class, Inequality, and Political Order.* New York: Praeger.

Pateman, Carole. 1988. *The Sexual Contract.* Cambridge: Polity, 1988.

Peterson, Paul E. 1995. *The Price of Federalism.* Washington, D.C.: The Brookings Institution.

Peterson, Paul E., and Mark Rom, 1989. "American Federalism, Welfare Policy, and Residential Choices." *American Political Science Review* 83: 711–28.

Peterson, Richard R. 1996. "A Re-evaluation of the Economic Consequences of Divorce." *American Sociological Review* 61: 528–36.

Pettit, Philip. 1997. *Republicanism: A Theory of Freedom and Government.* New York: Oxford University Press.

———. 1999. "Republican Freedom and Contestatory Democratization." In *Democracy's Value*, edited by Ian Shapiro and Casiano Hacker-Cordón. Cambridge: Cambridge University Press.

———. 2000. "Democracy, Electoral and Contestatory." In *NOMOS XLII: Designing Democratic Institutions*, edited by Ian Shapiro and Stephen Macedo. New York: New York University Press.

Phillips, Kevin. 2002. *Wealth and Democracy: A Political History of the American Rich.* New York: Broadway Books.

Pierson, Paul. 1996. *Dismantling the Welfare State? Regan, Thatcher and the Politics of Retrenchment.* Cambridge: Cambridge University Press.

Piketty, Thomas. 1995. "Social Mobility and Redistributive Politics." *Quarterly Journal of Economics* 110: 551–84.

Pitkin, Hanna. 1972. *The Concept of Representation.* Berkeley and Los Angeles: University of California Press.

Plato. 1974. *The Republic.* Translated by Desmond Lee. 2d rev. ed. Harmondsworth: Penguin.

Pocock, J.G.A. 1975. *The Machiavellian Moment: Florentine Political Thought and the Atlantic Republican Tradition.* Princeton: Princeton University Press.

Pogge, Thomas. 1992. "Cosmopolitanism and Sovereignty." *Ethics* 103: 48–75.

Polsby, Nelson. 1960. "How to Study Community Power." *Journal of Politics* 22: 474–84.

———. 1963. *Community Power and Political Theory.* New Haven: Yale University Press.

———. 1980. *Community Power and Political Theory: A Further Look at Problems of Evidence and Inference.* 2d ed. New Haven: Yale University Press.

Posner, Richard. 1985a. "An Economic Theory of the Criminal Law." *Columbia Law Review* 85, no. 6: 1193–1231.

———. 1985b. *The Federal Courts: Crisis and Reform.* Cambridge: Harvard University Press.

Powell, G. Bingham. 2000. *Elections as Instruments of Democracy: Majoritarian and Proportional Visions.* New Haven: Yale University Press.

Powers, Nancy R. 2001. *Grassroots Expectations of Democracy and Economy: Argentina in Comparative Perspective.* Pittsburgh: University of Pittsburgh Press.

Przeworski, Adam. 1991. *Democracy and the Market.* Cambridge: Cambridge University Press.

———. 1999. "Minimalist Conception of Democracy: A Defense." In *Democracy's Value*, edited by Ian Shapiro and Casiano Hacker-Cordón. Cambridge: Cambridge University Press.

———. 2001. "Democracy as an Equilibrium." Mimeo. New York University.

165

Przeworski, Adam, Michael Alvarez, Jose Cheibub, and Fernando Limongi. 2000. *Democracy and Development: Political Institutions and Well-Being in the World, 1950–1990.* Cambridge: Cambridge University Press.

Przeworski, Adam, and Michael Wallerstein. 1988. "Structural Dependence of the State on Capital." *American Political Science Review* 82, no. 1: 11–29.

Putnam, Robert D. 1993a. *Making Democracy Work: Civic Traditions in Modern Italy.* Princeton: Princeton University Press.

———. 1993b. "The Prosperous Community: Social Capital and Public Affairs." *American Prospect* 13: 35–42.

———. 2000. *Bowling Alone: The Collapse and Revival of American Community.* New York: Simon and Schuster.

Rae, Douglas W. 1967. *The Political Consequences of Electoral Rules.* New Haven: Yale University Press.

———. 1969. "Decision-Rules and Individual Values in Constitutional Choice." *American Political Science Review* 63: 40–56.

———. 1975. "The Limits of Consensual Decision." *American Political Science Review* 69: 1270–94.

———. 1995. "Using District Magnitude to Regulate Political Party Competition." *Journal of Economic Perspectives* 9, no. 1: 65–75.

———. 1999. "Democratic Liberty and Tyrannies of Place." In *Democracy's Edges*, edited by Ian Shapiro and Casiano Hacker-Cordón. Cambridge: Cambridge University Press.

———. 2003. *The End of Urbanism.* New Haven: Yale University Press.

Rae, Douglas W., with Douglas Yates, Jennifer Hochschild, Joseph Morone, and Carol Fessler. 1981. *Equalities.* Cambridge: Harvard University Press.

Ranney, Austin. 1975. *Curing the Mischiefs of Faction: Party Reform in America.* Berkeley and Los Angeles: University of California Press.

Rawls, John. 1971. *A Theory of Justice.* Cambridge: Harvard University Press.

———. 1993. *Political Liberalism.* New York: Columbia University Press.

———. 1995. "Reconcilation through the Public Use of Reason." *Journal of Philosophy* 92, no. 3: 132–80.

Ribar, David C., and Mark O. Wilhelm. 1996. "Welfare Generosity: The Importance of Administrative Efficiency, Community Values, and Genuine Benevolence." *Applied Economics* 28, no. 8: 1045–54.

———. 1999. "The Demand for Welfare Generosity." *Review of Economics and Statistics* 81. no. 1: 96–108.

Rich, Michael J. 1991. *Federal Policy-Making and the Poor: National Goals, Local Choices, and Distributional Outcomes.* Princeton: Princeton University Press.

Riker, William H. 1982. *Liberalism against Populism: A Confrontation between the Theory of Democracy and the Theory of Social Choice.* San Francisco: W. H. Freeman.

Riker, William H., and Barry W. Weingast. 1988. "Constitutional Regulation of Legislative Choice: The Political Consequences of Judicial Deference to Legislatures." *Virginia Law Review* 74: 373–401.

Rinne, Tim. 1995. "The Rise and Fall of Single-Payer Health Care in Nebraska." *Action for Universal Health Care* 3, no. 10: 4–5.

Roemer, John. 1995. "Should Marxists Be Interested in Exploitation?" *Philosophy and Public Affairs* 14: 30–65.

———. 1998. "Why the Poor Do Not Expropriate the Rich: An Old Argument in New Garb." *Journal of Public Economics* 70, no. 3: 399–424.

———. 1999. "Does Democracy Engender Justice?" In *Democracy's Value*, edited by Ian Shapiro and Casiano Hacker-Cordón. Cambridge: Cambridge University Press.

Roemer, John, and Woojin Lee. 2002. "Racialism and Redistribution in the US: 1972–1996" (forthcoming).

Rousseau, Jean-Jacques. [1762] 1968. *The Social Contract*. Harmondsworth: Penguin.

Rueschemeyer, Dietrich, Evelyne Huber Stephens, and John D. Stephens. 1992. *Capitalist Development and Democracy*. Oxford : Polity.

Runciman, W. G. 1966. *Relative Deprivation and Social Justice*. Routledge & Kegan Paul.

Sabetti, Filippo. 1996. "Path Dependency and Civic Culture: Some Lessons from Italy about Interpreting Social Experiments." *Politics and Society* 24: 19–44.

Sandel, Michael. 1982. *Liberalism and the Limits of Justice*. Cambridge: Cambridge University Press.

———. 1996. *Democracy's Discontents*. Cambridge: Harvard University Press.

Schelling, Thomas C. 1960. *The Strategy of Conflict*. Cambridge: Harvard University Press.

Schumpeter, Joseph. 1942. *Capitalism, Socialism, and Democracy*. New York: Harper.

Scott, James. 1985. *Weapons of the Weak*. New Haven: Yale University Press.

———. 1990. *Domination and the Arts of Resistance*. New Haven: Yale University Press.

Sen, Amartya. 1992. *Inequality Reexamined*. New York: Russell Sage; Cambridge: Harvard University Press.

Shammas, Carol. 1993. "A New Look at Long Term Trends in Wealth Inequality in the United States." *American Historical Review* 98, no. 2: 412–31.

Shapiro, Ian. 1986. *The Evolution of Rights in Liberal Theory*. Cambridge: Cambridge University Press.

———. 1987. "Richard Posner's Praxis," *Ohio State Law Review* 48, no. 4: 1009–26.

———. 1990a. "J.G.A. Pocock's Republicanism and Political Theory: A Critique and Reinterpretation." *Critical Review* 4, no. 3: 433–71.

Shapiro, Ian. 1990b. *Political Criticism*. Berkeley and Los Angeles: University of California Press.

———. 1993. "Democratic Innovation: South Africa in Comparative Context." *World Politics* 46: 121–50.

———. 1996. *Democracy's Place*. Ithaca: Cornell University Press.

———. 1999a. *Democratic Justice*. New Haven: Yale University Press.

———. 1999b. "Enough of Deliberation: Politics Is about Interests and Power." In *Deliberative Politics: Essays on Democracy and Disagreement*, edited by Stephen Macedo. Oxford: Oxford University Press.

———. 1999c. "Group Aspirations and Democratic Politics." In *Democracy's Edges*, edited by Ian Shapiro and Casiano Hacker-Cordón. Cambridge: Cambridge University Press.

———. 2001a. *Abortion: The Supreme Court Decisions 1965–2000*. 2d ed. Indianapolis: Hackett.

———. 2001b. "The State of Democratic Theory." In *Political Science: The State of the Discipline*, edited by Ira Katznelson and Helen Milner. New York and London: W. W. Norton; Washington, D.C.: American Political Science Association.

———. 2002a. "Democratic Justice and Multicultural Recognition." In *Multiculturalism Reconsidered*, edited by David Held and Paul Kelly. Cambridge: Polity.

———. 2002b. "Optimal Deliberation?" *Journal of Political Philosophy* 10, no. 2 (June): 196–211.

Shapiro, Ian, and Mayling Birney. 2002. "Death and Taxes? The Estate Tax Repeal and American Democracy." Mimeo. Yale University.

Shapiro, Ian, and Casiano Hacker-Cordón, eds. 1999a. *Democracy's Edges*. Cambridge: Cambridge University Press.

———. 1999b. *Democracy's Value*. Cambridge: Cambridge University Press.

Shapiro, Ian, and Courtney Jung. 1996. "South African Democracy Revisited: A Reply to Koelble and Reynolds." *Politics and Society* 24: 237–47.

Shepsle, Kenneth, and Barry Weingast. 1981. "Structure Induced Equilibrium and Legislative Choice." *Public Choice* 37, no. 3: 503–19.

Shiffrin, Steven. 1998. *Dissent, Injustice, and the Meanings of America*. Princeton: Princeton University Press.

Shklar, Judith. 1989. "The Liberalism of Fear." In *Liberalism and Moral Life*, edited by Nancy Rosenblum. Cambridge: Harvard University Press.

Shorter, Edward. 1997. *A History of Psychiatry: From the Era of the Asylum to the Age of Prozac*. New York: John Wiley & Sons.

Shugart, Matthew, and John M. Carey. 1992. *Presidents and Assemblies: Constitutional Design and Electoral Dynamics*. New York: Cambridge University Press.

Simon, Adam. 2000. "Assessing Deliberation in Small Groups." Paper presented at the Midwest Political Science Association Annual Meeting, Chicago, Ill.

Sirianni, Carmen. 1993. "Learning Pluralism: Democracy and Diversity in Feminist Organizations." In *Democratic Community: NOMOS XXXV*, edited by Ian Shapiro and John Chapman. New York: New York University Press.

———. 2001. *Civic Innovation in America*. Berkeley and Los Angeles: University of California Press.

Skocpol, Theda. 1991. "Targeting within Universalism." In *The Urban Underclass*, edited by Christopher Jencks and Paul E. Peterson. Washington, D.C.: The Brookings Institution.

———. 1995. *Social Policy in the United States: Future Possibilities in Historical Perspective*. Princeton: Princeton University Press.

———. 1997. *Boomerang: Clinton's Health Security Effort and the Turn against Government in the U.S.* New York: W. W. Norton.

Smith, Adam. [1776] 1937. *An Inquiry into the Nature and Causes of the Wealth of Nations*. New York: Modern Library.

Smith, Heather, and Tom Tyler. 1996. "Justice and Power: When Will Justice Concerns Encourage the Disadvantaged to Support Policies Which Redistribute Economic Resources and the Disadvantaged Willingly to Obey the Law?" *European Journal of Social Psychology* 26: 171–200.

Smith, Richard. H., et al. 1996. "Envy and Schadenfreude." *Personality and Social Psychology Bulletin* 22: 158–68.

Smith, Rogers. 1985. *Liberalism and American Constitutional Law*. Cambridge: Harvard University Press.

———. 1997. *Civic Ideals: Conflicting Visions of Citizenship in U.S. History.* New Haven: Yale University Press.

Snyder, James M., and Gerald Kramer. 1988. "Fairness, Self-Interest, and the Politics of the Progressive Income Tax." *Journal of Public Economics* 36: 197–230.

Sobin, Dennis. 1973. *The Working Poor*. Port Washington, N.Y.: Kennikat.

Spears, Ian. 2000. "Understanding Inclusive Peace Agreements in Africa: The Problems of Sharing Power." *Third World Quarterly* 21 (February): 105–18.

———. 2002. "Africa: The Limits of Power Sharing," *Journal of Democracy* 13, no. 3: 123–36.

Steen, Jennifer A., and Ian Shapiro. 2002. "Walking Both Sides of the Street: PAC Contributions and Political Competition." Paper presented at the annual meeting of the American Political Science Association. Boston, Mass., August.

Steinmo, Sven 1993. *Taxation and Democracy.* New Haven: Yale University Press.

Stokes, Susan C. 1996. "Accountability and Policy Switch in Latin America's Democracies." Paper prepared for the New York–Chicago Seminar on Democracy conference, "Democracy and Accountability," New York University.

Sugrue, Thomas J. 1993. "The Structures of Urban Poverty: The Reorganization of Space and Work in Three Periods of American History." In *The "Underclass" Debate: Views from History*, edited by Michael Katz. Princeton: Princeton University Press.

Sunstein, Cass. 2002. "The Law of Group Polarization." *Journal of Political Philosophy* 10, no. 1: 175–95.

Swenson, Peter. 1991. "Bringing Capital Back In, or Social Democracy Reconsidered." *World Politics* 43, no. 4: 513–44.

Swenson, Peter. 2002. *Capitalists against Markets: The Making of Labor Markets and Welfare States in the United States and Sweden.* Oxford: Oxford University Press.

Swenson, Peter, and Scott Greer. 2002. "Foul Weather Friends: Big Business and Health Care Reform in the 1990s in Historical Perspective." *Journal of Health Politics, Policy and Law* 27, no. 4 (August): 605–38.

Tangian, A. S. 2000. "Unlikelihood of Condorcet's Paradox in a Large Society," *Social Choice and Welfare* 17: 337–65.

Taylor, Charles. 1989. *Sources of the Self.* Cambridge: Harvard University Press.

Taylor, Donald M., Fathali Moghaddam, Ian Gamble, and Evelyn Zeller. 1987. "Disadvantaged Group Responses to Perceived Inequality." *Journal of Social Psychology* 127, no. 3: 259–72.

Taylor, D. M., Stephen Wright, F. M. Moghaddam, and Richard Lalonde. 1990. "The Personal/Group Discrimination Discrepancy: Perceiving My Group, But Not Myself, as a Target for Discrimination" *Personality and Social Psychology Bulletin* 16: 256–62.

Taylor, Michael. 1969. "Proof of a Theorem on Majority Rule." *Behavioral Science* 14: 228–31.

Thomson, Judith Jarvis. 1971. "A Defense of Abortion." *Philosophy and Public Affairs* 1: 47–66.

Tobin, James. 1988. "Roundtable Discussion: Politics, Economics and Welfare." In *Power, Inequality and Democratic Politics: Essays in Honor of Robert Dahl,* edited by Ian Shapiro and Grant Reeher. Boulder, Colo.: Westview.

Tocqueville, Alexis de. [1835] 1969. *Democracy in America.* Edited by J. P. Mayer. Translated by George Lawrence. Vol. 1. New York: Harper Perennial.

———[1840] 1969.*Democracy in America.* Edited by J. P. Mayer. Translated by George Lawrence. Vol. 2. New York: Harper Perennial.

Treisman, Daniel. 2000. "Decentralization and Inflation: Commitment, Collective Action, or Continuity?" *American Political Science Review* 94, no. 4: 837–57.

Tribe, Lawrence. 1978. *American Constitutional Law.* New York: Foundation Press.

Tsebelis, George. 1995. "Decision-Making in Political Systems: Veto-Players in Multicameralism, Presidentialism, and Multipartyism." *British Journal of Political Science* 25: 289–325.

———. 2002. *Veto Players: How Political Institutions Work.* Princeton: Princeton University Press.

Tullock, Gordon. 1981. "Why So Much Stability?" *Public Choice* 37, no. 2: 189–202.

Tushnet, Mark. 1999. *Taking the Constitution Away from the Courts.* Princeton: Princeton University Press.

Tversky, Amos, and Daniel Kahneman. 1981. "The Framing of Decisions and the Rationality of Choice." *Science* 211: 543–58.

Tweedie, Jack. 1994. "Resources Rather Than Needs: A State-Centered Model of Welfare Policy Making." *American Journal of Political Science* 38, no. 3: 651–71.

Uggen, Christopher. 2002. "Barriers to Democratic Participation." Working Discussion Paper for the Urban Institute's Reentry Roundtable: Washington, D.C.: The Urban Institute.

United Nations. 2002. *Human Development Report 2002: Deepening Democracy in a Fragmented World*. Oxford: Oxford University Press.

Vail, Leroy, ed. 1989. *The Creation of Tribalism in South Africa*. Berkeley and Los Angeles: University of California Press.

Van Parijs, Philippe. 1995. *Real Freedom for All: What (If Anything) Can Justify Capitalism?* Oxford: Oxford University Press.

———. 1996. "Justice and Democracy: Are They Incompatible?" *Journal of Political Philosophy* 4, no. 2: 101–17.

———. 1999. "Contestatory Democracy versus Real Freedom for All." In *Democracy's Value*, edited by Ian Shapiro and Casiano Hacker-Cordón, 191–98. Cambridge: Cambridge University Press.

Verba, Sidney, and Gary R. Orren. 1985. *Equality in America: The View from the Top*. Cambridge: Harvard University Press.

Verba, Sidney, Kay Schlozman, and Henry Brady. 1995. *Voice and Equality: Civic Voluntarism in American Politics*. Cambridge: Harvard University Press.

Vreeland, James. 2003. *The IMF and Economic Development*. Cambridge: Cambridge University Press.

Walzer, Michael. 1983. *Spheres of Justice: A Defense of Pluralism and Equality*. New York: Basic Books.

———. 1987. *Interpretation and Social Criticism*. Harvard University Press.

Weber, Max. 1947. *Theories of Social and Economic Organization*. New York. Free Press.

———. [1914] 1968. *Economy and Society*. Edited by Guenther Roth and Claus Wittich. Berkeley and Los Angeles: University of California Press.

———. 1997. *From Max Weber: Essays in Sociology*. Edited by H. H. Gerth and C. Wright Mills. New York: Routledge.

———. 1998. "The Profession and Vocation of Politics." In Max Weber, *Political Writings*, edited by Peter Lassman and Ronald Speirs. Cambridge: Cambridge University Press.

Weitzman, Leonore. 1985. *The Divorce Revolution*. New York: Free Press.

Wendt, Alexander. 1994. "Collective Identity-Formation and the International State." *American Political Science Review* 88 no. 2: 384–96.

———. 1999. "A Comment on Held's Cosmopolitanism." In *Democracy's Edges*, edited by Ian Shapiro and Casiano Hacker-Cordón. Cambridge: Cambridge University Press.

West, Robin. 1988. "Jurisprudence and Gender." *University of Chicago Law Review* 55, no. 1: 67–70.

Wilkinson, Richard. 2001. *Mind the Gap: Hierarchies, Health, and Human Evolution*. New Haven: Yale University Press.

Williamson, Jeffrey G., and Peter H. Lindert. 1980. *American Inequality: A Macroeconomic History.* New York: Academic Press.

Wilson, William Julius. 1996. *When Work Disappears: The World of the New Urban Poor.* New York: Knopf.

Winnick, Andrew J. 1989. *Toward Two Societies: The Changing Distribution of Income and Wealth in the United States since 1960.* New York: Praeger.

Witte, John. 1985. *The Politics and Development of the Federal Income Tax.* Madison: University of Wisconsin Press.

Wittman, Donald A. 1973. "Parties as Utility Maximizers." *American Political Science Review* 67: 490–98.

Wolff, Edward N. 1994. "Trends in Household Wealth in the United States," *Review of Income and Wealth* 40, no. 2: 143–74.

Wollheim, Richard. 1962. "A Paradox in the Theory of Democracy." In *Philosophy, Politics, and Society,* edited by Peter Laslett and W. G. Runciman, 2d ser. Oxford: Blackwell.

Wright, Stephen. 1997. "Ambiguity, Social Influence, and Collective Action: Generating Collective Protest in Response to Tokenism." *Personality and Social Psychology Bulletin* 23, no. 12: 1277–90.

Wright, Stephen, Donald Taylor, and Fathali Moghaddam. 1990. "Responding to Membership in a Disadvantaged Group: From Acceptance to Collective Protest." *Journal of Personality and Social Psychology* 58, no. 6: 994–1003.

Young, Iris M. 1990. *Justice and the Politics of Difference.* Princeton: Princeton University Press.

Yunker, James A. 1983. "Optimal Redistribution with Interdependent Utility Functions." *Public Finance* 28, no. 1: 132–55.

Index